Indians Are Us?

Indians Are Us?

Culture and Genocide in Native North America

Ward Churchill

Common Courage Press   Monroe, Maine 04951

Library of Congress Cataloging-in-Publication Data

Churchill, Ward.
Indians are us? : culture and genocide in native
North America / Ward Churchill.
p.   cm.
Includes bibliographical references and index.
ISBN 1-56751-021-3 — ISBN 1-56751-020-5 (pbk.)
1. Indians of North America--Public opinion.
2. Indians of North America--Social conditions.
3. Indians of North America--Philosophy.
4. Public opinion--United States. I. Title.
E98.P99C48   1994
973.0497--dc20   93-28922

Common Courage Press
P.O. Box 702
Monroe, ME 04951
207-525-0900
fax: 207-525-3068

First Printing

Other Books by Ward Churchill

Authored

Fantasies of the Master Race (1992)

Struggle for the Land (1993)

Coauthored

Culture versus Economism (with Elisabeth R. Lloyd, 1984)

Agents of Repression (with Jim Vander Wall, 1988)

The COINTELPRO Papers (with Jim Vander Wall, 1990)

Edited

Marxism and Native Americans (1983)

Critical Issues in Native North America (1989)

Critical Issues in Native North America, Vol. II (1990)

Coedited

Cages of Steel (with J.J. Vander Wall, 1992)

Dedication

This one's for the Bear,
partner, friend, lover, ally...

Acknowledgments

A number of people—activists, academics, and friends—have made contributions along the way to the material included in this book. Among these are Nilak Butler, Bobby Castillo, Chrystos, Dan Debo, Vine Deloria, Jr., Jimmie Durham, Don Grinde, Bucky Harjo, Norb and Charlie Hill, Michael Hunter, M. Annette Jaimes, Sandy Janis, Winona LaDuke, Sage LaPeña, Adrian C. Lewis, Lucy Lippard, Joe and Vivian Locust, George Martin, Russ Means, Dian Million, Glenn T. Morris, Simon J. Ortiz, Jim Page, Bob Robideau, Nantiki Rose, Ted Roy, Inez Talamantez, Brian St. Laurent, George Tinker, John Trudell, Jim and Jennie Vander Wall, Sharon Venne, "White Bob," and Elizabeth Woody. To them, and to the many others who've helped shape what I've had to say herein, my appreciation is certainly due. Thanks, too, to Flic Shooter and Greg Bates at Common Courage Press for their fine work and faith in the worthiness of the current project.

Thanks are also due in a perverse sort of way to a whole herd of hang-around-the-forts, sell-outs and "nickel" Indians, whose collective negative example has done much to propel this book to completion. Prominent among these are Vernon Bellecourt, Ben "Nightmare" Campbell, David Bradley, Andreas Carmen, Tim Giago, Antonio Gonzales, Suzan Shown Harjo, the International Indian Treaty Council, Fern Mathias, "Cahuilla Red Elk," Carole Standing Elk, Chuey Varella, and Roberta Wilson. To them I say: "Keep it up, guys. You illustrate perfectly certain of the points I wish to make, and the very nature of your braying, rumor-mongering, and backbiting serves to make me look better and better to anyone possessed of a mind."

The same can be said for certain non-Indian organizations and individuals, notably the Anti-Defamation League of B'nai Brith, Bob Black, "Li'l Lawrence" from Berkeley, and the editorial page crew—Vinnie Carroll and "Shiftless Dave" Shifflet—of the *Rocky Mountain News*.

Chrystos's poem "He Burnt" is included in her collection *Dream On* (Vancouver: Press Gang Publishers, 1991), and reprinted by permission. Earlier versions of several of the essays contained herein have been published elsewhere. "Renegades, Terrorists, and Revolutionaries" first saw the light of day in *Propaganda Review*. "Let's Spread the 'Fun' Around" and "In the Matter of Julius Streicher" were published together under the title "Crimes Against Humanity" in *Z Magazine*. "Nobody's Pet Poodle" also ran in *Z*, as well as in *Crazy Horse Spirit*. "Another Dry White Season" and "'P' is for Plagiarism" appeared in *Bloomsbury Review*. "Naming Our Destiny" came out initially in *Global Justice*. "The Real Revisionism" was put forth in *American Indian Quarterly* and "Do It Yourself Indianism" was first published in *High Plains Quarterly*.

Contents

He Burnt

a swastika on her grass
He was drunk   he said he didn't know
that her family died in the nazi Holocaust
burning through the sod   Cries of burning bodies
children whose hollow eyes are caught briefly
in old newspaper photographs being loaded to die
Music burnt   Philosophy burnt   Memory burnt
burning through us the stench of kerosene
Could we continue
to live here
digging up the black remains near rosebushes
Always the grass will have a faint trace
unless it is entirely dug up & replanted
Every morning as her children go to school
she glances there with a burning shudder
putting sandwiches in bags
She remembers her mother's memories
of Rosa   Sarah   Claire   Hannah   Nora   Ruth
Judith
She remembers their flight to south america
where the nazis followed
when it seemed they had lost
Their symbol covering jackets of teenagers on street corners
my eyes burn   I know the nazis won
as the slaveowners have
We see the evidence of their victories
in every morning's paper burning with a stench
that fills our lives
Not so long ago some other boys burnt a cross
on the grass of a Black family
less than thirty miles from the grass of my home
I have dead I carry on my own
I'm sorry   he said   I didn't know what I was doing
Oh but
he did

—Chrystos
(Menominee)

Bringing the Law Home

Application of the Genocide Convention in the United States

The fact that domestic law does not punish an act which is an international crime does not free the perpetrator of such crime from responsibility under international law.

—International Law Commission
Report of Principles,
UN Doc. A/1706, Dec. 13, 1950

The following is a brief supporting a motion to dismiss charges against Ward Churchill, Russell Means, Glenn T. Morris, and Cahuilla Red Elk (a.k.a.: Margaret Martinez), leaders of the American Indian Movement of Colorado, for having halted a Columbus Day celebratory parade near the Colorado State Capitol Building in Denver, on October 12, 1991. Having stopped the parade for approximately forty-five minutes, the defendants— supported by more than three hundred other protestors—refused police directives to remove themselves from the street until they were arrested. They were then charged with refusing to obey a lawful police order, obstructing a public thoroughfare, and disturbing the peace, offenses carrying a combined

$1,500 fine and six months' incarceration.

The defendants contend that they were engaged in entirely lawful conduct on October 12, 1991, and that such charges as are presently lodged against them as a result of their actions on that date are invalid. They anchor this contention in various elements of international law and legal doctrine, most specifically the United Nations 1948 Convention on Punishment and Prevention of the Crime of Genocide, to which the United States is by its own comportment and assertion(s) bound.

Genocide and the Genocide Convention

The crime of genocide is usually understood in the United States as being almost exclusively associated with nazi Germany in its drive to exterminate such *untermenschen* ("subhuman peoples") as the Poles, Slavs, Gypsies, and, especially, the Jews. This is an entirely erroneous view. The meaning of the term, coined by the Polish jurist Raphael Lemkin in 1944, is very much broader, both in temporal scope and in terms of the techniques employed. Although the word itself was constructed by combining the Greek *genos* ("race" or "tribe") and the Latin *cide* ("killing"), according to Lemkin it describes a process considerably more multifaceted and sophisticated than simple mass murder. Indeed, mass murder may or may not be present within the genocidal context:

> Generally speaking, genocide does not necessarily mean the immediate destruction of a nation, *except when* accomplished by mass killing of all the members of a nation. It is intended rather to signify a coordinated plan of different actions

aimed at destruction of the essential foundations of the life of national groups, with the aim of annihilating the groups themselves. The objective of such a plan would be disintegration of the political and social institutions, of culture, language, national feelings, religion, and the economic existence of national groups, and the destruction of personal security, liberty, health, dignity, and the lives of individuals belonging to such groups. Genocide is the destruction of the national group as an entity, and the actions involved are directed against individuals, not in their individual capacity but as members of the national group (emphasis added).[1]

Lemkin observes that "Genocide has two phases: one, destruction of the national pattern of the oppressed group: the other, the imposition of the national pattern of the oppressor."[2] Clearly, the latter imposition could not occur if all or even most members of the oppressed group have to be killed in order for a defined "genocide" to have transpired. To the contrary, as it was put by the Lebanese delegate to the United Nations (U.N.) committee which produced the Draft Convention on Punishment and Prevention of the Crime of Genocide in 1947, what is at issue is the "destruction of a [recognizably distinct] human group, *even though the individual members survive* (emphasis added)."[3]

This concept of genocide as the creation of conditions which bring about the destruction of discrete cultural entities resulted in a formulation in the initial U.N. Draft Convention on Genocide which focused not only upon mass killing, but upon actions and policies which brought about the "disintegration of the political, social or economic structure of a group or nation" and the "systematic moral debasement of a group, people, or nation."[4] In the subsequent Draft Convention produced by the U.N. Secretariat in 1948, genocide was defined in a two-fold way, as "destruction of a group" and as "preventing its preservation and development."[5]

Overall, the construction of international law expressly prohibiting genocidal conduct followed, as the Lebanese delegate put it at the time, the idea that distinct human groups should be treated as "absolute entities...which it would be criminal to attack."[6] In the end, Article II of the U.N.'s 1948 Convention on Punishment and Prevention of the Crime of Genocide (UN GOAR Res. 260A (III) 9 December 1948; effective 21 January 1951) specifies five categories of activity to be genocidal when directed against an identified "national, ethnical, racial, or religious group," and therefore criminal under international law. Only one of these involves outright killing,

a) Killing members of the group;

b) Causing serious bodily or mental harm to members of the group;

c) Deliberately inflicting on the group conditions of life calculated to bring about its physical destruction in whole or in part;

d) Imposing measures intended to prevent births within the group;

e) Forcibly transferring children of the group to another group.

Under Article III, the Convention makes the following acts punishable under the law:

a) Genocide;

b) Conspiracy to commit genocide;

c) Direct and public incitement to commit genocide;

d) Attempt to commit genocide;

e) Complicity in genocide.

Article IV states that all persons shall be held accountable for acts committed under Article III, "whether they are constitutionally responsible rulers, public officials, or private individuals." Article V calls upon the nations of the world to enact "the necessary legislation to give effect to the present Convention and, in particular, to provide effective penalties for persons guilty of genocide or any of the other acts enumerated in Article III." The Convention was intended to prevent as well as punish commission of genocide. Thus a broad latitude of meaning, centering on notions of "advocacy," has been associated with the provisions concerning incitement of (Article III (c)) and complicity in (Article III (e)) genocide and/or genocidal processes.[7] In situations where there is disagreement as to the meaning of such terms, or in which a given government professes confusion concerning the substance of the law, the Convention provides, under Article IX, for interpretation and adjudication by the International Court of Justice (ICJ).

U.S. Response to the Genocide Convention

It is instructive that, although most nations rapidly ratified the Genocide Convention, the United States declined to do so for forty years. The reason for this extensive delay resides primarily, as is revealed in the records of Senate debates on the Genocide Convention since it was referred to that body by President Truman in 1950, in congressional concern that a broad range of federal policies vis-à-vis minority populations in the U.S. might be viewed as genocidally criminal under international law.[8] Considerable anxiety was expressed by various senators and expert witnesses over the years that certain activities of subordinate (state and local) governments and private parties, each of them sanctioned and/or protected by the federal government, might well violate the terms of the Convention.

Examples include the persistence of "Jim Crow" laws in various southern states, despite the extreme and well-recognized mental harm such statutes imposed upon African-American and other readily identifiable minority populations.[9] Another illustration is official toleration of the organizing activities of the Ku Klux Klan and comparable groups, despite their advocacy of patently genocidal principles and frequent resort to physical violence against racially-defined target groups (e.g., more than 1,000 lynchings of blacks between 1930 and 1960).[10] Other issues specifically concerning American Indians, such as involuntary sterilization programs and the massive forced transfer of children, will be covered below.

When the United States Senate finally ratified

the Genocide Convention during the closing days of the 100th Congress, it was largely on the basis of a growing belief that the U.S. was forfeiting "moral leadership" in world affairs as a result of its nonratification,[11] and on the basis of the Genocide Convention Implementation Act of 1988 (Title 18, Part I, U.S.C.; otherwise known as "The Proxmire Act"), a statute which incorporated certain language designed to narrow the intent of the internationally-accepted convention in its application to the United States.[12] Further, the instrument of treaty ratification which the Senate instructed President Ronald Reagan to deposit with the U.N. Secretary-General in November of 1988 contained a "Resolution of Ratification" (S. Exec. Rep. 2, 99th Cong., 1st Sess. 26-27 (1985), adopted on February 19, 1986; often referred to as "The Lugar-Helms-Hatch Sovereignty Package"). The resolution contained a reservation (Article I (2)) stating:

> [N]othing in the Convention requires or authorizes legislation or other action by the United States of America prohibited by the Constitution of the United States as interpreted by the United States.

It is thus plain that the Senate sought, even while enacting legislation to "implement" the Genocide Convention and effecting a corresponding ratification of its terms by treaty, to exempt the U.S. from the implications of international law, custom, and convention. In effect, it sought to elevate the U.S. Constitution to a status above that of the Laws of Nations. As has been noted elsewhere, "the acknowledged purpose of the Sovereignty Package was to reduce the convention to nothing more than a mere symbol of opposition to genocide. This fact alone raises the question of whether the United States ratified in good faith."[13] The Package has been described by a Senate Committee as an "embarrassment to the United States" insofar as it clearly suggests that the U.S. formally seeks to retain prerogatives to engage in or sanction policies and activities commonly understood as being genocidal, even while professing to condemn genocide.[14]

Legal Validity of the U.S. Posture on Genocide

There is abundant evidence that the Senate was aware, even as it advanced its "Sovereignty Package" purporting to subordinate the Genocide Convention to the U.S. Constitution, that the gesture contradicted the requirements of the constitution itself. Not the least indicator of this lies in the testimony of an expert witness, American Bar Association representative George Finch, in his testimony before the Senate Foreign Affairs Committee during its 1950 hearings on the matter. After observing that a formal treaty would be required in order for the U.S. to become a party of record in the Convention, Finch observed that "By the United States Constitution [Article VI, Section 2] treaties are 'the supreme law of the land, and the judges in every State shall be bound thereby, anything in the Constitution or laws of any State to the contrary notwithstanding.'"[15] In other words, the government would be unable to unilaterally legislate exceptions for itself with regard to the terms, provisions, and understandings of the Genocide Convention if it were ratified by treaty.

On its face, the problem might seem to have

been resolved, domestically at least, by a Supreme Court opinion rendered in *Reid v. Covert* (354 U.S. 1, 1957) that "any treaty provision that is inconsistent with the United States Constitution would simply be invalid under national law." Under Article 27 of the 1969 Vienna Convention on the Law of Treaties, however, no country can invoke the provisions of its internal law as a reason for not abiding by a treaty obligation.[16] Although the United States is not yet a signatory to the Vienna Convention, it has officially recognized it as being the "definitive" promulgation of the Laws of Nations with regard to treaty relations.[17] Hence, the Senate's attempt to carve out exemptions for the U.S. from the force of international law has no international legal integrity, and is subject to protest or renunciation by other parties to the Genocide Convention.

This was spelled out at least as early as 1978, when the rapporteur of a U.N. Economic and Social Council (ECOSOC) working group studying problems in the Genocide Convention's implementation worldwide reviewed the preliminary language framing proposed U.S. "reservations" and "understandings" on the issue. He officially concluded that, because it failed to conform to Vienna Convention requirements, Article I(2) of the Senate draft was invalid.[18] A virtually unaltered version of the U.S. Sovereignty Package was nonetheless submitted to the U.N. Secretariat a decade later, with the result that by December 1989 nine European allies of the United States—Denmark, Finland, Ireland, Italy, the Netherlands, Norway, Spain, Sweden, and the United Kingdom—had entered formal objections to Article I(2). Three of these nations—Denmark, the

Netherlands, and the United Kingdom—also entered strong objections to Article I(1) of the Package, in which the Senate attempted to reserve unto itself the "right" to determine when and if the ICJ might have authority in dispute resolution involving the U.S. The Netherlands declined to recognize the United States as a party to the Genocide Convention until such time as these "difficulties" are corrected. The other eight nations elected to hold this matter in abeyance, pending "discussions."[19] As has been observed elsewhere:

> [T]he convention has already been ratified by over one hundred states [none of which attached qualifications remotely comparable to those demanded by the United States], and under international rules of treaty law these states have a say in determining whether or not the U.S. conditions are acceptable...[B]y insisting on adoption of the Sovereignty Package, the Senate effectively gutted U.S. ratification of the convention.[20]

Moreover, it is legally irrelevant whether or not the United States ever attempted to ratify the Genocide Convention, or whether it manages to accomplish such ratification in a valid fashion in the future. Genocide has come to be seen as a crime within customary international law, and the Convention is thus binding upon the U.S. whether or not it chooses to formally acknowledge the fact.[21] This is tacitly recognized by the federal government itself, as is indicated in the authoritative *Restatement of the Foreign Relations Law of the United States* (1987).[22] Further, the Charter of the United Nations, to which the U.S. is a signatory, assumes that the organization can declare principles of international law which are binding, even upon nonmember nations.[23]

> The concept of offenses against the [customary] law of nations (*delicti juris gentium*) was recognized by the classical text-writers on international law and has been employed in national constitutions and statutes. It was regarded as sufficiently tangible in the eighteenth century so that United States Federal Courts sustained indictments charging acts as an offense against the law of nations, even if there were no statutes defining the offense. Early in the nineteenth century it was held that criminal jurisdiction of federal courts rested only on statutes though the definition of crimes denounced by statutes might be left largely to international law. Thus "piracy as defined by the law of nations" is an indictable offense in federal courts and all offenses against the law of nations are indictable at common law in state courts.[24]

Perhaps the clearest U.S. recognition of this principle came during the preparation for the trial of the major nazi criminals at Nuremberg, a process almost exclusively initiated, and subsequently spearheaded, by the United States.[25] It was determined by a U.S. legal task force headed by Supreme Court Justice Robert H. Jackson that the nazi leadership should be held accountable to the "full measure of international law," despite the fact that much of what was at issue had never seen formal codification, never mind official acceptance by Germany.[26] Following (very loosely) from a passage in the 1907 Hague (IV) Convention, the Jackson group stipulated that:

> International law shall be taken to include the
> principles of the law of nations as they result
> from usages established among civilized people,
> from the laws of humanity, and the dictates of
> public conscience.[27]

This precedent-setting formulation of "customary international law" was "laid before the representatives of Britain, France, and Soviet Russia at the London Conference in June 1945 and served as the foundation of the London Charter," the international agreement which established the juridical predication upon which the nazis were later tried.[28] In an interesting role reversal, Justice Jackson served as Chief U.S. Prosecutor in the Nuremberg Trial of 1946-47, while Attorney General Francis Biddle served as senior U.S. Tribunal member (Judge).[29] Jackson was thus mandated to articulate his government's formal international legal positions through presentations against the nazi defendants, while Biddle was charged with validating and implementing these articulations through his rulings on points of law, votes as to the guilt or innocence of the defendants on specific charges, and votes concerning imposition(s) of sentence on those convicted.[30]

Both men consistently went on record during the proceedings as rejecting arguments entered by counsel for the defendants that the charges against their clients were invalid because they represented enforcement of ex post facto law (*nullem crimen sine lege* or *nulla poena sine lege previa*).[31] The U.S. position was based on the principle that customary international law was binding upon all governments. It is worthy of note that neither this posture, nor any other adopted by its representatives during the trial, has ever been renounced by the United States. Rather, a dictum elaborated by Justice Jackson during his opening remarks to the Tribunal—that in order for the standards of legality enunciated at Nuremberg to have integrity, they must be applied at least as equally to the victors as to the vanquished—has seen continuous and approving reiteration by U.S. jurists and officials.[32] The implication is obvious: having articulated international legal doctrine upon which others were tried, convicted, and sentenced, the United States is bound both legally and morally to comply with its strictures.[33]

Consequently, the apparent intent of the Senate's Sovereignty Package, to allow "the United States [to] set its own agenda and be accountable to no one" with regard to its comportment on genocide, has no basis on either constitutional or international legal grounds.[34] Further, while doing nothing to alter the force or substance of international legality, such a stance carries with it obvious overtones of Hitlerian jurisprudence and diplomacy. This compounds the impression abroad, already engendered by the Reagan Administration's 1986 disavowal of even minimal ICJ authority vis-à-vis U.S. foreign policy, that the United States is becoming (or has already become) an "outlaw" nation.[35] It is, of course, incumbent upon the courts at every level to constrain government to adhere to the rule of law, international no less than any other, rather than to seek unrestricted prerogatives of power. Any other course of conduct on the part of the judiciary would be repugnant to both the letter and spirit of U.S. juridical doctrine.

The Question of First Amendment Rights

Implicit to the charges against the present defendants is a contention by the City of Denver that those against whom the accused directed their actions of October 12, 1991, were engaged in lawful activities protected by the First Amendment of the U.S. Constitution. The defendants contest this assumption on the basis that First Amendment guarantees of free speech and peaceful assembly are not absolute or unqualified. Such rights must be balanced against, among other things, the Fourteenth Amendment guarantees of the right to equitable social treatment of all citizens. Other constraints center in the famous dictum that it is illegal for one to falsely shout "Fire!" in a crowded theater. Similarly, it is well-established law that it is criminally actionable behavior to make statements which threaten the life of the President of the United States or other officials, and so forth. A range of existing statutes and regulations, long upheld by U.S. courts, concerning "hate speech," harassment, verbal assault, and misrepresentation might also be cited in this regard.[36]

The defendants, all American Indians, maintain that the Columbus Day festivities which were conducted in Denver on October 12, 1991, constituted a celebration of the genocide perpetrated against their people, beginning with the Columbian landfall on October 12, 1492 (details supporting their belief will be provided in the following section). Insofar as this is true, it follows that the Columbus Day celebration constitutes advocacy of (or incitement of) genocide within the meaning of Article III(c) of the Genocide Convention. Further, to the extent that at least some of the elements of the genocidal process initiated by Columbus remain in evidence, the celebration constitutes complicity in genocide within the meaning of Article III(e) of the Convention. Such activities, of course, are unlawful by accepted international definition, binding upon the the United States and its various levels of government. Thus, not only did the participants in the Columbus Day celebration lack a lawful right to engage in the activities at issue, the City of Denver lacked legal authority to grant them a permit for this purpose.

It will no doubt be argued by the prosecution that the defendants overreach in these contentions, and that the juridical waters they seek to navigate are in any event uncharted. This is untrue. Precedents, accruing from the first Nuremberg Trial,[37] do exist in which the United States clearly revealed its doctrinal posture with regard to the specific actions (offenses) alleged here. These precedents must be considered binding upon American courts at every level. Three examples will be used as illustration.

- In the case brought by the United States against Nazi Party ideologist *Alfred Rosenberg* at Nuremberg, Justice Jackson argued at length that the defendant was guilty of "Crimes Against Humanity" on the basis of his articulation during the 1930s of ideological/philosophical theses which "laid the theoretical foundation for" and helped "shape public opinion to accept" a policy of genocide which emerged during the following decade. It is instructive that, although the British, French, and Soviet members of the Tribunal declined to convict Rosenberg on this basis, the U.S. member, Francis Biddle, entered a guilty verdict in behalf of his government. Rosenberg was ultimately convicted and hanged for his subsequent role in implementing criminal policies during the nazi occupation of the western USSR in the 1940s.[38]

- A similar case was brought by Jackson against prewar Hitler Youth leader *Baldur von Schirach*, because of his role in indoctrinating German young people to accept the premises which led to genocide and aggressive war; "ideological and emotional preparation...was the central issue" of the American case. In this instance, Biddle joined the other Tribunal members in voting to acquit, but only on the basis that the case had not been made (rather than because he felt the charges to be misguided). Von Schirach was ultimately sentenced to twenty year' imprisonment because of his wartime role in deporting Jews to extermination facilities while serving as head of the nazi regime in Vienna.[39]

- Jackson made an almost identical Crimes Against Humanity case against propagandist *Julius Streicher*, despite the fact that he was aware Streicher "was never a member of the inner ring" of nazis, and "had nothing to do with the formulation of Nazi policy." The accusations against him consisted solely of his

having sometimes penned and often published virulently antisemitic materials.
Insofar as he was found to have participated directly in no aspect of the physical
extermination of the Jews, he was convicted by vote of all four Tribunal members only of having participated in the
"psychological conditioning of the
German public" which led to a genocidal
outcome. On this basis, he was hanged
(for further details, see "In the Matter of
Julius Streicher").[40]

On the basis of these cases, it seems indis-
putable that the United States government, through
participating judicial officials, committed itself firmly to both a conception and implementation of international law which proscribes advocacy of genocide
even when the immediate physical implementation
of genocidal policies is absent. In part, this can only
be attributed to a desire, explained by Justice
Jackson in his predication to the Nuremberg
Tribunal's creation, not simply to punish those
guilty of given offenses, but to establish an international legal "groundwork barring revival of such
power" as led to the nazi genocide.[41] In the latter
connection, matters of advocacy become an all-
important consideration. For this reason, the United
States, along with the other three allied powers,
complemented the proceedings at Nuremberg by
implementing occupation regulations—subsequently
incorporated into German domestic law at the be-
hest of the occupying powers—prohibiting all celebratory demonstrations of nazism (including, most
prominently, parades and speeches), the display of

nazi symbols and regalia, portraits of Adolf Hitler and other nazi leaders, and so forth. The premise of these laws and regulations was/is that celebration of a perpetrator of genocide can only be construed as advocacy or endorsement of the genocide itself.[42]

Columbus and the Beginning of Genocide in the "New World"

It has been contended by those who would celebrate Columbus that accusations concerning his perpetration of genocide are distortive "revisions" of history. Whatever the process unleashed by his "discovery" of the "New World," it is said, the discoverer himself cannot be blamed. Whatever his defects and offenses, they are surpassed by the luster of his achievements; however "tragic" or "unfortunate" certain dimensions of his legacy may be, they are more than offset by the benefits—even for the victims—of the resulting blossoming of a "superior civilization" in the Americas.[43] Essentially the same arguments might be advanced with regard to Adolf Hitler: Hitler caused the Volkswagen to be created, after all, and the autobahn. His leadership of Germany led to jet propulsion, significant advances in rocket telemetry, laid the foundation for genetic engineering. Why not celebrate his bona fide accomplishments on behalf of humanity rather than "dwelling" so persistently on the genocidal by-products of his policies?

To be fair, Columbus was never a head of state. Comparisons of him to nazi SS leader Heinrich Himmler, rather than Hitler, are therefore more accurate and appropriate. It is time to delve into the substance of the defendants' assertion that Columbus and Himmler, nazi *lebensraumpolitik* (conquest of "living space" in eastern Europe) and the "settlement of the New World" bear more than casual resemblance to one another. This has nothing to do with the Columbian "discovery," not that this in itself is completely irrelevant. Columbus did not sally forth upon the Atlantic for reasons of "neutral science" or altruism. He went, as his own diaries, reports, and letters make clear, fully expecting to encounter wealth belonging to others. It was his stated purpose to seize this wealth, by whatever means necessary and available, in order to enrich both his sponsors and himself.[44] Plainly, he prefigured, both in design and by intent, what came next. To this extent, he not only symbolizes the process of conquest and genocide which eventually consumed the indigenous peoples of America, but bears the personal responsibility of having participated in it. Still, if this were all there was to it, the defendants would be inclined to dismiss him as a mere thug along the lines of Al Capone rather than viewing him as a counterpart to Himmler.

The 1492 "voyage of discovery" is, however, hardly all that is at issue. In 1493 Columbus returned with an invasion force of seventeen ships, appointed at his own request by the Spanish Crown to install himself as "viceroy and governor of [the Caribbean islands] and the mainland" of America, a position he held until 1500.[45] Setting up shop on the large island he called Española (today Haiti and the Dominican Republic), he promptly instituted policies of slavery (*encomiendo*) and systematic extermination against the native Taino population.[46] Columbus's programs reduced Taino numbers from as many as eight million at the outset of his regime to about three million in 1496.[47] Perhaps 100,000 were left by the time of the governor's departure. His policies, however, remained, with the result that by 1514 the Spanish census of the island showed barely 22,000 Indians remaining alive. In 1542, only two hundred were recorded.[48] Thereafter, they were considered extinct, as were Indians throughout the Caribbean Basin, an aggregate population which totalled more than fifteen million at the point of first contact with the Admiral of the Ocean Sea, as Columbus was known.[49]

This, to be sure, constitutes an attrition of population in real numbers every bit as great as the toll of twelve to fifteen million—about half of them Jewish—most commonly attributed to Himmler's slaughter mills. Moreover, the proportion of indigenous Caribbean population destroyed by the Spanish in a single generation is, no matter how the figures are twisted, far greater than the seventy-five percent of European Jews usually said to have been exterminated by the nazis.[50] Worst of all, these data apply *only* to the Caribbean Basin; the process of genocide in the Americas was only just beginning at the point such statistics become operant, not ending, as they did upon the fall of the Third Reich. All told, it is probable that more than one hundred million native people were "eliminated" in the course of Europe's ongoing "civilization" of the Western Hemisphere.[51]

It has long been asserted by "responsible scholars" that this decimation of American Indians which accompanied the European invasion resulted primarily from disease rather than direct killing or conscious policy.[52] There is a certain truth to this, although starvation may have proven just as lethal in the end. It must be borne in mind when considering such facts that a considerable portion of those who perished in the nazi death camps died, not as the victims of bullets and gas, but from starvation, as well as epidemics of typhus, dysentery, and the like. Their keepers, who could not be said to have killed these people directly, were nonetheless found to have been culpable in their deaths by way of deliberately imposing the conditions which led to the proliferation of starvation and disease among them.[53] Certainly, the same can be said of Columbus's regime, under which the original residents were, as a first order of business, permanently dispossessed of their abundant cultivated fields while being converted into chattel, ultimately to be worked to death for the wealth and "glory" of Spain.[54]

Nor should more direct means of extermination be relegated to incidental status. As the matter is put by Kirkpatrick Sale in his recent book, *The Conquest of Paradise*:

> The tribute system, instituted by the Governor sometime in 1495, was a simple and brutal way of fulfilling the Spanish lust for gold while acknowledging the Spanish distaste for labor. Every Taino over the age of fourteen had to supply the rulers with a hawk's bell of gold every three months (or, in gold-deficient areas, twenty-five pounds of spun cotton); those who did were given a token to wear around their necks as proof that they had made their payment; those who did not were, as [Columbus's brother, Fernando] says discreetly, "punished" – by having their hands cut off, as [the priest, Bartolomé de] las Casas says less discreetly, and left to bleed to death.[55]

31

INDIANS ARE US?

It is entirely likely that upwards of 10,000 Indians were killed in this fashion alone, on Española alone, as a matter of policy, during Columbus's tenure as governor. Las Casas' *Brevísima relación,* among other contemporaneous sources,[56] is also replete with accounts of Spanish colonists (*hidalgos*) hanging Tainos *en masse,* roasting them on spits or burning them at the stake (often a dozen or more at a time), hacking their children into pieces to be used as dog feed and so forth, all of it to instill in the natives a "proper attitude of respect" toward their Spanish "superiors."

> [The Spaniards] made bets as to who would slit a man in two, or cut off his head at one blow; or they opened up his bowels. They tore the babes from their mother's breast by their feet and dashed their heads against the rocks...They spitted the bodies of other babes, together with their mothers and all who were before them, on their swords.[57]

No SS trooper could be expected to comport himself with a more unrelenting viciousness. And there is more. All of this was coupled to wholesale and persistent massacres:

> A Spaniard...suddenly drew his sword. Then the whole hundred drew theirs and began to rip open the bellies, to cut and kill [a group of Tainos assembled for this purpose] – men, women, children and old folk, all of whom were seated, off guard and frightened...And within two credos, not a man of them there remains alive. The Spaniards enter the large house nearby, for this was happening at its door, and in the same way, with cuts and stabs, began to kill as many as were found

there, so that a stream of blood was running, as if a great number of cows had perished.[58]

Elsewhere, las Casas went on to recount how

in this time, the greatest outrages and slaughterings of people were perpetrated, whole villages being depopulated...The Indians saw that without any offense on their part they were despoiled of their kingdoms, their lands and liberties and of their lives, their wives, and homes. As they saw themselves each day perishing by the cruel and inhuman treatment of the Spaniards, crushed to earth by the horses, cut in pieces by swords, eaten and torn by dogs, many buried alive and suffering all kinds of exquisite tortures...[many surrendered to their fate, while the survivors] fled to the mountains [to starve].[59]

Such descriptions correspond almost perfectly to those of systematic nazi atrocities in the western USSR offered by William Shirer in Chapter 27 of his *The Rise and Fall of the Third Reich*.[60] But, unlike the nazi extermination campaigns of World War II, the Columbian butchery on Española continued until there were no Tainos left to butcher.

Evolution of the Columbian Legacy

Nor was this by any means the end of it. The genocidal model for conquest and colonization established by Columbus was to a large extent replicated by others such as Cortez (in Mexico) and Pizarro (in Peru) during the following half-century.[61] During the same period, expeditions—such as those of Ponce de Leon in 1513, Coronado in 1540, and de Soto during the same year—were launched with an eye towards effecting the same pattern on the North American continent proper.[62] In the latter sphere, the Spanish example was followed and in certain ways intensified by the British, beginning at Roanoake in 1607 and Plymouth in 1620.[63] Overall, the process of English colonization along the Atlantic Coast was marked by a series of massacres of native people as relentless and devastating as any perpetrated by the Spaniards. One of the best-known illustrations—drawn from among hundreds—was the slaughter of some 800 Pequots at present-day Mystic, Connecticut, on the night of May 26, 1637.[64]

During the latter portion of the seventeenth century, and throughout most of the eighteenth, Great Britain battled France for colonial primacy in North America. The resulting sequence of four "French and Indian Wars" greatly accelerated the liquidation of indigenous people as far west as the Ohio River Valley. During the last of these, concluded in 1763, history's first documentable case of biological warfare occurred against Pontiac's Algonkian Confederacy, a powerful military alliance aligned with the French.

> Sir Jeffrey Amherst, commander-in-chief of the British forces...wrote in a postscript of a letter to Bouquet [a subordinate] that smallpox be sent among the disaffected tribes. Bouquet replied, also in a postscript, "I will try to [contaminate] them...with some blankets that may fall into their hands, and take care not to get the disease myself."...To Bouquet's postscript Amherst replied, "You will do well to [infect] the Indians by means of blankets as well as to try every other method that can serve to extirpate this execrable

race." On June 24, Captain Ecuyer, of the Royal Americans, noted in his journal: "...we gave them two blankets and a handkerchief out of the small-pox hospital. I hope it will have the desired effect."[65]

It did. Over the next few months, the disease spread like wildfire among the Mingo, Delaware, Shawnee, and other Ohio River nations, killing perhaps 100,000 people.[66] The example of Amherst's action does much to dispel the myth that the post-contact attrition of Indian people through disease introduced by Europeans was necessarily unintentional and unavoidable. There are a number of earlier instances in which native people felt disease had been deliberately inculcated among them. For example, the so-called "King Philip's War" of 1675-76 was fought largely because the Wampanoag and Narragansett nations believed English traders had consciously contaminated certain of their villages with smallpox.[67] Such tactics were also continued by the United States after the American Revolution. At Fort Clark on the upper Missouri River, for instance, the U.S. Army distributed smallpox-laden blankets as gifts among the Mandan. The blankets had been gathered from a military infirmary in St. Louis where troops infected with the disease were quarantined. Although the medical practice of the day required the precise opposite procedure, army doctors ordered the Mandans to disperse once they exhibited symptoms of infection. The result was a pandemic among the Plains Indian nations which claimed at least 125,000 lives, and may have reached a toll several times that number.[68]

Contemporaneously with the events at Fort

Clark, the U.S. was also engaged in a policy of wholesale "removal" of indigenous nations east of the Mississippi River, "clearing" the land of its native population so that it might be "settled" by "racially superior" Anglo-Saxon "pioneers."[69] This resulted in a series of extended forced marches—some more than a thousand miles in length—in which entire peoples were walked at bayonet-point to locations west of the Mississippi. Rations and medical attention were poor, shelter at times all but nonexistent. Attrition among the victims was correspondingly high. As many as fifty-five percent of all Cherokees, for example, are known to have died during or as an immediate result of that people's "Trail of Tears."[70] The Creeks and Seminoles also lost about half their existing populations as a direct consequence of being "removed."[71] It was the example of nineteenth-century U.S. Indian Removal policy upon which Adolf Hitler relied for a practical model when articulating and implementing his *Lebensraumpolitik* during the 1930s and '40s.[72]

By the 1850s, U.S. policymakers had adopted a popular philosophy called "Manifest Destiny" by which they imagined themselves enjoying a divinely ordained right to possess *all* native property, including everything west of the Mississippi.[73] This was coupled to what has been termed a "rhetoric of extermination" by which governmental and corporate leaders sought to shape public sentiment to embrace the eradication of American Indians.[74] The professed goal of this physical reduction of "inferior" indigenous populations was to open up land for "superior" Euroamerican "pioneers."[75] One outcome of this dual articulation was a series of general massacres perpetrated by the United States military.

A bare sampling of some of the worst must include the 1854 massacre of perhaps 150 Lakotas at Blue River (Nebraska), the 1863 Bear River (Idaho) Massacre of some 500 Western Shoshones, the 1864 Sand Creek (Colorado) Massacre of as many as 250 Cheyennes and Arapahoes, the 1868 massacre of another 300 Cheyennes at the Washita River (Oklahoma), the 1875 massacre of about 75 Cheyennes along the Sappa Creek (Kansas), the 1878 massacre of still another 100 Cheyennes at Camp Robinson (Nebraska), and the 1890 massacre of more than 300 Lakotas at Wounded Knee (South Dakota).[76]

Related phenomena included the army's internment of the bulk of all Navajos for four years (1864-68) under abysmal conditions at the Bosque Redondo, during which upwards of a third of the population of this nation is known to have perished of starvation and disease.[77] Even worse in some ways was the unleashing of Euroamerican civilians to kill Indians at whim, and sometimes for profit. In Texas, for example, an official bounty on native scalps—*any* native scalps—was maintained until well into the 1870s. The result was that the indigenous population of this state, once the densest in all of North America, had been reduced to near zero by 1880. As it has been put elsewhere, "The facts of history are plain: Most Texas Indians were exterminated or brought to the brink of oblivion by [civilians] who often had no more regard for the life of an Indian than they had for that of a dog, sometimes less."[78] Similarly, in California, "the enormous decrease [in indigenous population] from about a quarter-million [in 1800] to less than 20,000 is due chiefly to the cruelties and wholesale massacres perpetrated by miners and early settlers."[79]

> Much of the killing in California and southern Oregon Territory resulted, directly and indirectly, from the discovery of gold in 1849 and the subsequent influx of miners and settlers. Newspaper accounts document the atrocities, as do oral histories of the California Indians today. It was not uncommon for small groups or villages to be attacked by immigrants...and virtually wiped out overnight.[80]

All told, the North American Indian population within the area of the forty-eight contiguous states of the United States, an aggregate group which had probably numbered in excess of twelve million in the year 1500, was reduced by official estimate to barely more than 237,000 four centuries later.[81] This vast genocide—historically paralleled in its magnitude and degree only by that which occurred in the Caribbean Basin—is the most sustained on record. Corresponding almost perfectly with this upper-ninetieth-percentile erosion of indigenous population by 1900 was the expropriation of about 97.5 percent of native land by 1920.[82] The situation in Canada was/is entirely comparable.[83] Plainly, the nazi-esque dynamics set in motion by Columbus in 1492 continued, and were not ultimately consummated until the present century.

The Columbian Legacy in the United States

While it is arguable that the worst of the genocidal programs directed against Native North America had ended by the twentieth century, it seems undeniable that several continue into the present. One obvious illustration is the massive compulsory transfer of American Indian children from their families, communities, and societies to Euroamerican families and institutions, a policy which is quite blatant in its disregard for Article I(e) of the 1948 Convention. Effected through such mechanisms as the U.S. Bureau of Indian Affairs (BIA) boarding school system,[84] and a pervasive policy of placing Indian children for adoption (including "blind" adoption) with non-Indians, such circumstances have been visited upon more than three-quarters of all indigenous youth in some generations after 1900.[85] The stated goal of such policies has been to bring about the "assimilation" of native people into the value orientations and belief system of their conquerors.[86] Rephrased, the objective has been to bring about the disappearance of indigenous societies as such, a patent violation of the terms, provisions, and intent of the Genocide Convention (Article I(c)).

An even clearer example is a program of involuntary sterilization of American Indian women by the BIA's Indian Health Service (IHS) during the 1970s. The federal government announced that the program had been terminated, and acknowledged having performed several thousand such sterilizations. Independent researchers have concluded that as many as forty-two percent of all native women of childbearing age in the United States had been sterilized by that point.[87] That the program represented a rather stark—and very recent—violation of Article I(d) of the 1948 Convention seems beyond all reasonable doubt.

INDIANS ARE US?

More broadly, implications of genocide are quite apparent in the federal government's self-assigned exercise of "plenary power" and concomitant "trust" prerogatives over the residual Indian land base pursuant to the *Lonewolf v. Hitchcock* case (187 U.S. 553 (1903)). This has worked, with rather predictable results, to systematically deny native people the benefit of their remaining material assets. At present, the approximately 1.6 million Indians recognized by the government as residing within the U.S., when divided into the fifty-million-odd acres nominally reserved for their use and occupancy, remain the continent's largest landholders on a per capita basis.[88] Moreover, the reservation lands have proven to be extraordinarily resource rich, holding an estimated two-thirds of all U.S. "domestic" uranium reserves, about a quarter of the readily accessible low-sulfur coal, as much as a fifth of the oil and natural gas, as well as substantial deposits of copper, iron, gold, and zeolites.[89] By any rational definition, the U.S. Indian population should thus be one of the wealthiest—if not *the* richest—population sectors in North America.

Instead, by the federal government's own statistics, they comprise far and away the poorest. As of 1980, American Indians experienced, by a decided margin, the lowest annual and lifetime incomes on a per capita basis of any ethnic or racial group on the continent. Correlated to this are all the standard indices of extreme poverty: the highest rates of infant mortality, death by exposure and malnutrition, incidence of tuberculosis and other plague diseases. Indians experience the highest level of unemployment, year after year, and the lowest level of educational attainment. The overall quality of life is so dismal that alcoholism and other forms of substance abuse are endemic; the rate of teen suicide is also several times that of the nation as a whole. The average life expectancy of a reservation-based Native American male is less than 45 years; that of a reservation-based female less than three years longer.[90]

It's not that reservation resources are not being exploited, or profits accrued. To the contrary, virtually all uranium mining and milling occurred on or immediately adjacent to reservation land during the life of the Atomic Energy Commission's ore-buying program, 1952-81.[91] The largest remaining enclave of traditional Indians in North America is currently undergoing forced relocation in order that coal may be mined on the Navajo Reservation.[92] Alaska native peoples are being converted into landless "village corporations" in order that the oil under their territories can be tapped; and so on.[93] Rather, the BIA has utilized its plenary and trust capacities to negotiate contracts with major mining corporations "in behalf of" its "Indian wards" which pay pennies on the dollar of conventional mineral royalty rates.[94] Further, the BIA has typically exempted such corporations from an obligation to reclaim whatever reservation lands have been mined, or even to perform basic environmental cleanup of nuclear and other forms of waste. One outcome has been that the National Institute for Science has recommended that the two locales within the U.S. most heavily populated by native people—the Four Corners Region and the Black Hills Region—be designated as "National Sacrifice Areas."[95] Indians have responded that this would mean their being converted

41

into "national sacrifice *peoples*."[96]

Even such seemingly innocuous federal policies as those concerning Indian identification criteria carry with them an evident genocidal potential. In clinging insistently to a variation of a eugenics formulation—dubbed "blood-quantum"—ushered in by the 1887 General Allotment Act, while implementing such policies as the Federal Indian Relocation Program (1956-1982), the government has set the stage for a "statistical extermination" of the indigenous population within its borders.[97] As the noted western historian, Patricia Nelson Limerick, has observed: "Set the blood-quantum at one-quarter, hold to it as a rigid definition of Indians, let intermarriage proceed...and eventually Indians will be defined out of existence. When that happens, the federal government will finally be freed from its persistent 'Indian problem'."[98] Ultimately, there is precious little difference, other than matters of style, between this and what was once called the "Final Solution of the Jewish Problem."

Confronting Genocide in America

Were the genocide of American Indians initiated by Christopher Columbus and carried on with increasing ferocity by his successors a matter of only historical significance—as with the nazi extermination campaigns—it would be utterly inappropriate, and unlawful, to celebrate it. Insofar as aspects of the genocide at issue are demonstrably ongoing—not just here, but in Central and South America as well—this becomes all the more true.[99] The indigenous people of the Americas have an unquestionable, absolute, and vitally urgent need to

42

alter the physical and political circumstances which have been and continue to be imposed upon them. In the alternative, we face, collectively, a final eradication through a number of means.

Given contemporary demographic disparities between indigenous and non-indigenous populations in the Americas, and the power relations which attend these, it seems self-evident that a crucial aspect of native survival must go to altering the non-Indian sensibilities which contribute to—either by affirming the rightness of, or acquiescing in—the continuing genocide against Native America. Very high on any list of those expressions of non-indigenous sensibility which contribute to the perpetuation of genocidal policies against Indians are the annual Columbus Day celebrations, events in which it is baldly asserted that the process, events, and circumstances described above are, at best, either acceptable or unimportant. More often, the sentiments expressed by participants are, quite frankly, that the fate of Native America embodied in Columbus and the Columbian legacy is a matter to be openly and enthusiastically applauded as an unrivaled "boon to all mankind."[100] Undeniably, the situation of American Indians will not—in fact, *cannot*—change for the better so long as such attitudes are deemed socially acceptable by the mainstream populace. Hence, such celebrations as Columbus Day *must* be stopped.

Within the scope of the Genocide Convention and other elements of international law, custom, and convention, American Indians have a right to expect the support of all levels of governance in the United States, from the federal executive to local mayors, in putting a stop to celebration/advocacy/incitement of our destruction. It follows that we have the same right to expect support from the judiciary, from the Supreme Court to county and municipal courts. Again, we have the same right to expect support from the various law enforcement agencies in this country, from the Federal Bureau of Investigation and U.S. Marshals Service to the Denver Police Department. In other words, under the law, the City of Denver *should* under no circumstances have issued a permit for the conducting of activities celebrating Columbus Day on October 12, 1991. The courts *should* have intervened to enjoin such activities, and the police *should* have enforced the prohibition of such activities against anyone attempting to violate it. Of course, none of these official actions occurred. The executive dimension of government, the courts, and the police all defaulted upon their legal responsibilities. The illegal activities of the participants in the public celebration of Columbus Day in Denver, Colorado, were not only allowed, but to all appearances endorsed, by those mandated to prevent them.[101]

The rights and responsibilities of individual citizens in such situations are not mysterious. During the course of the Nuremberg proceedings, Justice Jackson and his associates repeatedly queried how it was that "average Germans" had simply "stood by" while their government pursued a policy of Crimes Against Humanity.[102] Given the legitimation of precisely these crimes under then-prevailing German law, one can only conclude that Jackson meant individual German citizens had shirked a binding obligation under a higher (international) law

44

to physically prevent such crimes from occurring. Such a principle is not inconsistent with domestic laws concerning the right to effect "citizens' arrests" and so forth.[103] Moreover, it is now universally embodied in covenants relieving all persons, including active-duty soldiers and police, of any "responsibility" to comply with unlawful orders, regulations, or statutes.[104] Indeed, it is arguable that, after Nuremberg, a legal requirement was incurred by each individual citizen to vigorously—and, when necessary, *physically*—oppose the commission of a Crime Against Humanity by *any* party, official or otherwise.[105] As Ben Whitaker, senior American diplomat, framed the matter before the United Nations in 1985:

> [S]ince wider public education about this doctrine is highly crucial for the aversion of future genocide...explicit wording should be added to the Convention, perhaps at the end of Article III, that "In judging culpability, a plea of superior orders is not an excusing defense." Similarly, wider publicity should be given to the principle in national codes governing armed forces, prison staffs, police officers, doctors, and others, to advise and warn them that it is not only their right to disobey orders violating human rights, such as to carry out genocide or torture, but their legal duty to disobey. Such precepts should be taught in the schools, and the United Nations Educational, Scientific and Cultural Organization might be asked to encourage this internationally.[106]

In essence, then, the defendants cannot be convicted of any crime in the instant case insofar as they comported themselves in an entirely lawful manner. We cannot have refused to obey a lawful order by a police official insofar as the order in question—to allow an illegal activity to proceed unhampered—was itself unlawful. It was therefore our legal *duty* to disobey it. We cannot have obstructed a public thoroughfare insofar as said thoroughfare was already obstructed by an illegal assembly. We merely met the legal requirement of attempting to put a stop to the unlawful activity already occurring. We cannot have disturbed the peace insofar as the peace was already disturbed by the aforementioned unlawful assembly, which included, among other things, brass bands. Again, we simply met the legal requirement of attempting to halt the commission of a Crime Against Humanity. In addition, we were engaged in a form of the very "educational" activity vis-à-vis the Genocide Convention called for by Mr. Whitaker. There being no basis to the charges leveled against the defendants, we collectively demand that all charges be immediately dismissed.

Editor's Note: The charges were not dismissed. Put to a Denver jury, however, the arguments contained in this brief resulted in the acquittal of the defendants on all counts on June 26, 1992. In post-verdict statements to the press, the jurors clearly indicated that they had been convinced by the defense that it was the Columbus Day celebrants and various collaborating officials, rather than the defendants, who had engaged in wrongful activities. For further details, see M. Annette Jaimes, "The Trial of the 'Columbus Day Four'," *Lies of Our Times*, Vol. 3, No. 9, September 1992, pp. 8-9.

Notes

1. Raphael Lemkin, *Axis Rule in Occupied Europe* (Concord, NH: Carnegie Endowment for International Peace/Rumford Press, 1944, p. 79).

2. *Ibid.*

3. U.N. Doc. E/A.C. 25/S.R. 1-28.

4. Report of the United Nations Economic and Social Council, 1947, 6th Part; quoted in Robert Davis and Mark Zannis, *The Genocide Machine in Canada: The Pacification of the North* (Montréal: Black Rose Books, 1973, p. 19).

5. U.N. Doc. A/36, 1948.

6. U.N. Doc. E/A.C. 25/S.R. 1-28.

7. See, for example, Maxwell Cohen, *Canadian Civil Liberties Association Brief to the Senate Standing Committee on Legal and Constitutional Affairs on Hate Propaganda*, Ottawa, April 22, 1969: "[B]ecause Canadian law already forbids most substantive aspects of genocide in that it prohibits homicide or murder vis-à-vis individuals, and because it may be undesirable to have the same acts forbidden under two different legal categories, we deem it advisable that the Canadian legislation [on genocide], which we urge as a symbol of our country's dedication to the rights set out in the Convention, should be confined to 'advocating and promoting genocide,' acts which are not forbidden at present by the Criminal Code."

8. An exhaustive analysis of these debates may be found in Lawrence J. LeBlanc, *The United States and the Genocide Convention* (Durham, NC: Duke University Press, 1991).

9. This is well covered in LeBlanc, *op. cit.*, pp. 99-115. Also see C. Vann Woodward, *The Strange Career of Jim Crow* (New York: Oxford University Press, [3rd ed., revised] 1974) and William L. Patterson, ed., *We*

Charge Genocide: The Historic Petition to the United Nations for Relief from a Crime of the United States Government Against the Negro People (New York: International Publishers, 1970).

10. Again, a broad literature exists. Perhaps the most focused for purposes of this presentation is Wyn Craig Wade, *The Fiery Cross: The Ku Klux Klan in America* (New York: Simon and Schuster Publishers, 1987). Also see Leonard Zeskind, *The Christian Identity Movement: A Theological Justification for Racist and Anti-Semitic Violence* (New York: Division of Church and Society of the National Council of Churches of Christ in the U.S., 1986).

11. See 132 *Congressional Record* S1253-77, February 18, 1986. Also see U.S. Senate, *Hearings on the Genocide Convention Before the Senate Committee on Foreign Relations* (97th Cong., 1st Sess) (U.S. Government Printing Office, Washington, D.C., 1985.)

12. U.S. Senate, *Hearing on Legislation to Implement the Genocide Convention Before the Senate Committee on the Judiciary (S. 1851)* (Washington, D.C.: 100th Cong., 2d Sess., U.S. Government Printing Office, 1989).

13. LeBlanc, *op. cit.*, p. 98.

14. S. Exec. Rep. No. 2, 99th Cong., 1st Sess., 1987, p. 32; the report also points out that "a question arises as to what the United States is really seeking to accomplish by attaching this understanding. The language suggests the United States fears it has something to hide."

15. U.S. Senate, *Hearings on the Genocide Convention Before a Subcommittee of the Senate Committee on Foreign Relations* (Washington, D.C.: 81st Cong., 2d Sess., U.S. Government Printing Office, 1978, p. 217).

16. The text of the Vienna Convention may be found in L.

Henkin, et al., *International Law: Cases and Materials*, (Charlottesville, VA: The Michie Company, 1980, p. 264).

17. See Michla Pomerance, *The Advisory Function of the International Court in the League and U.N. Eras* (Baltimore: Johns Hopkins University Press, 1973, pp. 115-25.

18. U.N. Economic and Social Council, *Study of the Question of the Prevention and Punishment of the Crime of Genocide*, UN Doc. E/CN.4/Sub.2/416 (1978), Note 9, pp. 46-7. For interpretation of the 1969 Convention itself, see Sir Ian Sinclair, *The Vienna Convention on the Law of Treaties* (Manchester: Manchester University Press, [2nd edition] 1984).

19. U.N. Secretariat, *Multilateral Treaties Deposited with the Secretary-General: (Status as of 31 December 1989*, St/Leg/Ser. E/8, 1990, Note 2, pp. 102-4. Also see Jonathan Leich, "Contemporary Practice of the United States Relating to International Law," *American Journal of International Law*, No. 82, 1988, pp. 337-40.

20. LeBlanc, *op. cit.*, pp. 7-8.

21. International Court of Justice, *Advisory Opinions and Orders*, "Reservations to the Convention on Prevention and Punishment of the Crime of Genocide," 1951, pp. 15-69.

22. According to Section 701, the United States is bound by the international customary law of human rights (p. 153). In Section 702, genocide is recognized as a violation of customary international human rights law (pp. 161-3).

23. The text of the U.N. Charter may be found in Ian Brownlie, ed., *Basic Documents on Human Rights* (Oxford: Clarendon Press, 1981).

24. Quincy Wright, "The Law of the Nuremberg Trial," in Jay W. Baird, ed., *From Nuremberg to My Lai*

(Lexington, MA: D.C. Heath and Company, 1972, p. 37).

25. An exhaustive analysis of the decisively central role played by the United States in creating what became known as "Nuremberg Doctrine" may be found in Bradley F. Smith, *The Road to Nuremberg* (New York: Basic Books, 1981).

26. Henry L. Stimson, "The Nuremberg Trial, Landmark in Law," *Foreign Affairs*, Vol. XXV, January 1947, pp. 179-89. Also see U.N. War Crimes Commission, *History of the United Nations War Crimes Commission and the Development of the Laws of War* (London: His Majesty's Stationery Office, 1948).

27. Quoted in Smith, *op. cit.*, p. 241.

28. For the official interpretation of the extent of the U.S. role in this connection, Robert H. Jackson, *Report of Robert H. Jackson, United States Representative to the International Conference on Military Trials, London, 1945* (Washington, D.C.: Department of State Publication 3080, U.S. Government Printing Office, 1949; the text of the Charter is included therein). The London Charter assumed the force of international law by virtue of its endorsement and subsequent ratification by twenty-three nations pursuant to the London Conference.

29. See Eugene C. Gerhart, *America's Advocate: Robert H. Jackson* (Indianapolis: Bobbs-Merrill Publishers, 1958) and Francis Biddle, *In Brief Authority* (New York: Alfred A. Knopf Publishers, 1962).

30. For a thorough examination of the structure of U.S. participation during the trial, see Bradley F. Smith, *Reaching Judgment at Nuremberg* (New York: Basic Books, 1977).

31. For the German arguments in this regard, see International Military Tribunal, *Trial of the Major War Criminals before the International Military Tribunal*, 42 Vols., (Blue Series), Nuremberg, 1949, Vol. 1,

168-70, 458-94.

32. Justice Jackson's opening remarks are contained in International Military Tribunal, *Trial of the Major War Criminals before the International Military Tribunal*, 42 Vols., (Blue Series), Nuremberg, 1949, Vol. 2, pp. 98-155.

33. It should be noted that the same principles pertain to the prosecution of major Japanese criminals following World War II. See Arnold C. Brackman, *The Other Nuremberg: The Untold Story of the Tokyo War Crimes Trials* (New York: Quill/William Morrow Publishers, 1987) and Philip Piccagallo, *The Japanese on Trial* (Austin: University of Texas Press, 1979). Also see Jarritus Wolfinger, *Preliminary Inventory of the Record of the International Military Tribunal for the Far East* (Washington, D.C.: National Archives and Record Service Doc. No. PI 180/RG 238, General Services Administration, n.d.).

34. LeBlanc, *op. cit.*, p. 55.

35. In October 1985, President Ronald Reagan withdrew a 1946 U.S. declaration accepting ICJ jurisdiction in all matters of "international dispute." The withdrawal took effect in April 1986. This was in response to the ICJ determination in *Nicaragua v. United States*, the first substantive case ever brought before it to which the U.S. was a party. The ICJ ruled the U.S. action of mining Nicaraguan harbors in times of peace to be unlawful. The Reagan Administration formally rejected the authority of the ICJ to decide the matter (but removed the mines). It is undoubtedly significant that the Reagan instrument contained a clause accepting continued ICJ jurisdiction over matters pertaining to "international commercial relationships," thus attempting to convert the world court into a mechanism for mere trade arbitration. See *U.S. Terminates Acceptance of ICJ Compulsory Jurisdiction* (Washington, D.C.: Department of State

Bulletin No. 86, January 1986).

36. One such statute, on the books in Boulder, Colorado, for example, makes it a felonious offense to engage in verbal assault containing racial epithets such as "nigger."

37. There was actually a series of "Nuremberg Tribunals" conducted from 1945-49, beginning with the trial of the nazi leadership, in which we are most interested here. For summaries of the others, including those of the German industrialists and judiciary, nazi doctors, etc., see John Alan Appleman, *Military Tribunals and International Crimes* (Greenwood, CT: Greenwood Press, 1954).

38. As Smith puts it (*Reaching Judgment at Nuremberg, op. cit.*, p. 192), "The American prosecution spent endless hours asserting...that Rosenberg's theoretical writings had been significant in the nazi rise to power and that his work in education had played a vital role in preparing German youth for [the crimes which were to follow]." For further detail, see International Military Tribunal, *Trial of the Major War Criminals before the International Military Tribunal* (Blue Series), Nuremberg, 1949, Vols. 4-5.

39. The quote is from Smith, *Reaching Judgment at Nuremberg, op. cit.*, p. 236. At p. 233, Smith observes that "[Von Schirach's prewar] position required him to perform two main tasks: to undermine and finally eliminate all independent youth groups, and to gather the overwhelming majority of young Germans into the Hitler Youth and related organizations, where they could receive massive doses of nazi indoctrination....The [American] prosecution made a vigorous effort to Hitler's general plans by stressing the importance the Führer attached to the indoctrination of youth and by showing that the...ideological training that [von] Schirach had provided in the Hitler Youth fitted in with the nazi 'blueprint' for aggression." For

further detail, see the relevant portions of International Military Tribunal, *Trial of the Major War Criminals before the International Military Tribunal* (Blue Series).

40. The description of Streicher's place (or lack of it) within the nazi hierarchy is taken from a defendant memorandum prepared by staff member Robert Stewart for Justice Jackson during the summer of 1946. It is quoted in Smith, *Reaching Judgment at Nuremberg, op. cit.,* p. 200. At p. 201, Smith observes that Streicher was charged only as an "anti-Semitic agitator," and that the "core of the case against [him] came down to a question of whether he had advocated and encouraged extermination of the Jews while knowing, or having reason to believe, that such extermination was the settled policy of the nazi government." For further detail, see the relevant portions of International Military Tribunal, *Trial of the Major War Criminals before the International Military Tribunal* (Blue Series).

41. Quoted in Smith, *Reaching Judgment at Nuremberg, op. cit.,* p. 47.

42. John Gimble, *The American Occupation of Germany* (Stanford, CA: Stanford University Press, 1968). Also see John J. McCloy, "The Present Order of German Government" (Washington, D.C.: *Department of State Bulletin,* June 11, 1951), and General Lucius D. Clay, "The Present State of Denazification, 1950," in Constantine Fitzgibbon, ed., *Denazification* (New York: W.W. Norton Publishers, 1969). These proscriptions were, under U.S. "tutelage," built into the constitution and statutory code of the German Republic during the early 1950s as an expedient to "attaining true democracy." Surely, this performance bespeaks something of an official posture of the United States with regard to "First Amendment Guarantees" where celebration/advocacy/incitement

of genocide is concerned.

43. A survey of opinion pieces from *Time* and *Newsweek* magazines, June through August 1991, will abundantly illustrate this point.

44. See Samuel Eliot Morison, ed. and trans., *Journals and Other Documents on the Life and Voyages of Christopher Columbus* (New York: Heritage Publishers, 1963).

45. The letter of appointment to these positions, signed by Ferdinand and Isabella, and dated May 28, 1493, is quoted in full in Benjamin Keen, trans., *The Life of the Admiral Christopher Columbus by His Son Ferdinand* (New Brunswick, NJ: Rutgers University Press, 1959, pp. 105-6).

46. The best sources on Columbus's policies are Troy Floyd, *The Columbus Dynasty in the Caribbean, 1492-1526* (Albuquerque: University of New Mexico Press, 1973) and Stuart B. Schwartz, *The Iberian Mediterranean and Atlantic Traditions in the Formation of Columbus as a Colonizer* (Minneapolis: University of Minnesota Press, 1986).

47. Regarding the eight million figure, see Sherburn F. Cook and Woodrow Borah, *Essays in Population History, Vol. I* (Berkeley: University of California Press, 1971, esp. Chap. VI). The 3 million figure pertaining to the year 1496 derives from a survey conducted by Bartolomé de las Casas in that year, covered in J.B. Thatcher, *Christopher Columbus, Vol. 2* (New York: Putnam's Sons Publishers, 1903-1904, pp. 348ff).

48. For summaries of the Spanish census records, see Lewis Hanke, *The Spanish Struggle for Justice in the Conquest of America* (Philadelphia: University of Pennsylvania Press, 1947, pp. 200ff). Also see Salvador de Madariaga, *The Rise of the Spanish American Empire* (London: Hollis and Carter Publishers, 1947).

49. For aggregate estimates of the precontact indigenous population of the Caribbean Basin, see William Denevan, ed., *The Native Population of the Americas in 1492* (Madison: University of Wisconsin Press, 1976), Henry F. Dobyns, *Their Numbers Become Thinned: Native American Population Dynamics in Eastern North America* (Knoxville: University of Tennessee Press, 1983) and Russell Thornton, *American Indian Holocaust and Survival: A Population History Since 1492* (Norman: University of Oklahoma Press, 1987). For additional information, see Dobyns's bibliographic *Native American Historical Demography* (Bloomington/Indianapolis: University of Indiana Press, 1976).

50. These figures are utilized in numerous studies. One of the more immediately accessible is Leo Kuper, *Genocide: Its Political Use in the Twentieth Century* (New Haven, CT: Yale University Press, 1981).

51. See Henry F. Dobyns, "Estimating American Aboriginal Population: An Appraisal of Techniques with a New Hemispheric Estimate," *Current Anthropology*, No. VII, 1966, pp. 395-416.

52. An overall pursuit of this theme will be found in P.M. Ashburn, *The Ranks of Death* (New York: Coward Publishers, 1947). Also see John Duffy, *Epidemics in Colonial America* (Baton Rouge: Louisiana State University Press, 1953). Broader and more sophisticated articulations of the same idea are embodied in Alfred W. Crosby, Jr.,*The Columbian Exchange: Biological and Cultural Consequences of 1492* (Westport, CT: Greenwood Press, 1972) and *Ecological Imperialism: The Biological Expansion of Europe, 900-1900* (Melbourne: Cambridge University Press, 1986).

53. *Reaching Judgment at Nuremberg, op. cit.*

54. See Tzvetan Todorov, *The Conquest of America* (New York: Harper and Row Publishers, 1984).

55. Kirkpatrick Sale, *The Conquest of Paradise: Christopher Columbus and the Columbian Legacy* (New York: Alfred A. Knopf Publishers, 1990, p. 155).

56. Far from the "revisionist historian" he was described as being in the July 15, 1991 edition of *Newsweek*, las Casas was the *first* historian of the New World. There was no one for him to revise. Consequently, those who seek to counter or deny his accounts— "mainstream" historians all—are the actual revisionists seeking to maintain a "politically correct interpretation" of events.

57. Bartolomé de las Casas, *The Spanish Colonie* (*Brevísima relación*), University Microfilms reprint, 1966.

58. Bartolomé de las Casas, *Historia de las Indias, Vol. 3*, (Mexico City: Fondo de Cultura Económica, 1951; esp. Chap. 29).

59. Las Casas, quoted in Thatcher, *op. cit.*, pp. 348ff.

60. For instance, quoting an affidavit by SS *Obergruppenführer* Otto Ohlendorf: "The Einsatz [killing] unit would enter a village or town and order the prominent Jewish citizens to call together all Jews....Then they were shot, kneeling or standing, by firing squads in a military manner." See William Shirer, *The Rise and Fall of the Third Reich: A History of Nazi Germany* (New York: Simon and Schuster Publishers, 1960, p. 959).

61. Todorov, *op. cit.*

62. See Charles Gibson, ed., *The Spanish Tradition in America* (New York: Harper and Row Publishers, 1968).

63. For detailed examination of the conceptual linkages and differentiations between Spanish and English practices in the New World, see Williams, *op. cit.*

64. The estimate of Pequot casualties—most of them women, children, and old people—accrues from a conservative source. See Robert M. Utley and

Wilcomb E. Washburn, *Indian Wars* (Boston: Houghton Mifflin Publishers, 1977, p. 42).

65. E. Wagner and Allen E. Stearn, *The Effects of Smallpox on the Destiny of the Amerindian* (Boston: Bruce Humphries, Inc., 1945, pp. 44-5).

66. *Ibid.*

67. Sherburn F. Cook, "The Significance of Disease in the Extinction of the New England Indians," *Human Biology*, No. 45, 1973, pp. 485-508.

68. The Fort Clark incident is covered in Thornton, *op. cit.*, pp. 94-6.

69. Donald E. Green, *The Politics of Indian Removal: Creek Government and Society in Crisis* (Lincoln: University of Nebraska Press, 1977).

70. Russell Thornton, "Cherokee Population Losses During the Trail of Tears: A New Perspective and a New Estimate," *Ethnohistory*, No. 31, 1984, pp. 289-300.

71. *Ibid.*, p. 293. Also see Grant Foreman, *Indian Removal: The Immigration of the Five Civilized Tribes* (Norman: University of Oklahoma Press, 1953).

72. Perhaps the very clearest articulation of the conceptual and practical linkages between nazi performance in eastern Europe and the prototypical U.S. Indian Removal policy may be found in a lengthy memorandum prepared by Colonel Friedrich Hossbach to record the content of a Führer Conference conducted on November 5, 1937; the relevant portion is contained in *Trial of the Major War Criminals before the International Military Tribunal, op. cit.*, pp. 386-PS, 25:402 ff.

73. This too played directly into the nazi formulation of *Lebensraumpolitik*. See Frank Parella's M.A. thesis, *Lebensraum and Manifest Destiny: A Comparative Study in the Justification of Expansionism* (Washington, D.C.: Georgetown University, 1950).

74. David Svaldi, *Sand Creek and the Rhetoric of Extermination: A Case-Study in Indian-White Relations* (Washington, D.C.: University Press of America, 1989). The comparisons to nazi rhetoric are obvious.

75. Reginald S. Horsman, *Race and Manifest Destiny: The Origins of Racial Anglo-Saxonism* (Cambridge, MA: Harvard University Press, 1981). Also see Richard Drinnon, *Facing West: The Metaphysics of Indian Hating and Empire Building* (New York: Schocken Books, [2nd edition] 1990).

76. Lenore Stiffarm and Phil Lane, Jr., "The Demography of Native North America: A Question of American Indian Survival," in M. Annette Jaimes, ed., *The State of Native America: Genocide, Colonization, and Resistance* (Boston: South End Press, 1992, p. 34).

77. Lawrence C. Kelly, *Navajo Roundup* (Boulder, CO: Pruett Publishing, 1970). Also see Roberto Mario Salmón, "The Disease Complaint at Bosque Redondo (1864-1868)," *The Indian Historian*, No. 9, 1976.

78. W.W. Newcome, Jr., *The Indians of Texas* (Austin: University of Texas Press, 1961, p. 334).

79. James M. Mooney, "Population," in Frederick W. Dodge, ed., *Handbook of the Indians North of Mexico, Vol. 2* (Washington, D.C.: Bureau of American Ethnology Bulletin No. 30, Smithsonian Institution, 1910, pp. 286-7).

80. *American Indian Holocaust and Survival, op. cit.*, p. 107. Also see Robert F. Heizer, ed., *The Destruction of the California Indians* (Salt Lake City/Santa Barbara: Peregrine Smith Publishers, 1974).

81. U.S. Bureau of the Census, *Fifteenth Census of the United States, 1930: The Indian Population of the United States and Alaska* (Washington, D.C.: U.S. Government Printing Office, 1937, p. 3; Table II: "Indian Population by Divisions and States, 1890-1930").

82. The official record of the cumulative reductions in native land base leading to this general result may be found in Charles C. Royce, *Indian Land Cessions in the United States: 18th Annual Report, 1896-1897* (Washington, D.C.: Smithsonian Institution, 1899). An additional 100 million acres were also being expropriated under provision of the 1887 General Allotment Act (ch. 341, 24 *Stat.* 362, 365, now codified at 25 U.S.C. 331 *et seq.*), even as Royce completed his study; this left Indians with about 50 million acres total, or approximately 2.5 percent of their original land base. On allotment, see Janet A. McDonnell, *The Dispossession of the American Indian, 1887-1934* (Bloomington/Indianapolis: Indiana University Press, 1991).

83. James M. Mooney, *The Aboriginal Population of America North of Mexico* (Washington, D.C.: Smithsonian Miscellaneous Collections, LXXX, No. 7, 1928, p. 33). For a more contemporary assessment of the situation in Canada, see Davis and Zannis, *op. cit.*

84. On the boarding school system, see Jorgé Noriega, "American Indian Education in the United States: Indoctrination for Subordination to Colonialism," in Jaimes, *op. cit.*, pp. 371-402.

85. On adoption policies, see Tillie Blackbear, "American Indian Children: Foster Care and Adoptions," in Office of Educational Research and Development, National Institute of Education, *Conference on Educational and Occupational Needs of American Indian Women, October 1976* (Washington, D.C.: U.S. Department of Education, 1980, pp. 185-210). "Blind" adoptions are those in which the court orders adoption records permanently sealed in order that the person adopted can never know the identity of his/her parents or cultural heritage.

86. The goals of U.S. Assimilation Policy were summed

up by Indian Commissioner Francis Leupp as "a mighty pulverizing engine for breaking up [the last vestiges of] the tribal mass"; see his *The Indian and His Problem* (New York: Charles Scribner's Sons, 1910, p. 93). Superintendent of Indian Education Daniel Dorcester described the objectives of his office as being to "develop the type of school that would destroy tribal ways"; quoted in Evelyn C. Adams, *American Indian Education: Government Schools and Economic Programs* (New York: King's Crown Press, 1946, p. 70). See generally, Henry E. Fritz, *The Movement for Indian Assimilation, 1860-1890* (Philadelphia: University of Pennsylvania Press, 1963), and Francis Paul Prucha, ed., *Americanizing the American Indian: Writings by the "Friends of the Indian," 1880-1890* (Cambridge, MA: Harvard University Press, 1973).

87. Brint Dillingham, "Indian Women and IHS Sterilization Practice," *American Indian Journal*, Vol. 3, No. 1, January 1977, pp. 27-8. Also see Janet Larson, "And Then There Were None: IHS Sterilization Practice," *Christian Century*, No. 94, January 26, 1976; and Bill Wagner, "Lo, the Poor and Sterilized Indian," *America*, No. 136, January 29, 1977. It should be noted that the government has conducted a comparable program against Puerto Rican and, to a somewhat lesser extent, African-American women. See *Women Under Attack: Abortion, Sterilization Abuse, and Reproductive Freedom* (New York: Committee for Abortion Rights and Against Sterilization Abuse, 1979).

88. U.S. Bureau of the Census, *1980 Census of the Population, Supplementary Report: American Indian Areas and Alaska Native Villages* (Washington, D.C.: U.S. Government Printing Office, 1984).

89. See Joseph G. Jorgenson, ed., *American Indians and Energy Development II* (Cambridge, MA: Anthropology

Resource Center/Seventh Generation Fund, 1984).

90. These data derive from several sources, among them U.S. Senate, Committee on Labor and Human Resources, Subcommittee on Employment and Productivity, *Guaranteed Job Opportunity Act: Hearing on S. 777* (Washington, D.C.: 100th Cong., 1st Sess., U.S. Government Printing Office, 1980); U.S. Congress, Office of Technology Assessment, *Indian Health Care* (Washington, D.C.: U.S. Government Printing Office, 1986; Ser. No. OTA-H-290); and U.S. Department of Health and Human Services, *Chart Series Book* (Washington, D.C.: Public Health Service Rep. No. HE20.9409.988, 1988). Also see *Conference on Educational and Occupational Needs of American Indian Women, op. cit.*

91. Ward Churchill and Winona LaDuke, "Native America: The Political Economy of Radioactive Colonization," in Jaimes, *op. cit.*, pp. 241-66.

92. Jerry Kammer, *The Second Long Walk: The Navajo-Hopi Land Dispute* (Albuquerque: University of New Mexico Press, 1980). Also see Anita Parlow, *Cry, Sacred Ground: Big Mountain, USA* (Washington, D.C.: Christic Institute, Washington, D.C., 1988).

93. M.C. Barry, *The Alaska Pipeline: The Politics of Oil and Native Land Claims* (Bloomington/ Indianapolis: Indiana University Press, 1975).

94. See Michael Garitty, "The U.S. Colonial Empire is as Near as the Nearest Reservation," in Holly Sklar, ed., *Trilateralism: The Trilateral Commission and Elite Planning for World Management* (Boston: South End Press, 1980, pp. 238-68).

95. As the Los Alamos Scientific Laboratory put it in its February 1978 *Mini-Report:* "Perhaps the solution to the radon emission problem is to zone the land into uranium mining and milling districts so as to forbid human habitation."

96. Russell Means, "The Same Old Song," in Ward Churchill, ed., *Marxism and Native Americans* (Boston: South End Press, 1983, p. 25).

97. The 1887 "standard" was "one-half or more degree of Indian blood." This was subsequently lowered to one-quarter for "educational" purposes at the end of World War I (Act of May 25, 1918; 40 *Stat. L.* 564). On the origins of the Relocation Program and its effects of scattering Indians among the non-Indian population, see Donald L. Fixico, *Termination and Relocation: Federal Indian Policy, 1945-1960* (Albuquerque: University of New Mexico Press, 1986). The term "statistical extermination" comes from M. Annette Jaimes, "Federal Indian Identification Policy," in Jaimes, *op. cit.*, p. 137.

98. Patricia Nelson Limerick, *The Legacy of Conquest: The Unbroken Past of the American West* (New York: W.W. Norton Publishers, 1987, p. 338).

99. See, for example, Richard Arens, ed., *Genocide in Paraguay* (Philadelphia: Temple University Press, 1976). Also see John Hemming, *Red Gold: The Conquest of the Brazilian Indians* (London: Macmillan Publishers, 1978) and Rigoberta Menchú, *I, Rigoberta Menchú: An Indian Woman in Guatemala* (London/New York: Verso Press, 1984).

100. Letter to the editor, *Rocky Mountain News*, October 13, 1991.

101. This contention is readily borne out in a video tape prepared by University of Colorado media student Lori Windle, submitted as evidence in the present case.

102. See, for example, Justice Jackson's remarks in the trial in Smith, *Reaching Judgment at Nuremberg*, *op. cit.*, quoted throughout. Another U.S. prosecutor at Nuremberg, Telford Taylor, also takes up the issue in his book, *Nuremberg and Vietnam: An American Tragedy* (New York: Quadrangle Books, 1970).

103. Consider, for example, the instruction of Judge Paul F. Larrazolo to the jury at the end of the 1968 trial of participants in the celebrated "Tierra Amarilla Courthouse Raid," in New Mexico: "[A]nyone, including a state police officer, who intentionally interferes with a citizen's arrest does so at his own peril., since the arresting citizens are entitled under the law to use whatever force is reasonably necessary to effect said citizen's arrest and to use whatever force is necessary to defend themsellves in the process of making said citizen's arrest." The defendants had shot a state trooper in the chest when he attempted to prevent them from arresting a state's attorney they felt was violating their rights. The jury acquitted them of all charges. Quoted in Peter Nabakov, *Tijerina and the Courthouse Raid* (Albuquerque: University of New Mexico Press, 1969, p. 246).

104. For instance, U.S. diplomat Ben Whitaker, Rapporteur of a 1985 U.N. study on implementation of the Genocide Convention, notes that this principle was "not new at [the Nuremberg] trial," and "was perfectly familiar in national legal systems [including that of the United States]." Consequently, "the doctrine was...not one invented de novo by the victors at Nuremberg," and there is "little doubt that courts today would hold that the concept of individual responsibility will override any defense of superior orders"; U.N. Economic and Social Council, Revised and Updated Report on the Question of the Prevention and Punishment of the Crime of Genocide Prepared by Mr. B. Whitaker, 25-26 UN Doc. E/CN.4/Sub.2/1985/6 (1985), p. 24.

105. This position is articulated quite well in John Duffett, ed., *Against the Crime of Silence: Proceedings of the International War Crimes Tribunal* (New York: Clarion Books, 1970).

106. Whitaker, *op. cit.*, p. 26.

Let's Spread the "Fun" Around

The Issue of Sports Team Names and Mascots

If people are genuinely interested in honoring
Indians, try getting your government to live up
to the more than 400 treaties it signed with our
nations. Try respecting our religious freedom
which has been repeatedly denied in federal
courts. Try stopping the ongoing theft of Indian
water and other natural resources. Try reversing
your colonial process that relegates us to the
most impoverished, polluted, and desperate
conditions in this country....Try understanding
that the mascot issue is only the tip of a very
huge problem of continuing racism against
American Indians. Then maybe your ["honors"]
will mean something. Until then, it's just so
much superficial, hypocritical puffery. People
should remember that an honor isn't born when
it parts the honorer's lips, it is born when it is
accepted in the honoree's ear.

—Glenn T. Morris
Colorado AIM

During the past couple of seasons, there has
been an increasing wave of controversy regarding
the names of professional sports teams like the
Atlanta "Braves," Cleveland "Indians," Washington

"Redskins," and Kansas City "Chiefs." The issue extends to the names of college teams like Florida State University "Seminoles," University of Illinois "Fighting Illini," and so on, right on down to high school outfits like the Lamar (Colorado) "Savages." Also involved have been team adoption of "mascots," replete with feathers, buckskins, beads, spears, and "warpaint" (some fans have opted to adorn themselves in the same fashion), and nifty little "pep" gestures like the "Indian Chant" and "Tomahawk Chop."

A substantial number of American Indians have protested that use of native names, images, and symbols as sports team mascots and the like is, by definition, a virulently racist practice. Given the historical relationship between Indians and non-Indians during what has been called the "Conquest of America," American Indian Movement leader (and American Indian Anti-Defamation Council founder) Russell Means has compared the practice to contemporary Germans naming their soccer teams the "Jews," "Hebrews," and "Yids," while adorning their uniforms with grotesque caricatures of Jewish faces taken from the nazis' antisemitic propaganda of the 1930s. Numerous demonstrations have occurred in conjunction with games—most notably during the November 15, 1992, match-up between the Chiefs and Redskins in Kansas City—by angry Indians and their supporters.

In response, a number of players—especially African-Americans and other minority athletes—have been trotted out by professional team owners like Ted Turner, as well as university and public school officials, to announce that they mean not to insult, but instead to "honor," native people. They have been joined by the television networks and most major newspapers, all of which have editorialized that Indian discomfort with the situation is "no big deal," insisting that the whole thing is just "good, clean fun." The country needs more such fun, they've argued, and "a few disgruntled Native Americans" have no right to undermine the nation's enjoyment of its leisure time by complaining. This is especially the case, some have contended, "in hard times like these." It has even been contended that Indian outrage at being systematically degraded—rather than the degradation itself—creates "a serious barrier to the sort of intergroup communication so necessary in a multicultural society such as ours."

Okay, let's communicate. We may be frankly dubious that those advancing such positions really believe in their own rhetoric, but, just for the sake of argument, let's accept the premise that they are sincere. If what they are saying is true in any way at all, then isn't it time we spread such "inoffensiveness" and "good cheer" around among *all* groups so that *everybody* can participate *equally* in fostering the round of national laughs they call for? Sure it is—the country can't have too *much* fun or "intergroup involvement"—so the more, the merrier. Simple consistency demands that anyone who thinks the Tomahawk Chop is a swell pastime must be just as hearty in their endorsement of the following ideas, which—by the "logic" used to defend the defamation of American Indians—should help us all *really* start yukking it up.

First, as a counterpart to the Redskins, we need

an NFL team called "Niggers" to "honor" Afroamerica. Halftime festivities for fans might include a simulated stewing of the opposing coach in a large pot while players and cheerleaders dance around it, garbed in leopard skins and wearing fake bones in their noses. This concept obviously goes along with the kind of gaiety attending the Chop, but also with the actions of the Kansas City Chiefs, whose team members—prominently including black team members—lately appeared on a poster looking "fierce" and "savage" by way of wearing Indian regalia. Just a bit of harmless "morale boosting," says the Chiefs' front office. You bet.

So that the newly-formed "Niggers" sports club won't end up too out of sync while expressing the "spirit" and "identity" of Afroamericans in the above fashion, a baseball franchise—let's call this one the "Sambos"—should be formed. How about a basket-ball team called the "Spearchuckers"? A hockey team called the "Jungle Bunnies"? Maybe the "essence" of these teams could be depicted by images of tiny black faces adorned with huge pairs of lips. The players could appear on TV every week or so gnawing on chicken legs and spitting water-melon seeds at one another. Catchy, eh? Well, there's "nothing to be upset about," according to those who love wearing "war bonnets" to the Super Bowl or having "Chief Illiniwik" dance around the sports arenas of Urbana, Illinois.

And why stop there? There are plenty of other groups to include. "Hispanics"? They can be "repre-sented" by the Galveston "Greasers" and San Diego "Spics," at least until the Wisconsin "Wetbacks" and Baltimore "Beaners" get off the ground. Asian

Let's Spread the "Fun" Around

Americans? How about the "Slopes," "Dinks," "Gooks," and "Zipperheads"? Owners of the latter teams might get their logo ideas from editorial page cartoons printed in the nation's newspapers during World War II: slant-eyes, buck teeth, big glasses, but nothing racially insulting or derogatory, according to the editors and artists involved at the time. Indeed, this Second World War-vintage stuff can be seen as just another barrel of laughs, at least by what current editors say are their "local standards" concerning American Indians.

Let's see. Who's been left out? Teams like the Kansas City "Kikes," Hanover "Honkies," San Leandro "Shylocks," Daytona "Dagos," and Pittsburgh "Polacks" will fill a certain social void among white folk. Have a religious belief? Let's all go for the gusto and gear up the Milwaukee "Mackerel Snappers" and Hollywood "Holy Rollers." The Fighting Irish of Notre Dame can be rechristened the "Drunken Irish" or "Papist Pigs." Issues of gender and sexual preference can be addressed through creation of teams like the St. Louis "Sluts," Boston "Bimbos," Detroit "Dykes," and the Fresno "Faggots." How about the Gainesville "Gimps" and Richmond "Retards," so the physically and mentally impaired won't be excluded from our fun and games?

Now, don't go getting "overly sensitive" out there. *None* of this is demeaning or insulting, at least not when it's being done to Indians. Just ask the folks who are doing it, or their apologists like Andy Rooney in the national media. They'll tell you—as in fact they *have* been telling you—that there's been no harm done, regardless of what their victims think, feel, or say. The situation is exactly the same as when those with precisely the same mentality used to insist that Step'n'Fetchit was okay, or Rochester on the *Jack Benny Show*, or Amos and Andy, Charlie Chan, the Frito Bandito, or any of the other cutesey symbols making up the lexicon of American racism. Have we communicated yet?

Let's get just a little bit real here. The notion of "fun" embodied in rituals like the Tomahawk Chop must be understood for what it is. There's not a single non-Indian example deployed above which can be considered socially acceptable in even the most marginal sense. The reasons are obvious enough. So why is it different where American Indians are concerned? One can only conclude that, in contrast to the other groups at issue, Indians are (falsely) perceived as being too few, and therefore too weak, to defend themselves effectively against racist and otherwise offensive behavior. The sensibilities of those who take pleasure in things like the Chop are thus akin to those of schoolyard bullies and those twisted individuals who like to torture cats. At another level, their perspectives have much in common with those manifested more literally—and therefore more honestly—by groups like the nazis, aryan nations, and ku klux klan. Those who suggest this is "okay" should be treated accordingly by anyone who opposes nazism and comparable belief systems.

Fortunately, there are a few glimmers of hope that this may become the case. A few teams and their fans have gotten the message and have responded appropriately. One illustration is Stanford University, which opted to drop the name "Indians" with regard to its sports teams (and, con-

Let's Spread the "Fun" Around

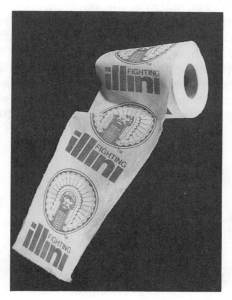

trary to the myth perpetrated by those who enjoy insulting Native Americans, Stanford has experienced *no* resulting drop-off in attendance at its games). Meanwhile, the local newspaper in Portland, Oregon, recently decided its long-standing editorial policy prohibiting use of racial epithets should include derogatory sports team names. The Redskins, for instance, are now simply referred to as being "the Washington team," and will continue to be described in this way until the franchise adopts an inoffensive moniker (newspaper sales in Portland have suffered no decline as a result).

Such examples are to be applauded and encouraged. They stand as figurative beacons in the night, proving beyond all doubt that it is quite possible to indulge in the pleasure of athletics without accepting blatant racism into the bargain. The extent to which they do not represent the norm of American attitudes and behavior is exactly the extent to which America remains afflicted with an ugly reality which is far different from the noble and enlightened "moral leadership" it professes to show the world. Clearly, the United States has a very long way to go before it measures up to such an image of itself.

In the Matter of Julius Streicher

Applying Nuremberg Precedents in the United States

On October 16, 1946, a man named Julius Streicher mounted the gallows. Moments later he was dead, the sentence of an international tribunal comprised of representatives of the United States, France, Great Britain, and the Soviet Union having been imposed. Streicher's body was cremated, and—so horrendous were his crimes thought to have been—his ashes dumped into an unspecified German river so that "no one should ever know a particular place to go for reasons of mourning his memory."[1]

Julius Streicher was convicted at Nuremberg, Germany, of what were termed "Crimes Against Humanity."[2] The lead prosecutor in his case—Justice Robert Jackson of the United States Supreme Court—did not argue that the defendant had killed anyone, nor that he had committed any especially violent act. Nor was it contended that Streicher held any particularly important position in the German government during the period when the "Third Reich" exterminated 6,000,000 Jews, as well as several million Gypsies, Poles, Slavs, homosexuals, and other *untermenschen* ("subhumans").[3]

Indeed, the sole offense for which the accused was ordered put to death was having served as publisher/editor of a Bavarian tabloid entitled *Der Stürmer* during the early-to-mid-1930s, years before the nazi genocide actually began. In this capacity, he had penned a long series of virulently anti-semitic editorials and "news" stories, usually accompanied by cartoons and images graphically depicting Jews in an extraordinarily derogatory fashion.[4] This, the prosecution asserted, had done much to "dehumanize" the Jews in the mind of the German public. Such dehumanization had made it possible—or at least easier—for average Germans to later indulge in the outright liquidation of Jewish "vermin." The tribunal agreed, holding that Streicher was therefore complicit in genocide and deserved death by hanging.[5]

During the trial, Justice Jackson observed that, in implementing its sentences, the participating powers were morally and legally binding themselves to adhere forever after to the same standards of conduct being applied to Streicher and other nazi leaders. In the alternative, he said, the victorious allies would be committing "pure murder" at Nuremburg—no different in substance from that committed by those they presumed to judge—rather than establishing the "permanent benchmark of justice" which was intended.[6] U.S. Secretary of War Henry L. Stimson publicly concurred, asserting in the pages of *Foreign Affairs* that "a standard has been raised to which Americans, at least, must repair; for it is only as this standard is accepted, supported, and enforced that we can move onward to a world of law and peace."[7]

Yet in the United States of Robert Jackson and Henry Stimson, the indigenous American Indian population had already been reduced, in a process which is ongoing to this day, from 12.5 to fifteen million in the year 1500 to fewer than 250,000 by the beginning of the twentieth century.[8] This was accomplished, according to both official and unofficial sources, "largely through the cruelty of [Euroamerican] settlers," and a sometimes informal but nonetheless clear and consistent governmental policy which made it an articulated goal to "exterminate these red vermin," or at least whole segments of them.[9]

Official bounties had been placed on the scalps of Indians—*any* Indians— in places as diverse as Georgia, Kentucky, Texas, the Dakotas, Oregon, and California. They remained in effect until resident Indian populations were decimated or disappeared. Entire peoples such as the Cherokee were reduced by half through a policy of forced removal from their homelands east of the Mississippi River to less preferable areas in the West. Others, such as the Navajo, while concentrated under military guard, suffered much the same fate. The United States Army and cooperating militias perpetrated wholesale massacres of native people at places like Fallen Timbers, Horseshoe Bend, Bear River, Sand Creek, the Washita River, the Marias River, Camp Robinson and Wounded Knee Creek.[10]

Through it all, hundreds of dime novels—each competing with the next to make Indians appear more grotesque, menacing, and inhuman—were sold in the tens of millions of copies.[11] Plainly, the

Euroamerican public was being conditioned to see Indians in such a way as to allow their eradication to continue. And continue it did until the "Manifest Destiny" of the U.S.—a direct precursor to what Adolf Hitler would subsequently call *Lebensraumpolitik* ("the politics of living space")—was consummated.[12]

By 1900, the national project of "clearing" Native Americans from their land and replacing them with "superior" Anglo-American settlers was complete. The indigenous population had been reduced by as much as 98 percent. Approximately 97.5 percent of their original territory had "passed" to the invaders.[13] The survivors were concentrated, out of sight and mind of the public, on scattered "reservations," all of them under the self-assigned "plenary" (full) power of the federal government.[14] There was, of course, no tribunal comparable to that at Nuremberg passing judgement on those who had created such circumstances in North America. No U.S. official or private citizen was ever imprisoned— never mind hanged—for implementing or propagandizing what had been done. Nor had the process of genocide against Indians been completed. Instead, it merely changed form.

Between the 1880s and the 1980s, more than half of all American Indian children were coercively transferred from their own families, communities, and cultures to those of the conquering society. This was done through compulsory attendance at remote boarding schools, often hundreds of miles from their homes. Native children were kept for years and systematically "deculturated": indoctrinated to think and act in the manner of Euroamericans rather than as Indians.[15] It was also accomplished through a pervasive foster home and adoption program—including "blind" adoptions, where children would be permanently denied information about their origins—placing native youth in non-Indian homes.[16]

The express purpose of all this was to facilitate a U.S. governmental policy to bring about the "assimilation" (dissolution) of indigenous societies. In other words, Indian cultures *as such* were to be caused to disappear.[17] Such policy objectives are in direct violation of the second article of the United Nations 1948 Convention on Punishment and Prevention of the Crime of Genocide—an element of international law arising from the Nuremberg proceedings—under which the forced "transfer of the children" of a targeted "racial, ethnical, national, or religious group" is explicitly prohibited as a genocidal activity.

Article II of the Genocide Convention also expressly prohibits involuntary sterilization as a means of "preventing births among" a targeted population. Yet, in 1976, it was conceded by the U.S. government that its "Indian Health Service" (IHS), then a subpart of the Bureau of Indian Affairs (BIA), was even then conducting a secret program of involuntary sterilization which had affected approximately forty percent of all Indian women of childbearing age.[18] The program was allegedly discontinued, and the IHS was transferred to the Public Health Service, but *no one was punished*. Hence, business as usual has continued in the "health" sphere: in 1990, for example, it came out that the IHS was inoculating Inuit children in Alaska with Hepatitis-B vaccine. The vaccine had already been banned by the World Health Organization as having a demonstrated correlation with the HIV-virus which is itself correlated to AIDS. As this is being written, a "field test" of Hepatitis-A vaccine, also HIV-correlated, is being conducted on Indian reservations in the northern Plains region.[19]

The Genocide Convention makes it a Crime Against Humanity to create conditions leading to the destruction of an identifiable human group. Yet the BIA has utilized the government's plenary prerogatives to negotiate mineral leases "on behalf of" Indian peoples paying a fraction of standard royalty rates for their natural resources. The result has been "super profits" for a number of preferred U.S. corporations.[20] Meanwhile, Indians, whose reservations ironically turned out to be in some of the most mineral-rich areas of North America, a matter which makes us the nominally *wealthiest* segment of the continent's population, live in dire poverty.

By the government's own data in the mid-1980s, Indians received the lowest annual and lifetime per capita incomes of any aggregate population group in the United States. Concomitantly, we suffer the highest rate of infant mortality, death by exposure and malnutrition, plague disease, and the like. Under such circumstances, alcoholism and other escapist forms of substance abuse are endemic in the Indian community. This situation leads both to a general physical debilitation of the population and a catastrophic accident rate. Teen suicide among Indians is several times the national average. The average life expectancy of a reservation-based Native American man is less than 45 years; women can expect to live less than three years longer.[21] This, in a country where average life-expectancy exceeds 70 years.

Such itemizations could be continued at great length, including matters like the radioactive contamination of large portions of contemporary Indian Country, the forced relocation of traditional Navajos to make way for massive coal stripping operations around Big Mountain (Arizona), and so on.[22] But the point should be made: Genocide, as defined in "black letter" international law, is a persistent fact of day-to-day life—and death—for North America's native peoples. Yet there has been (and is) only the barest flicker of public concern about, or even consciousness of, this reality. Serious expression of public outrage is absent. No one is punished and the process continues.

A salient reason for public acquiescence to the ongoing holocaust in Native North America has been a continuation of the dime novel legacy, often through more effective media. Since 1925, Hollywood has released more than 2,000 films, many of them rerun frequently on television, portraying Indians as strange, perverted, ridiculous, and often very dangerous *things of the past*.[23] We are habitually presented to mass audiences in a one-dimensional manner, devoid of recognizable human motivations and emotions, thoroughly and systematically dehumanized. Temporally, we have been consigned to another dimension entirely, drifting as myths through the vast panorama of Americana.

Nor is this the extent of it. Everywhere, we are used as logos, as mascots, as jokes: "Big Chief" writing tablets, "Red Man" chewing tobacco, "Winnebago" campers, "Navajo" and "Cherokee" and

Cartoon image of a Jew,
Der Stermer, 1933.

Cleveland Indians Baseball Team
logo 1993.

"Pontiac" and "Cadillac" pickups and automobiles. There are the Cleveland "Indians," the Kansas City "Chiefs," the Atlanta "Braves," and the Washington "Redskins" professional sports teams—not to mention those in thousands of colleges, high schools, and elementary schools across the country—each with their own degrading caricatures and parodies of Indians and/or things Indian. Pop fiction continues in the same vein. There is an apparently unending stream of "New Age" manuals purporting to expose the "inner workings" of indigenous spirituality in everything from pseudo-philosophical to do-it-yourself-kind styles. Blond yuppies from Beverly Hills amble about the country purporting to be reincarnated seventeenth-century Cheyenne "shamans" ready to perform previously secret ceremonies for a fee.

A concerted, sustained, and in some ways accelerating effort has gone into making Indians unreal. It follows, therefore, that what has happened, is happening, and will *continue* to happen to Indians unless something is done to fundamentally alter the terms of our existence, is also unreal. And the unreal, of course, is purely a matter of entertainment in Euroamerican society, *not* a cause for attention or concern. As was established in the Streicher precedent at Nuremberg, the cause and effect relationship between racist propaganda on the one hand and genocidal policy implementation on the other is quite plain.

It is thus of obvious importance that the American public—plain, average, everyday U.S. citizens—begin to *think* about the implications of such things the next time they witness a swarm of face-painted and war-bonneted buffoons doing the "tom-ahawk chop" at a baseball or football game. It is necessary that they *think* about the implications of the grade-school teacher adorning their child in turkey feathers to commemorate Thanksgiving. *Think* about the significance of John Wayne or Charlton Heston killing a dozen "savages" with a single bullet the next time a western come on TV *Think* about why Land-o-Lakes finds it appropriate to market its butter through use of a stereotyped image of an "Indian Princess" on the wrapper. *Think* about what it means when non-Indian academics profess—as they often do—to "know more about Indians than Indians do themselves." *Think* about the significance of charlatans like Carlos Castaneda and Jamake Highwater and Mary Summer Rain and Lynn Andrews churning out "Indian" bestsellers, one after the other, while Indians typically can't get into print.

Think about the *real* situation of American Indians. *Think* about Julius Streicher. Remember Justice Jackson's admonition. *Understand* that the treatment of Indians in American popular culture is *not* "cute" or "amusing" or some sort of "good, clean fun." Know that it causes real pain and real suffering to real people. *Know* that it threatens our very survival. And *know* that this is just as much a Crime Against Humanity as anything the nazis ever did. It is likely that the indigenous people of the United States will never demand that those guilty of such criminal activity be punished for their deeds. But the least we have the right to expect—indeed, to *demand*—is that such practices finally be brought to a halt.

Notes

1. Probably the best biography of Streicher available in English is Randall L. Bytwerk, *Julius Streicher: The man who persuaded a nation to hate Jews* (New York: Dorset Press, 1983). Also see William Varga, *The Number One Nazi Jew Baiter* (New York: Carlton Press, 1981).

2. This was, at the time, a wholly new category of criminal behavior, the composition of which was devised mainly by legal theorists in the United States. For details on the evolution of the concept, see Bradley F. Smith, *The Road to Nuremberg* (New York: Basic Books, 1982). Also see Smith's *The American Road to Nuremberg: The Documentary Record, 1944-1945* (Stanford, CA: Hoover Institution Press, 1982).

3. Eugene Davidson, *The Trial of the Germans: Nuremberg, 1945-1946* (New York: Macmillan Publishers, 1966, pp. 39-58). Concerning Gypsies, Poles, Slavs, etc., see Michael Berenbaum, *A Mosaic of Victims: Non-Jews Persecuted and Murdered by the Nazis* (New York/London: New York University Press, 1990).

4. For specifics, see Office of United States Chief of Counsel for Prosecution of Axis Criminality, "Julius Streicher," *Nazi Conspiracy and Aggression, Vol. II* (Washington, D.C.: U.S. Government Printing Office, 1946, pp. 689-715).

5. See Klaus Kipphan, "Julius Streicher: Propagandist of the Holocaust," in Ralph Church and Klaus Kipphan, eds., *Juniata Studies: Peace, Justice and Conflict* (Huntington, PA: Juniata College, 1976). Also see George L. Mosse, *Toward the Final Solution* (New York: Howard Fertig Publisher, 1978).

6. In his opening statement to the tribunal on November 21, 1945, for instance, Jackson observed that "while this law is first applied against German aggressors...if it is to serve any useful purpose it

must condemn aggression by any other nations, including those which sit here now in judgement. We are able to do away with domestic tyranny and violence and aggression...only when we make all men answerable to the law"; Jay W. Baird, ed., *From Nuremberg to My Lai* (Lexington, MA: D.C. Heath and Co., 1972, p. 28). For further elaboration, see Robert H. Jackson, *The Nürnberg Case* (New York: Alfred A. Knopf Publishers, 1947).

7.   Henry L. Stimson, "The Nuremberg Trial: Landmark in Law," *Foreign Affairs*, January 1947, pp. 179-89.

8.   According to the U.S. Bureau of the Census, the actual count was 237, 196; see "Table II: Indian Population by Divisions and States, 1890-1930," *Fifteenth Census of the United States, 1930: The Indian Population of the United States and Alaska* (Washington, D.C.: U.S. Government Printing Office, 1937, p. 3). On preinvasion population levels, see Lenore A. Stiffarm and Phil Lane, Jr., "The Demography of Native North America: A Question of American Indian Survival," in M. Annette Jaimes, ed., *The State of Native America: Genocide, Colonization, and Resistance* (Boston: South End Press, 1992, pp. 23-53).

9.   The first quotation comes from James M. Mooney, "Population," in Frederick W. Dodge, ed., *Handbook of the Indians North of Mexico, Vol. 2* (Washington, D.C.: Bureau of Ethnology, Bulletin No. 30, Smithsonian Institution, 1910, pp. 286-7). Concerning the second quotation, see David Svaldi, *Sand Creek and the Rhetoric of Extermination: A Case Study in Indian-White Relations* (Lanham, MD: University Press of America, 1989).

10.   For a comprehensive overview of such processes on a hemispheric as well as U.S.-specific basis, see David E. Stannard, *American Holocaust: Columbus and the Conquest of the New World* (London/New York:

Oxford University Press, 1992). Also see M. Annette Jaimes, "Sand Creek: The Morning After," in *The State of Native America, op. cit.*, pp. 1-12.

11. Robert F. Berkhofer, Jr., *The White Man's Indian: Images of the American Indian from Columbus to the Present* (New York: Vintage Books, 1978). Also see Merle Curti, "Dime Novels and the American Tradition," *Yale Review*, No. XXVI, June 1937, pp. 761-78.

12. "Neither Spain nor Britain should be the models of German expansion, but the Nordics of North America, who had ruthlessly pushed aside an inferior race to win for themselves soil and territory for the future. To undertake this essential task, sometimes difficult, always cruel—this was Hitler's version of the White Man's Burden"; Norman Rich, *Hitler's War Aims: Ideology, the Nazi State, and the Course of Expansion* (New York: W.W. Norton & Co., 1973, p. 8). For an early and detailed examination of the conceptual and practical relationship between nazi and U.S. expansionism, see Frank Parella's M.A. thesis in political science, *Lebensraum and Manifest Destiny* (Washington, D.C.: Georgetown University, 1950).

13. After an exhaustive review of the record over a period of thirty years, the federal government's Indian Claims Commission officially estimated the original holdings of indigenous peoples within the United States to have been a little over two billion acres, of which approximately fifty million remain nominally under Indian control at present; Indian Claims Commission, *Final Report* (Washington, D.C.: U.S. Government Printing Office, 1978).

14. For analysis, see Charles Harvey, "Constitutional Law: Congressional Plenary Power Over Indian Affairs—A Doctrine Rooted in Prejudice," *American Indian Law Review*, No. 10, 1982, pp. 117-50.

15. U.S. Senate, Committee on Labor and Public Welfare,

Indian Education: A National Tragedy—A National Challenge (Washington, D.C.: 91st Cong., 1st Sess. [Report No. 95-501], U.S. Government Printing Office, 1969).

16. Tillie Walker Blackbear, "American Indian Children: Foster Care and Adoptions," in U.S. Department of Education, Office of Educational Research and Development, National Institute of Education, *Conference on Educational and Occupational Needs of American Indian Women* (Washington, D.C.: U.S. Government Printing Office, 1980, pp. 185-210).

17. The classic articulation of assimilation policy may be found in the words of Indian Commissioner Francis E. Leupp, in his *The Indian and His Problem* (New York: Charles Scribner's Sons, 1910; reprinted by Arno Press, New York, 1971, p. 93); in Leupp's view, it was a "mighty pulverizing engine for breaking up the tribal mass." For a detailed examination of the context of Leupp's sentiments, see Henry E. Fritz, *The Movement for Indian Assimilation, 1860-1890* (Philadelphia: University of Pennsylvania Press, 1963).

18. Brint Dillingham, "Indian Women and IHS Sterilization Practices," *American Indian Journal*, Vol. 3, No. 1, 1977, pp. 27-8.

19. Andrea Smith, "The HIV-Correlation to Hepatitis-A and B Vaccines," *WARN Newsletter* (Chicago: Women of All Red Nations, Summer 1992).

20. An excellent and succinct explanation of how this works may be found in Michael Garitty, "The U.S. Colonial Empire is as Close as the Nearest Reservation," in Holly Sklar, ed., *Trilateralism: The Trilateral Commission and Elite Planning for World Management.* (Boston: South End Press, 1980, pp. 236-68).

21. U.S. Bureau of the Census, Population Division, *A Statistical Profile of American Indian Population*

(Washington, D.C.: U.S. Government Printing Office, 1984); U.S. Department of Health and Human Services, *Chart Series Book* (Washington, D.C.: Public Health Service Report No. HE20.9409.988, 1988).

22. See the author's "Radioactive Colonization: Hidden Holocaust in Native North America," and "Genocide in Arizona? The 'Navajo-Hopi Land Dispute' in Perspective," in his *Struggle for the Land: Indigenous Resistance to Genocide, Ecocide and Expropriation in Contemporary North America* (Monroe, ME: Common Courage Press, 1992, pp. 143-96, 261-328).

23. Ralph and Natasha Friar, *The Only Good Indian...: The Hollywood Gospel* (New York: Drama Book Specialists, 1972). Also see Dan Georgakas, "They Have Not Spoken: American Indians in Film" (*Film Quarterly*, No. XXV, Spring 1972, pp. 26-32) and John A. Price, "The Stereotyping of North American Indians in Motion Pictures" (*Ethnohistory*, No. XX, Spring 1973, pp. 153-71).

Nobody's Pet Poodle

Jimmie Durham: An Artist for Native North America

> I've known Jimmie Durham for more than twenty years. He's personally never been anything but stone Indian the whole time, and I mean that in the fullest possible way. He's never done anything but good for Indian people. Anybody who wants to mess with Jimmie better be ready to talk to me. And I mean *that* too.
>
> —Russell Means, 1990

I have a vision—a recurrent hallucination, if you will—of an installation summing up the state of contemporary "American Indian art." It is of a life-sized plastic Indian man, seated in a director's chair and outfitted in the high Santa Fe style: abundant turquoise, fur and leather, genuine piñon-scented aftershave or cologne, fashionably long but neatly razor-cut black hair, a blanket-vest over an open-necked silk shirt, his medicine bag filled with cocaine, a $5,000 antique concho belt and Gucci loafers. Sometimes he wears a Billy-Jack hat. Altogether, looks like something of a combination of Rudy Gorman and Earl Biss, but thinner, sleeker, a bit firmer of jaw. In one hand, he holds a collection of sable artist's brushes, in the other a wad of hundred dollar bills. Tattooed in blue on his left buttock is the inscription "Government Inspected, U.S. Department of Interior Certified Grade-A Prime

89

Meat." Suspended from a genuine platinum Charles Loloma chain around his neck is a small laminated card reading "Federal Certificate of Degree of Indian Blood."

In my mind, the plastic Indian is flanked by a pair of stuffed poodles. Perhaps they are Afghan hounds. From chains around their necks, both dogs also sport *their* pedigree papers. Arrayed behind this triad is another, a row of rather shadowy and mysterious human forms. They are standing, heads bowed, representing, each in turn, certain other peoples who have been officially defined in accordance with eugenics codes during the present century. Around each of their necks is a noose of the coarsest hemp rope from which hangs a small spot-lit plaque. One bears a yellow Star-of-David symbol and reads "Jude." It was presented to the figure who wears it by the Ministry of Racial Purity of the Third Reich in 1936. The next, printed by South Africa's apartheid government in 1980 reads, with utter simplicity, "Colored." The third, more complex in design, offers its message in three languages. All translate as "Palestinian." It was issued in Israeli-occupied Gaza in 1991.

The plastic Indian in the foreground seems totally unaware of those standing behind him, whether human or canine. He may be conscious of them, but chooses to ignore their presence. He seems utterly resolute about focusing his attention elsewhere. After all, he has his money in hand and senses there is more to be had. Perhaps he will use some of it to buy another bracelet or some baskets from one of the old Pueblo women eking out a living down on the plaza. Or maybe the chump change will go for purchase of a bumper-sticker reading, "Indian and Proud." Who knows? Compensating for a sense of all-pervasive guilt—of downright psychological and spiritual *filthiness*—induced by selling out can be a very tricky business. And, make no mistake about it, the "Indian" in my installation knows, just like those he reflects in real life, deep down, where it counts most...he *knows* he's guilty. He *knows* he's sold his ass for a song. And he *knows* he's pandered his people, all of their heritage and whatever future they might have, for even less. Still, compulsively, he continues to wag his tail and lick the feet of whatever white patron comes before him.

Arithmetical Genocide

There is a basis to this idea which haunts me. It is called, in the sort of Orwellian turn of phrase so characteristic of colonizing bureaucracies, an "Act to Promote Development of Indian Arts and Crafts." Drafted by then-Representative (now Senator) Ben Nighthorse Campbell of Colorado in combination with Hawai'i Senator Daniel Inouye's Select Committee on Indian Affairs, the law, Public Law 101-644 (104 Stat. 4662), was signed into effect by George Bush on November 29, 1990.[1] P.L. 101-644 makes it a crime punishable by up to $1 million in fines and up to *fifteen years* in federal prison for anyone not federally recognized as being a Native American to "offer to display for sale or to sell any good, with or without a Government trademark, which...suggests it is Indian produced." For galleries, museums, and other "private concerns" which might elect to market or display as "Indian arts and crafts" the work of any person not meeting the federal definition of "Indianness," a fine of up to $5 million is imposed.

The government "standard" involved—usually called "blood quantum" within the lexicon of "scientific" racism—is that a person can be an "American Indian artist" only if he or she is "certifiably" of "one-quarter or more degree of Indian blood by birth." Alternatively, the artist may be enrolled as a member of one or another of the federally-sanctioned Indian "tribes" currently existing within the U.S. These entities' membership rolls originated in the prevailing federal racial criteria of the late 19th century. The initial U.S. motive in quantifying the number of Indians by blood was to minimize the number of land parcels it would have to assign native people under provision of the 1887 Dawes Act, thereby freeing up about two-thirds of all reservation land for "homesteading" by non-Indians or conversion into U.S. park and forest land. Tribal rolls have typically been maintained in this reductionist fashion ever since, a matter which has served to keep federal expenditures in meeting the government's obligations —often deriving from treaty relationships with indigenous nations—at a very low level.

Obviously involved is what the Juaneño/Yaqui scholar M. Annette Jaimes calls "a sort of statistical extermination" whereby the government seeks not only to keep costs associated with its discharge of Indian Affairs at the lowest possible level, but to eventually resolve its "Indian problem" altogether.[2] The thinking is simple. As the historian Patricia Nelson Limerick frames it: "Set the blood quantum at one-quarter, hold to it as a rigid definition of

Indians, let intermarriage proceed as it has for centuries, and eventually Indians will be defined out of existence."[3] Bearing out the validity of Jaimes's and Limerick's observations is the fact that, in 1900, about half of all Indians in this country were "full-bloods." By 1990, the proportion had shrunk to about twenty percent, and is dropping steadily. Among certain populous peoples, such as the Chippewas of Minnesota and Wisconsin, only about five percent of all tribal members are full-bloods. A third of all recognized Indians are at the quarter-blood cut-off point. Cherokee demographer Russell Thornton estimates that, given continued imposition of purely racial definitions, Native America as a whole will have disappeared by the year 2080.[4]

Probably the first consequence of the 1990 "Indian Arts and Crafts Act" was closure of the Cherokee National Museum in Muskogee, Oklahoma, a day after its passage. It seems that the late Willard Stone, whose large wood sculpture "The Trail of Tears"—incorporated into the Great Seal of the Cherokee Nation—serves as the museum's centerpiece display, failed to meet federal standards for being Indian. Stone, long considered the preeminent wood-carver in modern Cherokee history, was probably a full-blood or close to it. But he never deigned to register himself as such. The Cherokees always accepted him as Cherokee, treated him as an integral and important part of the community, and that was all that was necessary for Willard Stone. Cherokee leader Wilma Mankiller says the current tribal government will do whatever is necessary, given Stone's stature, to convey formal membership upon him posthumously.[5]

INDIANS ARE US?

But what of the thousands of other, lesser-known but still living, individuals who fall into the same category of circumstance?[6] What of the 200-odd native peoples—the Abenakis of Vermont, for example, or the Lumbees and Coatan of North Carolina—who continue to exist, but who have always been denied federal recognition? What of groups such as the Juaneño of the San Diego area, who were once recognized by the government, but whose rolls were closed after they were unilaterally declared "extinct" as a matter of convenience by the Department of Interior during the 1970s?[7] These are questions of no small magnitude and import. All told, as Jack Forbes and others have pointed out, there are probably upwards of seven million persons in the United States today with a legitimate claim to being American Indian by descent, by culture, or both. The U.S. Bureau of the Census admits to only about 1.6 million.[8] What is at issue is arithmetical genocide, the diminishment and ultimate elimination of an entire human group by accounting procedures rather than outright physical liquidation.

The Identity Police

What is ugliest about the Indian Arts and Crafts Act is that it is being passed off as something demanded by native people themselves. Indeed, its most vocal and vociferous advocates have been—by some definition or another—"Indians."[9] Specifically, the prime movers have been a rather small clique of low-talent and no-talent individuals in the Santa Fe area calling themselves the "Native American Artists Association," gathered around an alleged Chippewa and maudlin primitivist named David Bradley.[10]

Mainly, they are devoted to production of what the Luiseño artist Fritz Scholder once called "Bambi painting,"[11] and together, the NAAA—or "Bradley Group," as it is more often called—generates a truly amazing volume of prints and canvases depicting themes centered in virtually every sentimental Indian stereotype from the dime novel version of Hiawatha to Lynn Andrews's notion of spirit women. Mostly, their work is rendered with pictorial clumsiness, in the harmoniously cloying pastel tonalities so sought after by interior designers specializing in the décor of Southwest motel rooms and bank lobbies. They are, in a word, one step removed from those who stock "starving artists' sales" advertised in television commercials from coast to coast.[12]

The Bradley Group, of course, insists its goals are worthy enough: To prevent non-Indian artists, primarily Euroamericans, from "ripping-off native culture" by pretending to be Indians for commercial purposes. The facts, however, tell another story, suggesting strongly that the group's motive has always been about personal profit and that their targets have usually been other Indians. At least there is no record of their ever having found and exposed a bona fide white man masquerading as an Indian in order to sell his work. Instead, they have labored mightily and viciously to negate the genuine heritage of as many self-identified—and, often, community-recognized—Indian competitors as possible. Their objective was and is to restrict as closely as possible the definition of who might be viewed as an Indian artist, and therefore the definition of Indian art itself, to themselves and their various products. Anyone wishing, for whatever reason, to purchase a definably Indian art object will, so the theory goes, be compelled to buy it from them. The results of such a definitional scam stand to be quite lucrative for anyone on the inside track.

The saga began along about 1980, when Bradley was unaccountably afforded an opportunity to show a few of his small Carlos Castaneda-oriented canvases in Santa Fe's prestigious Elaine Horowitch Gallery. His problem, as he saw it, was that his work was displayed in proximity to the far superior pieces of another Indian, Randy Lee White, a mixed-blood Lakota Sun Dancer who was at the time exploring the motifs developed by his people in 19th century ledger book drawings. White's work sold steadily and at increasingly high prices. Bradley's material, even priced at a discount, moved slowly when it moved at all. Bradley was, to say the least, envious of White and thus goaded, genuine inspiration seems to have struck him for what may be the first and only time in his life. If only Randy White could be forced out of the gallery, he reasoned, his own work would increase in sales, both in terms of volume and by way of "price per unit." Bradley quickly became a "political organizer," sparking a series of pickets and newspaper editorials, television interviews and meetings with the Santa Fe Chamber of Commerce. White, mortified that what had been a source of true pride and commitment on his part had become the point of such contention, stopped identifying as who he was (and is).[13] The Bradleys had scored their first victory.

Considerable irony, some of it delicious and some of it the reverse, may be found in the outcome of the "Bradley/White controversy." On the tasty side, Randy Lee White, relocated from New Mexico to Los Angeles, successfully continued his life and career, and is widely recognized as an important contemporary painter. For his part, David Bradley also left the Horowitch Gallery for a time, but for different reasons. His work continued to bomb—most serious collectors declining to acquire such hack painting, regardless of the "ethnic flavor" attached to it—even after he had managed to eliminate what he saw as his major competitor. Sometimes a kind of natural justice does prevail. Much less palatable is the loss to Native America of White's substantial painterly talent, a loss which is balanced against nothing at all. Actually, the exchange amounts to much worse than nothing when it is considered that the schmaltz Bradley applies to canvas is the ostensible replacement for White's work in signifying the quality of art Native America is capable of generating these days.

Meanwhile, the NAAA had already set out to "clean up Santa Fe" more generally, stopping in at local exhibitions to demand "proof" by way of federal documentation as to the genetic pedigrees of other Indians and threatening harassment in the event that "real" native work (their own) wasn't included in gallery inventories. Their position also evolved to hold that native people from south of the Río Grande—most of them with blood quanta discernibly higher than that of many members of the Bradley Group, but none of whom are endowed with federal credentials to that effect—shouldn't be classified as Indians. Even a full-blood and traditionally-cultured Yaqui, Maya, or Turahumara would be better categorized as "Hispanic," from the

Bradley point-of-view. This novel interpretation of reality was followed by a heated questioning of the "authenticity" of Indians from Canada.[14]

This persistent and entirely self-serving narrowing of the criteria of Indianness conformed quite well with the earlier-mentioned needs of federal policy-makers eager to dispense with governmental obligations to Indians once and for all. Consequently, the Bradleys were "noticed" by those inhabiting the corridors of power. Shortly, they were anointed as "expert consultants" on matters of native art and identity to Inouye's select committee, enjoying a degree of influence with their colonizers they doubtless never envisioned at the outset of their crusade to crush the competition.[15] Small wonder that P.L. 101-644 reads like a script the Bradleys themselves might have written. For all practical purposes, they did. And, in the process, their people have been harmed, perhaps irreparably, as is always the case when important voices are stilled. The Bradley Group has acted, figuratively at least, in precisely the same fashion as the hang-around-the-fort Indians who helped assassinate Crazy Horse and Sitting Bull a century ago.

The Indigenous Alternative

It's not that there are no Indians who understand the nature and dynamics of the colonizing and genocidal processes to which we are subjected. Nor is it true that no Indians retain the courage and integrity necessary to stand up and resist against tremendous odds, regardless of personal cost or consequence. Numerous recent (and in some instances, current) examples spring readily to mind:

Anna Mae Aquash, Leonard Peltier, Marie Leggo, Joe Stuntz Killsright, Tina Trudell, Buddy Lamont, Bob Robideau and Dino Butler, Janet McCloud, Pedro Bissonette, David So Happy, Eddie Hatcher, the elders at Big Mountain, Standing Deer, Byron DeSersa, and many more. They, not the David Bradleys of the world, are the gut and sinew of that which has meaning in contemporary Indian life. These people, not some self-appointed identity police currying federal favor, represent the future of Native America. This is true, if indeed there is to be any native future at all.

The common denominator, aside from their intrinsic and undeniable Indianness, binding these individuals together is that each has been a member or supporter of the American Indian Movement over the past two decades. AIM, as is well known, has from its inception been constantly engaged, not only in the struggle for the survival of Native America, but in a struggle to attain its national liberation. So consistent is this pattern that members of the movement have come to be referred to in some circles as "the shock troops of Indian sovereignty in North America."[16] The effort has been grueling, its psychological and material costs in terms of personal comfort and often life itself extraordinarily high. AIM has changed substantially over the years, and has sustained a multitude of casualties, yet it has managed not merely to continue itself, but to grow in both size and strength. Today it exists in some form or another in virtually every native community on the North American continent.

Active participation in, or open support of, such a movement requires a certain outlook, a set of values and sensibilities which are deeply cynical with regard to the mores of the Eurocentric status quo, stubbornly combative yet able to find a certain irreverent humor in even the grimmest of circumstances, a quiet sense of spiritual grounding coupled to a willingness and ability to absorb considerable measures of pain and privation. Perseverance in a movement of this kind also demands an inclination to rethink the world as it is experienced, seeing it in terms of how it should be rather than as it is, an abiding sense of the rightness and wrongness of things and, perhaps most of all, an unshakable belief that the most fundamental sorts of justice can eventually be made to prevail. In sum, AIM—at least in its better moments—has truly embodied the indigenous alternative to U.S. business as usual, a living and viable American Indian worldview.[17]

Clearly, it is impossible to project the American Indian Movement as Bambi, to elaborate the essence of Wounded Knee, 1973, or the 1975 Oglala Firefight, in gentle contours or soft pastels. This can be done no more than a strip mine or slag heap can be transformed into the sort of tranquil landscape required for incorporation into Bambi art.[18] The movement has always been real, not red, at least not the red favored by buyers come to wax genteel in the glitz and glitter of the Santa Fe sunshine. One could as well reduce the horrors of Auschwitz or Babi Yar to a comfortable living room accent as to make AIM's sense of postcontact native reality, past or present, fit into such a mold. It follows that whatever AIM may be taken to be can be understood as an absolute antithesis of all and everything the NAAA stands for. It follows that the Bradleys stand in diametrical opposition to all that remains really Indian in Native America today.

Jimmie Durham

A major difficulty has been that there has been no one to say what has needed saying in the mode of discourse the Bradleys have sought to claim as their own. Fragments of AIM conceptualization have emerged from time to time during the 1970s and '80s, mainly through the verse of Simon J. Ortiz and Wendy Rose, the songs of Floyd Westerman, and the poetry, accompanied by traditional or rock music, of John Trudell. Elements of it have also been elucidated in the nonfiction books of writers such as Vine Deloria, Jr., the novels of Leslie Marmon Silko, and the stand-up comedic performances of Charlie Hill. But little of note has been done in the arenas of plastic or performance arts. In large part, this has been because those involved in AIM have been all but overwhelmed with the day-to-day demands of surviving as activists beset by some of the most virulent repression in U.S. history. To a lesser extent, it has been because, whenever time and opportunity presented themselves, AIM people concluded there were more important pursuits to claim their attention. This has been a substantial error in judgement on the part of the movement. It has given the Bradleys veritable command, however temporary, of a crucially important sphere of popular communications.

Since the late '70s, an exception to the rule has been Jimmie Durham, a mixed-blood Cherokee from western Arkansas. He came early to AIM and stayed with it as a member of organizational security and chief liaison to a nation-wide network of non-Indians called the Native American Support Committee during the worst governmental violence. From there, he went on to almost single-handedly create the International Indian Treaty Council, the movement's diplomatic arm and first indigenous group accepted as a non-governmental consultative organization by the United Nations. In 1977, he organized the first hemispheric delegation of native representatives to the Palace of Nations in Geneva, Switzerland. This led to formation of the U.N. Working Group on Indigenous Populations and the drafting, in 1992, of an element of international law entitled the "Universal Declaration of the Rights of Indigenous Peoples." Although IITC eventually collapsed as a functional entity, years after Durham's departure from its directorship in the early '80s, he had by then succeeded in using it as a vehicle upon which to establish a crucial and ongoing and formal indigenous presence within the community of nations.[19]

Seeking a change of venue after his stint as IITC director, and plainly possessed of an inordinate ability to articulate meanings and motives in the most complex intercultural settings, Durham opted to redeploy his insights and experiences in the context of aesthetic rather than directly political expression. Still, his first preoccupation has remained that of expressing the sublime contradictions of "modern life" in ways that motivate his audience to become involved in progressive social change. From the outset of his artistic career, Durham has sought to strip away the intellectual veil obscuring the mechanics of the structure of social knowledge itself, compelling those with whom he interacted through his work to confront the inconsistency of even their most axiomatic "understandings" of social reality. The goal of this endeavor is, in the manner of semiotics and left deconstructionism, optimistically cerebral. What is intended is to induce a certain cognitive dissonance among participants with regard to sets of comfortably familiar assumptions about the meaning of things, societally speaking. Such dissonance generates a marked mental discomfort and compels participants, in order for psychic reconciliation to be attained, to engage in some degree of critical rethinking of their core values and beliefs. His method has been described as amounting to "a conscious and deliberate, but merciful and constructive, exercise in psychological terrorism" designed to "produce a positive disordering of the existing social consensus."[20]

Towards this end, he has relied heavily upon a much-polished craft facility in combination with a biting satirical wit and acute sense of irony. He also demonstrates an uncanny knack for accentuating the tensions inherent between various aspects of his work, and a complete disregard for what are normally considered to be "the rules of the game." His initial work was emphatically sculptural, and to a certain extent remains so, consisting mostly of the creation of objects, often painted, integrating traditional materials (bone, stones, hair and feathers, etc.) with aspects of modern contexts (such as steel, plastic, chrome, and glass) in which they presently find themselves. Juxtaposition of these objects as a means of examining their relationality and dialectical unity quickly assumed an increasing importance. Such investigations soon came to be enhanced by incorporation of found objects, drawings or script, and photographs into the whole. Inevitably, this experimental coding of aggregations of objects led to their deployment in comprehensive mixed-media installations. [21]

Contextualization of the installations themselves—at least some of which have evolved to function as both literal and metaphorical environments—has dictated an ever more direct and active role for the artist himself in the presentation of his art. Such involvement often assumes the form of the artist's symbolically acting out, either theatrically or in more concrete ways, behavioral and/or attitudinal conceptions integral to a completion of a given work's intent. At other times, or simultaneously, the integration of art and artist requires an accompaniment to the physical display, some form of narrative elaboration, either written or verbal, sometimes both. It was this last dimension of his more general project which caused publication of a tightly-orchestrated exposition of Durham's verse and prose vignettes in book form, as a 1983 volume entitled *Columbus Day*.[22] It has also prompted a decade-long series of essays and interviews published in journals such as *The Third Text* and *Artforum*, and collections like Annette Jaimes's *The State of Native America*.[23]

Throughout the 1980s, Durham was largely sustained by the warm reception accorded his work in settings relatively free of the dominating and rigidly maintained colonialist construction of what art by American Indians "is supposed to be" enforced in the United States. Ireland continues to serve as an admirable case in point. Meanwhile, there is some indication that the established "art world," both in New York and in the Southwest, went out of its way to ignore him. Suffice it to say that the form and content of what Durham has to offer—most especially his extension of the AIM sensibility into a wholly new and different communicative dimension—has hardly endeared him to the sources of order and authority, governmental or aesthetic, in North America. Hence, any broad appreciation on this continent of the substance and depth of Durham's efforts has been much slower in coming, a matter which did not really begin to change for the better until his prominent inclusion in critic Lucy Lippard's 1990 book, *Mixed Blessings*.[24]

An Artist for Native North America

The dawning awareness in the U.S. of what Jimmie Durham is about, and the increasingly favorable attention paid to what he does, has of course captured the notice of the Bradley Group. Undoubtedly, they are horrified at the situation, knowing as they must, and at the most primal of levels, that a single completed project of Durham's— let's take "Museum of the American Indian" as an example—will greatly outweigh in durability and importance the collective accumulation of kitsch and clichés they will likely produce in their lifetimes. They are not so void of intellect as to be unable to perceive the dimension of threat posed by his sheer existence, that his presence alone, by way of content and contrast, stands to negate the very shallowness and petty pretension they have embraced and sought to make synonymous with things

Indian. Naturally enough, they have responded to this menace in the only way open to them, not by meeting Durham's conceptual and aesthetic challenges, but by making him a primary target of the insidious smear tactics at which they excel.

Predictably, the Bradleys' approach has been to assert that Jimmie Durham, all evidence to the contrary notwithstanding, "isn't Indian" and is therefore "not credible or qualified to address Indian subject matters." Equally predictably, the only basis for these assertions is that he—like Willard Stone and countless others, the author of this essay included—has never officially enrolled at Cherokee. The accusers, since they already know the answer to be "yes," have carefully avoided questioning whether he would be enrollable, were he to decide for some reason to sign up. Less have they been willing to address the stated reason why Durham—as well as imprisoned AIM leader Leonard Peltier and many of the others most actively engaged in the struggle for Indian self-determination—have declined to participate in federally-sponsored tribal enrollment procedures. As Peltier has put it:

> This is not our way. We never determined who our people were through numbers and lists. These are the rules of our colonizers, imposed for the benefit of our colonizers at our expense. They are meant to divide and weaken us. I will not comply with them.[25]

Durham himself has responded by applying the principle—so abundantly evident in both his art and in the indigenous traditions which inform it—of placing things in their proper perspective through the use of ridicule. Consider the sardonic "Artist's

Disclaimer" with which he now accompanies his exhibitions:

> The U.S. Congress recently passed a law which states that American Indian artists and galleries which show their work must present government-authorized documentation of the artist's "Indian-ness." Personally, I do not much like Congress, and feel that they do not have American Indians' interests at heart. Nevertheless, to protect myself and the gallery from Congressional wrath, I here-by swear to the truth of the following statement: I am a full-blood contemporary artist, of the sub-group (or clan) called sculptors. I am not an American Indian, nor have I ever seen or sworn loyalty to India. I am not a Native "American," nor do I feel that "America" has any right to either name me or un-name me. I have previously stated that I should be considered a mixed-blood: that is, I claim to be a male but in fact only one of my parents was male.

In the end, there is an undeniable, if utterly unintended, dimension of appropriateness to the Bradleys' identification of this man as their primary adversary. It can be explained in a number of ways, but perhaps Marx's notion of "the negation of the negation" best serves our purposes here: Insofar as Durham and his work may be taken as signifying nothing so much as the negation of all the NAAA stands for, and because they in turn can only be construed as signifying an attempted final negation of all that is truly native in America, then Durham *must* be seen as representing affirmation of that which is most alive and promising for the future of Indian people in the United States. The Bradleys *have*, no matter how inadvertently, been entirely correct in their assessment of Jimmie Durham. He *is*, unquestionably, an artist of, by, and for his people. By any reasonable assessment, his is the preeminent artistic voice of contemporary Native North America.

Notes

1. Ben "Nightmare" Campbell, who thinks he "might be" of three-eighths Northern Cheyenne blood quantum by birth, fashioned himself a lucrative career as an American Indian artist long before he sought tribal enrollment as part of a budding political career. Although Northern Cheyenne enrollment rules require positive proof of lineage, and Campbell by his own admission cannot provide it, these were apparently waived as part of a deal to make him the only "certified Indian in the U.S. Congress." The record of tribal enrollments nationalyl is replete with comparable examples of individuals being gratuitously added to or subtracted from the rolls for reasons other than any sort of tangible Indianness. In any event, according to his own statutory criteria, Campbell made himself an appreciable fortune "ripping off Indian artists" before getting himself certified as "real."

2. M. Annette Jaimes, "Federal Indian Identification Policy: A Usurpation of Indigenous Sovereignty in North America," in Ward Churchill, ed., *Critical Issues in Native North America* (Copenhagen: International Work Group on Indigenous Affairs, 1989, pp. 15-36). Also see Jaimes's much more extensive dissertation on the topic, *American Indian Identification-Eligibility Policy in Federal Indian Education Service Programs* (Ann Arbor: University Microfilms International, Dissertation Information Service, 1990 [Order No. 9101887]).

3. Patricia Nelson Limerick, *The Legacy of Conquest:*

The Unbroken Past of the American West (New York: W.W. Norton Co., 1987, p. 338).

4. Russell Thornton, *American Indian Holocaust and Survival: A Population History Since 1492* (Norman: University of Oklahoma Press, 1987, pp. 174-82).

5. See Lyn Nichols, "New Indian Art Regulations Shut Down Muskogee Museum," *San Francisco Examiner*, December 3, 1990.

6. Take, for example, the case of Jeanne Walker Rorex, a direct lineal descendant of Willard Stone, who was recently barred from participating in the American Indian Heritage Exhibition at the Philbrook Museum in Tulsa (where she won awards during the 1980s). As even conservative—and usually anti-Indian—columnist James J. Kilpatrick has observed, although she is undeniably a Cherokee, "Ms. Rorex is not a tribal member. She probably could get herself certified, but as a matter of principle she has refused to petition the Cherokee council. Her point is that many true Indian artists cannot obtain certification under the act"; see Kirkpatrick's 1992 column "Government Playing the Indian Game," distributed in photocopied form by the Thomas Jefferson Center, Charlottesville, VA.

7. For enumeration and analysis of these groups, see American Indian Policy Review Commission, Task Force Ten, *Report on Terminated and Nonfederally Recognized Tribes* (Washington, D.C.: U.S. Government Printing Office, 1976).

8. Jack D. Forbes, "Undercounting Native Americans: The 1980 Census and the Manipulation of Racial Identity in the United States," *Wicazo Sa Review*, Vol. VI, No. 1, Spring 1990, pp. 2-26. More generally, see Noel P. Gist and Anthony G. Dworkin, *The Blending of Races: Marginality and Identity in World Perspective* (New York: Wiley-Interscience Books, 1972).

INDIANS ARE US?

9. A classic example of this is Suzan Shown Harjo, for-
    mer director of the National Congress of American
    Indians, and currently a vociferous advocate of
    enrollment in general and the Arts and Crafts Act in
    particular. Interestingly, Harjo herself is a redhead
    who has come to rely rather heavily upon Lady
    Clairol to alter her appearance. Given that she was
    unable to engineer her own inclusion on the
    Southern Cheyenne roll until she was in her 40s—
    and well established politically—she herself would
    seem guilty of having spent much of her adult life
    engaged in the "fraud," to quote from one of her
    recent speeches, of "misrepresenting herself as an
    Indian for professional reasons." This is at least true
    under the standard of "Indianness" she is now so
    avid to impose on others. Moreover, she still identi-
    fies herself as being Muskogee as well as Cheyenne,
    yet remains unenrolled—and unenrollable—in the
    former "tribe." Consistency is plainly not one of the
    attributes of those comprising the identity police.

10. Bradley's is, in its way, a tragic and all-too-typical
    contemporary Indian story. A person of obviously
    mixed ancestry himself—he habitually wears sun-
    glasses to hide his blue eyes—he was adopted by
    non-Indians at an early age and apparently was
    unaware of his own native identity until fairly late in
    life. Hence, contrary to insinuations made in his
    recent public utterances, he was neither raised on a
    Chippewa reservation in Minnesota nor in any sort of
    traditional manner. Throughout his adult life, he has
    in fact chosen to remain in Santa Fe, a great dis-
    tance away from the people of whom he now claims
    to be a part. Profit aside, then, his present pose as a
    "super-Indian" seems motivated more than anything
    by a deep-seated psychological need to compensate
    for the degree of alienation and cultural disorienta-
    tion inflicted upon him by the dominant society over
    the years; see his rambling, inaccurate, and pro-

110

foundly illogical attempt at self-justification distributed by NAAA as a mimeographed "Columbus
Quincentennial Newsletter Update" on the campus of
the Institute of American Indian Arts (Santa Fe, NM)
during the fall of 1992.

11. Scholder is quoted to this effect in the introduction
to Anonymous, *Scholder/Indians* (Flagstaff, AZ:
Northland Press, 1972). Also see similar comments
in the introduction to Clinton Adams, *Fritz Scholder:
Lithographs* (New York: New York Graphic Society,
1975). For a study of alternatives in the sense that
Scholder, at least, intended them—artists such as
T.C. Cannon, Robert Penn, and Juane Quick-to-See
Smith—see Robert Ashton, Jr., and Jozefa Stuart,
Images of American Indian Art (New York: Walker and
Co., 1977).

12. For an in-depth examination of Bambi Art, see J.J.
Brody, *Indian Painters, White Patrons* (Albuquerque:
University of New Mexico Press, 1971). Also see
Jamake Highwater (Jay Marks), *Many Smokes, Many
Moons: A Chronology of American Indian History
Through Indian Art* (Philadelphia: J.B. Lippincott
Publishers, 1978) and *The Sweetgrass Lives On: Fifty
Contemporary American Indian Artists* (New York:
Lippencott and Crowell Publishers, 1980).

13. This reconstruction comes from the recollections of
participants, including Randy Lee White, discussions
with whom occurred during his exhibitions at the
McLaren-Markowitz Gallery (Boulder, CO) in 1985
and 1986, and at the Boulder Art Center in 1992.

14. The upshot of this in 1990 legislative terms is that a
formal disclaimer must be posted in connection with
exhibitions of Indian art from north or south of the
U.S. borders. Art by Mexican Indians resident to the
U.S. is—according to NAAA—only properly displayed
under the label "Chicano" (witness the organization's
1991 attempts to impose this description upon

Phoenix-area artist El Zarco Guerrero, who turned out to be enrolled in a southern California Mission Band).

15. Bradleyites were the only individuals queried on matters of "Indian arts and crafts" among the "over 1,000 interviews, by telephone and in person," of "federal employees, tribal members and others in the private sector who deal with Indian tribes," conducted by the Inouye Committee. For the count, see U.S. Senate, Select Committee on Indian Affairs, Special Committee on Investigations, *Federal Government's Relationship with American Indians* (Washington, D.C.: U.S. Government Printing Office, 1989, p. 3).

16. The description comes from a talk given by Janet McCloud during the 10th Annual Wounded Knee Memorial, Manderson, SD, March 1983.

17. For the best single overview of AIM and its implications, see Peter Matthiessen, *In the Spirit of Crazy Horse* (New York: Viking Press, 1983).

18. The "real, not red" formulation accrues from Fritz Scholder's explanation of his own aspirations in approaching American Indian imagery. See Adams, *op. cit.*

19. Durham's international work is covered to some extent in Vine Deloria, Jr., *Behind the Trail of Broken Treaties: An Indian Declaration of Independence* (Austin: University of Texas Press [2nd edition], 1984).

20. See the videotaped 1990 interview with Durham by the author, available under the title *What Follows* from the School of Fine Arts, University of Colorado at Boulder.

21. A fine analysis of Durham's work may be found in Lucy Lippard, "Jimmie Durham: Postmodernist 'Savage'," *Art in America*, February 1993, pp. 62-68. Also see Lippard's and other essays in the exhibition catalogue *Jimmie Durham: The Bishop's Moose and*

the Pinkerton Men (New York: Exit Art, 1989).

22. Jimmie Durham, *Columbus Day* (Minneapolis: West End Press, 1983). Also see his *American Indian Culture: Traditionalism and Spiritualism in Revolutionary Struggle* (Chicago: photocopied booklet, n.d.).

23. See, as examples, Jimmie Durham, "Here at the Centre of the World" (*The Third Text: Third World Perspectives on Contemporary Art and Culture*, No. 5, Winter 1988-89, pp. 21-32); Jimmie Durham and Jean Fisher, "The ground has been covered" (*Art Forum*, Summer 1989, pp. 99-105); and Jimmie Durham, "Cowboys and... Notes on Art, Literature and American Indians in the Modern American Mind," in M. Annette Jaimes, ed., *The State of Native America: Genocide, Colonization and Resistance* (Boston: South End Press, 1991, pp. 423-38).

24. Lucy Lippard, *Mixed Blessings: New Art in Multicultural America* (New York: Pantheon Books, 1990). Durham's work is discussed at pp. 48, 97, 183, 199, 204, 208-11.

25. Statement by Leonard Peltier to Paulette D'Auteuil Robideau at Leavenworth Federal Prison, June 1991. It should be noted that in 1988-89 David Bradley is reputed to have actively attempted to block Peltier's inclusion in Santa Fe art exhibits on the basis that the latter was a "Chicano" misrepresenting himself as a "real" Indian.

And They Did It Like Dogs in the Dirt...

An American Indian Analysis of
Black Robe

As we learned from movies like *A Man Called Horse*, the more "accurate" and "authentic" a film is said to be, the more extravagant it is likely to be in at least some aspects of its misrepresentation of Indians...the more "even-handed" or even "sympathetic" a movie is supposed to be in its portrayal of Indians, the more demeaning it's likely to be in the end....the more "sophisticated" the treatment of Indians, the more dangerous it's likely to be.

—Vine Deloria, Jr.
1978

Perhaps the only honest way to begin a review of Bruce Beresford's new film, *Black Robe* (Alliance Communications, 1991), is to acknowledge that, as cinema, it is a truly magnificent achievement. Beginning with Brian Moore's adaptation of his own 1985 novel of the same title,[1] the Australian director of such earlier efforts as *Breaker Morant*, *The Fringe Dwellers*, *Driving Miss Daisy,* and *Mr. Johnson*, has forged yet another work of obvious beauty and artistic integrity, capturing a certain sense of his subject matter in ways which are not so much atmospheric as environmental in their nuance and intensity. In arriving at such an accomplishment, he has been assisted quite ably by cinematographer Peter James, whose camerawork in this instance genuinely earns the overworked accolade of "brilliant."[2] Tim Wellburn also excelled, attaining a nearly perfect editing balance of pace and continuity, carrying the viewer along through the movie's spare one hundred minutes even while instilling the illusion that things are stretching out, incorporating a scope and dimension which, upon reflection, one finds to have been entirely absent.[3] The score, a superbly understated ensemble created by Georges Delerue, works with subtle efficiency to bind the whole package together.

Set in 1634 in that portion of Canada then known as "New France" (now Quebec), *Black Robe* purports to utilize the context of the period's Jesuit missions as a lens through which to explore the complexities of Indian/White interactions during the formative phase of European colonialism in North America. The film is expressly intended to convey a bedrock impression that what is depicted therein is "the way it *really* was," and no pain has been spared to obtain this result. As the producers put it, "Finding locations that looked remote enough for the film, as well as a river that was wide enough to double as the St. Laurence, with no buildings or power lines in sight, was the job of Location Manager François Sylvester. [He] spent months flying up and down Quebec rivers until he found the perfect site on the banks of the Saguenay and Lac St. Jean."[4] Thereafter, cast and crew spent eleven weeks under rugged conditions in the Canadian north pursuing the desired effect.

> Rushes show the cast paddling canoes in icy water (Beresford fell in twice), dragging canoes on slippery, icy snow along the riverbanks, stumbling through the forest, trudging through the brush. This is neither glamorous nor comfortable. The landscape...is a mix of wide valleys and mountains; ice has choked some of the rivers into narrow channels, and the light is steely grey.... The look of the film [moves] from the amber of autumn to the grey/green of winter, with cold blues, and gradually moving into the contrast of black and white as the snow thickens. As Peter James sees it, the trees and rivers are as much characters as the people; they look brighter or bleaker, and they contribute to the mood.[5]

Similarly, Herbert Pinter's production design is authentic to the minutest detail: "Some people said to me, 'It's the 17th Century, so who's going to remember?', but that's not how I work. I'd say 99 per cent of what you see is accurate. We really did a lot of research. It's actually easier this way, because if you do your homework, you avoid silly mistakes."[6]

> Pinter fashioned rectangular shovels out of birch bark, used shoulder bones of a moose for another digging implement, bound stone axes with spruce roots, knitted ropes of fibre and used cedar bark (obtained free from a merchant in Vancouver, but costing $37,000 in transport) to build the outer walls of huts....In the Huron village scene at the end of the film, Pinter created a strikingly authentic little chapel, lit only by candles waxed onto stones that are wedged into the fork of stag antlers.[7]

INDIANS ARE US?

The many extras used to represent the indigenous peoples involved are actually Indians, many of
them Crees from villages located in the general area
of the shoot. Native languages are spoken throughout the movie, and the corresponding subtitles deployed do no particular damage to the content of the
dialogue. The construction of both the Mohawk and
Huron villages used as sets—each of which took
about six weeks to complete—are accurate right
down to the cloying smoke persistently drifting
about the interior of buildings, a standard means by
which Indians traditionally repelled insects. The
inside of a Mohawk longhouse is adorned with
scores of real rabbit and goose carcasses strung
from racks, many of them slowly dripping blood
which begins to coagulate as a scene wears on.

The entire stew was completed with the deployment of an astutely selected combination of veteran
and first-time actors. They are headed by Lothaire
Bluteau, noted for his lead role in *Jesus of Montréal*,
who plays Father LaForge, *Black Robe*'s fictionalized
protagonist. Bluteau also appears to have served as
something of a "team captain" among the cast. As
critic Andrew Urban observed after visiting the location of the work-in-progress:

> Bluteau is...the most dedicated actor I have ever
> seen on a set. Whether he is called or not, he is
> there, absorbing, watching—and discussing
> details with Beresford, or James. He wants to
> know every frame, and has a possessive view of
> the film....He wants to know, and to agree with,
> all the major creative decisions. He wants it to be
> a film he endorses.[8]

Bluteau's devotion to his craft is ably complemented by that of the prolific August Shellenberg, who plays Chomina, a major Indian character. Several of the Indians who garnered support roles—Billy Two Bulls, Lawrence Bayne, Harrison Liu, and Tantoo Cardinal among them—are also long-time professionals who brought their well-refined and not insignificant talents to bear. These seasoned pros appear to have established a momentum which allowed several cinematic novices to transcend themselves in the quality of their performances. This is particularly true of Adan Young, an eighteen-year-old Canadian-born actor picked up during a casual audition in Australia to play Daniel (the main European character behind LaForge), and Sandrine Holt, a seventeen-year-old Eurasian from Toronto who was cast as Annuka, the Indian female lead. All told, the competence in acting displayed throughout the film lends an essential weight and substance to the sheer technical acumen embodied in its production.

"More Than Just a Movie"

It should be noted that the production of *Black Robe* was made possible only by virtue of a formal treaty allowing for large-scale cinematic collaboration between Canadian and Australian concerns. As Robert Lantos, whose Alliance Entertainment is the largest production and independent distribution house in Canada, put it, "We pursued, lobbied and pressured both governments to get it signed and we got good co-operation from Canada's Department of Communication."[9] This allowed the project to be underwritten with a budget of $12 million (U.S.), the highest ever—by a margin of more than twenty percent—for a "Canadian" undertaking.[10]

Given the sort of deadly seriousness with which the making of *Black Robe* was approached by all concerned, it was predictable that it would be treated as something more than just another movie by analysts. Indeed, from the outset, the mainstream media have rushed to accept at face value the pronouncements of Australian producer Sue Milliken, that the film is meant as an important tool for the understanding of "[Canada's] social history,"[11] and Lantos, that, because *Black Robe* was intended to be at least as much a work of history as of art, no attempt had been made to "tamper with its heart, its honesty."[12] Some papers have even gone so far as to enlist the services of professional historians to assess the picture on the basis of its historiography rather than its aesthetics.[13] Where this has not been the case, film critics themselves have postured as if they were suddenly possessed of an all-encompassing and scholarly historical competence.

Jay Scott of the *Toronto Globe and Mail*, for instance, immediately hailed *Black Robe* as an "honest, historically sound film," because it is handled with an appropriately "journalistic rather than moralistic...tone."[14] He then proceeded—while simply ignoring facts as obvious as that the Cree verbiage uttered throughout the flick was *not* the language spoken by *any* of the Indians to whom it is attributed—to offer his readers the sweeping assertion that the epic's "[sole] historical departure" is that "the actors playing the French characters... speak English."[15] Scott is joined in applauding the "evenhandedness" with which *Black Robe* unfolds by reviewers like Caryn James of the *New York*

Times, who concludes that it "pulls off a nearly impossible trick, combining high drama with high ideas."[16] James, in turn, is reinforced by Vincent Canby, also of the *Times*, who observes that, more than anything, Beresford's work is marked by its "historical authenticity."[17] The *New Yorker*, in its "Current Cinema" section, sums up the view of the status quo by proclaiming the film to be "a triumph" of unbiased cinematic presentation of history.[18]

Nor have reviewers writing for such periodicals been especially shy about what has motivated their praise. James, for example, is unequivocal in her contention that *Black Robe* stands as a useful and necessary counterbalance against what she describes as a wave of "Columbus bashing"—by which she means the assignment of some degree of tangible responsibility to Europeans and Euroamericans for their conduct during the conquest and colonization of the Americas over the past five centuries—currently sweeping the continent. The primary strength of Beresford's exposition, she argues, is that it presents an interpretation of early European colonialist thinking and behavior that embodies "no evil intentions." While one is free to disagree with or regret it in retrospect, one is compelled to acknowledge that, because they were "sincere," the colonists "must be respected for [their] motives" in perpetrating genocide, both cultural and physical, against American Indians.[19] Left conspicuously unmentioned in such formulations, of course, is the proposition that with only a minor shift in the frame-of-reference the same "logic" might be applied with equal validity to the nazis and their implementation of *Lebensraumpolitik* during the 1940s.

INDIANS ARE US?

Such use of *Black Robe* as a device in an establishmentarian drive to sanitize and rehabilitate the European heritage in America has been coupled directly to a similar effort to keep Indians "in their place" in the popular imagination. This has mainly assumed the form of juxtaposing Beresford's portrait of Native North America to that developed by Kevin Costner in *Dances With Wolves*, a movie which abandoned many of Euroamerica's most cherished falsehoods concerning how people lived their lives before the coming of the white man. *Washington Post* reporter Paul Valentine, to name one prominent example, took Costner to task in the most vituperative possible fashion for having presented what he called a "romantic view of Native Americans"[20] which lacked, among other things, reference to the following invented "facts":

> It is well documented, for example, that [Indians] stampeded herds of bison into death traps by igniting uncontrolled grass fires on the prairies....For many years afterward, animals could not find food in such burned-over areas, and starvation would finish the destruction [of buffalo herds]....Nomadic hunters and gatherers moved from spot to spot seeking food, strewing refuse in their wake....Women [were used to haul] the clumsy two-stick travois used to transport a family's belongings on the nomadic seasonal treks....[Indians] practiced....cannibalism.[21]

"*Black Robe* is no over-decorated, pumped-up boy's adventure yarn like *Dances With Wolves*," as Canby put it.[22] The *New Yorker* comments admiringly on the "straightforward, unromanticized...anthropological detachment" with which

Indians are portrayed by Beresford.[23] Scott goes even further, contending that the film is not so much a story about the onset of the European invasion as it is a true "exploration of North American aboriginal history" itself.[24] Having thus equipped his audience with the "inside scoop" on traditional Indian realities, Beresford can, as *Variety* put it, "lead us into unknown territory, and keep on pushing us further and further on, until, by the end, we find ourselves deep in the wilderness of the seventeenth-century consciousness."[25] There, we find, not good guys or bad guys, not right or wrong, but rather "well-meaning but ultimately devastating" European invaders doing various things to a native population which, through its own imperfections and "mystical" obstinacy, participates fully in bringing its eventual fate upon itself.[26]

It's just "one of those things," over which nobody had any genuine control, a "tragedy," no more. No one actually *did* anything to anyone, at least not with any discernible sense of malice. No one is culpable, there is no one to blame. Even at the level of cultural presumption, it's six of one, half-a-dozen of the other. The entire process was as natural, inevitable, and free of human responsibility, as glaciation. Or an earthquake. As James sums up, her own infatuation with *Black Robe* derives precisely from its accomplishment, through the most popular of all media, of the most desirable objective assigned to "responsible" historiography in contemporary North American society: Spin Control. In effect, Beresford successfully rationalizes the past in such a way as to let her, and everyone like her, off the hook; "[He] criticizes cultural imperialism," she says with evident satisfaction, "without creating villains."[27]

No Villains?

James's smug accolade is, to be sure, partly true. But it is at least equally false. What she really means is that *Black Robe* contains no *white* villains, and that this is what counts in her ever so "balanced" scheme of things. The handling of the indigenous victims of Europe's "cultural imperialism" is another matter entirely. The first whiff of this comes fairly early in the movie, when Father LaForge recalls a meeting in France with an earless and fingerless priest (based on real missionary Isaac Jogues), prior to his own departure for the New World. "The savages did this," the mutilated man points out, and the audience is left to let the horror of such atrocities settle into its collective subconscious. James explains the meaning of the scene as being motivational: "LaForge sees this as a compelling reason to bring his faith to a godless people."[28] Neither she nor Beresford allow so much as a hint that both clergymen are representatives of a church which had only just completed two centuries of inquisitions in which the refinement of torture had been carried to extraordinary lengths, and in which the pyres of burning heretics numbered in the tens of thousands.[29]

Even as the two men spoke, the Thirty Years War was raging in its full fury as Catholics and Protestants battled to the death over which side would dominate the spiritual, political, and economic life of the European subcontinent.[30] But nary a word is murmured on this score either. Nor is the fact that Jesuit missionaries were hardly acting on the basis of some pure religious fervor, no matter how misguided. Instead, as their own writings compiled in *The Jesuit Relations* and elsewhere make patently clear, they were consciously—one is tempted to say, cynically—using their faith as a medium through which to transform Indians, not just into ostensible Catholics, but into surrogate troops deployed as fodder by the French Crown in its struggle with Great Britain for imperial hegemony in North America (the series of four so-called "French and Indian Wars" commencing in 1689).[31]

In any event, the exchange between LaForge and his senior colleague serves as a prelude, a means of setting the psychic stage for the capture of the former, his interpreter (Daniel), and their party of Algonquin guides by "violent Iroquois" (Mohawks) while making their way along a 1,500-mile journey to the christianized Huron village of Ihonataria.[32] First the captive men are forced to "run the gauntlet" between two lengthy lines of blood-crazed warriors who beat them severely with all manner of stone clubs. Then, a leering "Mohawk chieftain"—a young male—brutally slashes the throat of an Algonquin child, announcing that the adults, men and women alike, will be ritually tortured to death in the morning. To further make his point, he calmly saws off one of LaForge's fingers with a clamshell. The condemned are at this point left to spend their last night under guard in a longhouse stuffed with the Mohawks' larder of recently killed game, most of it steadily oozing blood. Under the circumstances, the firelit interior scenes which follow take on an aura of nothing so much as a sequence from *The*

Texas Chainsaw Massacre. Only a sexual deception by Annuka allows the guard to be overpowered, and the survivors to escape their desperate plight.

Actually, Beresford softened portions of his characterization of the Mohawks in the interest of not driving away even moderately squeamish viewers. In Moore's original novel—a book the director and several of *Black Robe*'s producers found to be so "beautiful" that it simply *had* to be made into a movie—the body of the child is hacked up, boiled, and eaten while his family is forced to watch.[33] Even in its revised form, however, the matter is very far from the sort of "anthropological" accuracy, distance, and integrity attributed to it by most reviewers. It is, for starters, well established in even the most arcane anthropological sources that Iroquois village life was controlled, not by young men, but by elder women—who fail to appear anywhere in the film—known as Clan Mothers. The latitude of the women's decision-making included the disposition of captives, a circumstance which led invariably to children being adopted and raised as Mohawks rather than gratuitously slaughtered. By and large, the same rule would have applied to a young woman such as Annuka; she would have been mated to a Mohawk man, perhaps an unkind fate in the estimation of some, but certainly a substantially different fate than being dismembered and burned alive.[34]

In a project as exhaustively researched as Beresford's, it is unlikely to the point of impossibility that "errors" of such magnitude were unintentional. Hence, it is difficult to conclude that the extent to which the Mohawks were misrepresented, and the nature of that misrepresentation, were anything other than a deliberate exercise in vilification. Such a view is amply reinforced by the employment of more subtle means to convey the impression that these are, indeed, the bad guys. For example, all scenes of the Mohawk village are framed against an overcast and threatening sky, the pervasive darkness evoking a strong sense of the sinister. By contrast, when LaForge finally reaches Ihonataria, despite the fact that it is now much later in the winter than when the Mohawk sequence occurs, the setting is bathed in sunlight. To suggest that these subliminal cues were just "accidents" on the part of a veteran director who is known to do the most detailed storyboarding well in advance of his shoots would be insulting.

Ultimately, the Mohawks are used as mere props in a broader theme which is developed throughout the film. Beresford's play of good and evil goes much deeper than a simplistic notion that one particular group of Indians was "bad." Rather, the Mohawks are deployed only as the most dramatic illustration of a more-or-less subterranean message holding that that which is most emphatically resistant to the imposition of European values and belief systems—or, put another way, that which is most decisively *Indian*—is by definition evil. This is manifested most clearly in a confrontation between LaForge and an overtly anti-Christian Montaignais spiritual leader. The latter is personified as "a shaman (a nasty-spirited dwarf),"[35] his face continuously painted a vibrant ochre, standing in shocking contrast to the somber dignity of LaForge's attire and physical stature. The dwarf (indigenous spirituality) is self-serving, malicious, and vindictive, an altogether repulsive entity; LaForge (Christianity), on the other hand, is sensitive and selfless to the extent of self-flagellation and acceptance of martyrdom. Within such a consciously contrived scheme, there can be no question as to which tradition is most likely to win the sympathy of viewers.[36]

Nor do the Algonquins who serve as LaForge's guides, collaborating with the white man but unsure as to whether they should embrace his religion, escape such categorization. To the extent that they remain uncommitted to conversion, clinging somewhat pathetically to the vestiges of their own beliefs, they too are cast as being imbued with crude and sometimes bestial impulses. In his novel, Moore made the point by lacing their speech with obscenities for which there are no native counterparts (e.g., "Now we will all eat our fucking faces full"), contrasting this with LaForge's austere pursuit of purity. Once again, Beresford cleans things up a bit, substituting a tendency of the Indians to fart loudly throughout the night, the noise and the stench keeping the delicate Father LaForge awake until he is forced to witness an even more disturbing phenomenon.

This last has to do with Annuka's proclivity, fair and unmarried maiden though she is, to copulate voraciously with whatever male she happens to find convenient when the urge strikes. More shocking, she obviously prefers to do it in the dirt, on all fours, in what is colloquially referred to as "dog style" (like a dog, get it?). Well, if perchance viewers were too startled by such carnality to fully appreciate its significance the first time around, the director includes a second iteration. And, for those who are really slow to catch on, a third. The only deviation from such canine behavior is to be found in yet a fourth sex scene, when Annuka, Pocahontas-like,[37] falls in love with Daniel, LaForge's young French interpreter. In the best civilizing fashion (albeit still in the dirt, as befits a sin of the flesh), he teaches her the meaning of "the missionary position," still morally—and in some places, legally—defined as the only "unperverted" sexual posture in the United States, Canada, and Beresford's Australian homeland.[38]

When all is said and done, the only Indians exempted from what is plainly meant to be seen as the disgusting quality of indigenous existence are the Hurons, at least those who have converted to Christianity. Unfortunately, LaForge arrives at last to tend this promising flock only to find them mostly dead or dying from an unnamed "fever," perhaps smallpox, introduced by his predecessor. What an "irony" that in their "salvation" lay their extinction. Truly, God works in mysterious ways. Nothing to be done about it but carry on. That's progress, all for the best. Even for the victims, who might otherwise have been consigned to an eternity of farting and fornicating and wandering around at the command of yellow dwarfs. It is well that we remember, as *Black Robe* attempts to insure that we will, that however "mistaken, naïve," or even "wrongheaded" the invaders "may have been at times," they "did what they did for love [of humanity], nothing else, and that is nothing less than sheer nobility."[39]

Conclusion

Returning for a moment to the earlier-mentioned Holocaust metaphor, such a conclusion—which derives logically enough from Beresford's presentation—is quite comparable to a film's serving not only to rehabilitate but to ennoble the nazi exterminationist impulse through a systematic defamation of the Jewish *untermenschen* ("subhumans") based in such "historical documentation" as *The Protocols of the Elders of Zion*.[40] This, of course, was precisely the objective of Joseph Goebbels's propaganda ministry and its cooperating filmmakers in producing such works as *Die Rothschilds, Jud Süss,* and *Der ewige Jude* (*The Eternal Jew*) during the halcyon days of the Third Reich.[41] For all its pictorial beauty and technical sophistication (or because of them), *Black Robe* is different mainly in quality, not in kind.[42]

If there is a distinction to be drawn between the nazis' antisemitic cinema and the handling of indigenous subject matters in contemporary North America, it is that the former were designed to psychologically prepare an entire populace to accept a genocide which was even then on the verge of occurring. The latter is pitched more to rationalizing and redeeming a process of conquest and genocide which has already transpired. *Black Robe* is thus the sort of "sensitive" and "mature" cinematic exposition we might have expected of the nazis, had they won their war. Their state, much like the U.S. and Canada (and Australia, New Zealand, and South Africa, for that matter), would have been faced with the consequent necessity of achieving a complete psychic reconciliation of the horrors of victory experienced by the "Germanic settlers" upon whom it depended for consolidation of the *Lebensraum* gained through invasion and subsequent liquidation of native populations.[43]

In the context of the present Columbian Quincentennial, a symbolic period ripe with opportunity for wholesale reassessment of the evolution and current reality of Indian/immigrant relations in the Americas, and with the potential for some constructive redefinition of these relations, the form and function of films like *Black Robe* speak for themselves: "Nothing was really wrong with what happened," they proclaim. "Therefore, nothing really needs altering in the outcomes of what happened, nor in the continuing and constantly accelerating conduct of business as usual in this hemisphere. There is no guilt, no responsibility, nothing to atone for. Don't worry. Be happy. To the victors belong the spoils." Sieg Heil....

Note: A variation of this paper was presented under the title "*Black Robe*: Cinematic Imaging of Native America," at a conference entitled, sponsored by the Society for the Humanities, Cornell University, April 4, 1992.

Notes

1. Moore's earlier screenwriting credits include the script for Alfred Hitchcock's *Torn Curtain*.
2. James's credits include *Driving Miss Daisy* and *Mr. Johnson*.
3. Wellburn's credits include *The Fringe Dwellers*.
4. Alliance Communications press release, March 1991, p. 10.

5. Andrew L. Urban, "Black Robe," *Cinema Papers*, March 1991, pp. 6-12, quote at pp. 10-11.

6. Pinter's credits include *Breaker Morant*, *The Fringe Dwellers* and *Mr. Johnson*. The quote is taken from *ibid.*, p. 10.

7. *Ibid.*

8. *Ibid.*, p. 12.

9. "Black Robe: Anatomy of a Co-Production," *Moving Pictures International* (Special Supplement), September 5, 1991, p. viii.

10. *Ibid.* The Australian Film Finance Corporation committed thirty percent of the budget, Canada's Alliance Entertainment twenty percent. The balance was provided by Jake Eberts of the U.S.-based Allied Filmmakers.

11. Quoted in Urban, *op. cit.*, p. 10.

12. Alliance press release, *op. cit.*, p. 10.

13. See, for example, Antoinette Bosco, "Remembering Heaven-Bent Men Wearing Black Robes," *The Litchfield County Times*, February 14, 1992. Bosco is a nun who has authored two ostensibly non-fiction books on the Jesuit missionaries depicted in *Black Robe*.

14. Jay Scott, "A hideous piece of history wrapped in frosty, ebony shroud," *Toronto Globe and Mail*, September 5, 1991.

15. *Ibid.* In fact, Scott posits an inaccurate belief that Hurons and Montaignais actually spoke Cree: "the natives in *Black Robe* speak their own languages."

16. Caryn James, "Jesuits vs. Indians, With No Villains," *New York Times*, November 17, 1991.

17. Vincent Canby, "Saving the Huron Indians: A Disaster for Both Sides," *New York Times*, October 30, 1991. Canby also joins Scott and others in asserting that the movie's Indians "speak their own languages."

18. "True Believers," *New Yorker*, November 18, 1991, pp. 120-2; quote at p. 122.

19. James, *op. cit.*

20. Paul Valentine, "Dancing With Myths," *Washington Post*, April 7, 1991. Tellingly, a search of the indices reveal that Valentine has never, despite there being literally thousands of examples to choose from, published a review criticizing a filmmaker for engaging in a *negative* misrepresentation of Indians. Nor has he published anything critical of Hollywood's overwhelming romanticization of Euroamerican soldiers and "pioneers" engaged in the "Winning of the West." His agitation about Costner's allegedly "unbalanced portrayal" thus speaks for itself.

21. *Ibid.* Most of this is simply bizarre. For instance, it is a well-known principle of range management that burning off prairie grass in the fall causes it to grow back in the spring more luxuriously than ever. In fact, new grass tends to be choked out by dead material after a few years. Hence, occasional burn-offs—caused naturally by lightning strikes—are essential to the health of the prairies and, to the extent that Indians practiced this method of hunting at all (which is dubious in itself) they would have been enhancing rather than destroying buffalo graze. So much for their casually starving herds into extinction. Similarly, insofar as no one has suggested that inorganic substances had been created in precontact North America, exactly what sort of "refuse" are Indian "nomads" supposed to have "strewn in their wake"? Again, there is no substantiation at all for the notion that the travois was designed to be hauled by women. To the contrary, all indications are that it was meant to be and was in fact hauled by the dogs kept by every native group for that purpose. Finally, while there is no authentication whatsoever of a single incident of indigenous cannibalism anywhere in

the Americas, there are numerous documented cases in which Euroamericans adopted the practice. Witness, as but two illustrations drawn from the nineteenth century, the matter of Colorado's Alfred Packer, and of the notorious Donner Party.

22. Canby, *op. cit.*

23. "True Believers," *op. cit.*, p. 120.

24. Scott, *op. cit.*

25. "True Believers," *op. cit.*, p. 121.

26. "Toronto Fest: *Black Robe*," *Variety*, September 9, 1991, p. 65.

27. James, *op. cit.*

28. *Ibid.*

29. The author has had occasion to visit what is formally titled the Torture Museum, in Amsterdam, in which a number of the utensils developed for use in the French Catholic inquisition are displayed. Included are such items as the rack, the wheel, the iron maiden, the iron mask, special tongs for tearing out tongues, instruments used in drawing and quartering, and coarse-toothed saws created for dismembering living bodies. It is estimated that the Church caused such devices to be used on more than a quarter-million Europeans between 1400 and 1500. Suffice it to say that Native North America offered no remote counterpart to such ferocity, either quantitatively or technologically.

30. See Geoffrey Parker, *The Thirty Years' War* (New York: Military Heritage Press, [2nd ed.] 1978). For thorough (and classic) contextualization of this conflict in France, see James Westfall Thompson, *The Wars of Religion in France* (Chicago: Aldine Publishers, 1909).

31. See Rubin G. Twaites, ed., *The Jesuit Relations and Allied Documents* (Cleveland: Burrows Brothers Publishers, 1919; 73 vols.). Also see George M.

Wrong, *The Rise and Fall of New France* (New York: Macmillan Publishers, 1928; 2 vols.).

32. The description of the Iroquois as "violent" accrues from "Toronto Fest," *op. cit.* It is the *only* adjective used with reference to the Iroquois in this article, thus the author must have intended it to be definitive of their character.

33. Here we encounter the standard fable of Indian cannibalism once again. It is noteworthy that even a reputedly progressive publication like *In These Times* seems quite attached to this time-honored Eurocentric fantasy. At least it published a review by Pat Aufderheide ("Red and white blues in the *Black Robe*," November 20-26, 1991) in which Beresford's film, minus cannibalism, is thoroughly trashed in favor of Nelson Periera dos Santos' *How Tasty Was My Little Frenchman*. Stated reason? Because "the European is dinner" for a group of South American Indians.

34. All this has been common academic knowledge since at least as early as the publication of Lewis Henry Morgan's *The League of the Ho-De'-No-Sau-Nee, or Iroquois* (Rochester, NY: Sage & Brother, 1851).

35. "True Believers," *op. cit.*, p. 121.

36. This is a standard method of distorting native spirituality for non-Indian consumption. See L.C. Kleber, "Religion Among American Indians," *History Today*, No. 28, 1978.

37. The Pocahontas legend is, of course, one of the oldest and most hackneyed of the stereotypes foisted off on native women by Euroamerica. See Allison Bernstein, "Outgrowing the Pocahontas Myth: Toward a New History of American Indian Women," *Minority Notes*, Vol. 2, Nos. 1-2, Spring-Summer 1981.

38. The entire handling of indigenous sexuality in *Black Robe* is analogous to Ruth Beebe Hill's fetish with portraying Indians engaging in oral sex—also consid-

ered bestial and criminally perverse under Anglo-Saxon law—in her epic travesty, *Hanta Yo* (New York: Doubleday Publishers, 1979). For commentary, see Beatrice Medicine, "Hanta Yo: A New Phenomenon," *The Indian Historian*, Vol. 12, No. 2, Spring 1979.

39. Bosco, *op. cit.* Anyone inclined to buy into the good sister's interpretation of things should refer to the recent work of Osage/Cherokee theologian George Tinker. In a fine study entitled *Missionary Conquest: The Gospel and Native American Cultural Genocide* (Minneapolis: Fortress Press, 1993), he details not only the actions of, but the express motivations and underlying assumptions guiding four exemplary Christian proselytizers among "the savages of North America," each of them representing a particular period over a 200 year timespan.

40. The protocols—attributing a vast and carefully thought-out "anti-goyim" conspiracy to "World Jewry"—were fabricated and distributed by the Czarist political police in Russia during the early twentieth century as a means of whipping up anti-Jewish sentiments and consequent "solidarity" among the non-Jewish population. Subsequently, the utterly invented "historical document" was republished and disseminated by such antisemites as the nazis, and American industrialist Henry Ford, as a means of justifying programs directed against Jews in both Germany and the U.S. It is currently in circulation again in the United States after having been reprinted by various neonazi organizations.

41. See David Stewart Hull, *Film in the Third Reich: A Study of German Cinema, 1933-1945* (Berkeley: University of California Press, 1969, pp. 157-77). Also see Irwin Leiser, *Nazi Cinema* (New York: Macmillan Publishers, 1974, pp. 73-94).

42. Even the quasi-official rhetoric attending release of the nazi films was similar to that which has ac-

companied *Black Robe*. According to the minutes of a
Conference of Ministers at the Reich Propaganda
Ministry conducted on April 26, 1940, Goebbels
explained that the films should be reviewed in periodicals such as *Völkischer Beobachter* as if they were
utterly authentic in their depictions of Jews: The
"publicity campaign for *Jud Süss* and *Die Rothschilds*
should [make clear that they portray] Jewry as it
really is....If they seem antisemitic, this is not
because they are aiming at any particular bias." The
minutes are reproduced in full in Willi A. Boelcke,
*Secret Conferences of Dr. Goebbels: The Nazi
Propaganda War, 1939-1945* (New York: E.P. Dutton
Publishers, 1970). As Leiser (*op. cit.*, p. 76) observes,
Goebbels's instruction was motivated by a con-
viction—apparently shared by contemporary publicists in North America—that "propaganda only
achieves its desired objective when it is taken not for
propaganda but for truth. In a speech to the film
industry on 15 February 1941, Goebbels stated that
it was necessary to act on the principle that 'the
intention [of a picture] should not be revealed to
avoid irritating people,'" thus causing them to resist
or even reject inculcating the desired "message."

43. For more on what the nazis had in mind in this
regard, see Ihor Kamenetsky, *Secret Nazi Plans for
Eastern Europe: A Study of Lebensraum Policies* (New
York: Bookman Associates, 1961). On preliminary
implementation, see Alexander Dallin, *German Rule
in Russia, 1941-1944* (London: Macmillan
Publishers, 1957).

Another
Dry White Season

Jerry Mander's
In the Absence of the Sacred

The problem is one of cultural appropriation.
Eurocentric intellectuals habitually take the
knowledge of indigenous peoples and incorpo-
rate it into their own thinking, usually without
attribution. In the process, they tend to deform
it beyond recognition, bending it to suit their
own social, economic, and political objectives.
Unfortunately, this has, with very few exceptions, proven to be as true of professed "allies"
of native people as it has of their avowed enemies.

—M. Annette Jaimes
Alfred University 1990

They just can't help it. I swear, they really can't.
It's too deeply ingrained in the subconscious, a matter of subliminal presumption. No matter how well-
intentioned or insightful, regardless of how critical
of the dominant conceptual paradigm and "sensitive" to non-Western perspectives, the theoretical
writing of Euroamerican men—and most white
women as well—seems destined with a sort of sad
inevitability to become yet another exercise in intellectual appropriation, a reinforcement of the very

hegemony they purport to oppose. To expect otherwise, one supposes, would be to expect that a leopard will (or can) change its spots. This remains true despite the authors' most genuinely-held desires that things be otherwise, not to mention their oft and fervently-expressed assertions that, in their own cases at least, such wishes have already been fulfilled.

Take, as a prime example, Jerry Mander's book, *In the Absence of the Sacred: The Failure of Technology and the Survival of Indian Nations* (San Francisco: Sierra Club, 1992). There can be no question that the author's credentials as a proponent of fundamental and positive social change are impeccable. He is committed to reestablishing global ecological equilibrium and opposing the blatant anthropocentrism which, more than any other factor, signifies the Judeo-Christian ("Western" or European) tradition of "knowing." He is undoubtedly sincere in his contention, voiced throughout his treatise, that the only viable route forward is a wholesale abandonment of Eurosupremacist assumptions and a concomitant (re)assertion of what may be termed the "indigenous world view" on a planetary scale. He is articulate and effective—at times even eloquent—in elaborating his thesis. Yet, in many respects, the book embodies the worst of what he intends to oppose.

The book, Mander explains in the introduction, was originally conceived as two different projects: one about the technological fetishism of "mainstream culture," the other about contemporary indigenous societies. The first was "intended to raise questions about whether technological [Eurocentric]

140

society has lived up to its advertising, and also to address some grave concerns about its future direction....The second book was to be a kind of continuation and update of Dee Brown's *Bury My Heart At Wounded Knee*" (p. 4).[1] While "planning to write these two books," however, "it became apparent to me that their subjects were inseparable. They belonged together as one book. There is no way to understand the situation of the Indians, Eskimos, Aborigines, island peoples, or other native societies without understanding the outside societies that act upon them. And there is no way to understand the outside societies without understanding their relationships to native peoples and to nature itself" (p. 6).

> All things considered, it may be the central assumption of technological society that there is virtue in overpowering nature and native peoples....Save for such nascent movements as bioregionalism and Green politics, which have at least questioned the assumptions...most people in Western society are in agreement about our common superiority. So it becomes okay to humiliate—to find insignificant and thus subject to sacrifice—any way of life or thinking that stands in the way of the "progress" we have invented, which is scarcely a century old. In fact, having assumed such superiority, it becomes more than acceptable for us to bulldoze nature and native societies. To do so actually becomes desirable, inevitable, and possibly "divine" (pp. 6-7).

Formulated as a unified project, Mander's undertaking was therefore, in his own recounting, recast not only as a critique of what he apprehends as an hallucinatory and extremely dangerous "technotopianism" forming a core tenet of Eurocentrism, but as a means of addressing several other substantive questions: "Can we expect the situation to improve or worsen in the future? And what of the [native] people who always told us that this way would not work, and continue to say so now? Finally, which is the more 'romantic' viewpoint: that technology will fix itself and lead us to paradise, or that the answer is something far simpler?" (p. 7). In the latter connection, he implies that indigenous alternatives to the current Eurodominant status quo will be presented for consideration by readers. They will form a basis upon which the reader may form reasonable opinions as to which of the numerous options makes most sense. Fair enough. Even commendable. But the issue is how this worthy promise was approached, packaged, and presented by its author.

A Glimpse of the Technotopian Future

In terms of his first emphasis, upon the Western preoccupation with *techne* and its likely consequences, Mander succeeds admirably. His *tour de force* wholeheartedly embraces and gives non-fictional form to Kurt Vonnegut's sentiment that, "Just because some of us can read and write and do a little math, that doesn't mean we deserve to conquer the Universe."[2] He presents not only a summary of the analysis contained in his earlier *Four Arguments for the Elimination of Television*, but equally compelling chapters on biotechnology, the increasingly regimented corporate-state structure of "modern" society, computers, extraterrestrial exploration/ colonization, and nanotechnology.[3] Much useful corroborative information is arrayed with respect to nuclear technology, robotics, aerospace technology, and so on.

It is a devastating panorama overflowing with portraits of rampant technocratic insanity. To produce the cultural uniformity necessary for "maximally efficient product consumption," an increasingly somnambulistic humanity is permanently plugged by its alpha brain waves into electronic TV pulses.[4] Bacteriological/viral strains designed to target and eliminate specific human groups are unleashed as a vehicle of "species improvement" (a theme which raises the specter that the current world AIDS epidemic is an experiment of the U.S. military/intelligence community gone out of control). A quasi-human "master race" is genetically engineered and manufactured while "undesirable" racial/ethnic characteristics among the actual human population are suppressed through a variety of means. Entire new species of life, deemed "useful" by technocrats, are created while existing—or "useless"—species are eradicated at an ever greater rate. As a way of offsetting negative effects such as ozone depletion which accompany any permanent spiral of production and consumption, the molecular alteration ("re-engineering") of virtually the entire ecosphere is undertaken.[5]

The premise of technotopianism is that the natural world can and "must" be extinguished in its entirety, replaced with a marketable—and therefore "better"—artificial or "surrogate" environment.[6] This Doomsday Scenario is powerfully reinforced by the leading advocates of unrestrained technocracy spelling out their visions of our collective future. For

143

instance, Mander quotes the president of the RJR Nabisco Corporation:

[I am] looking forward to the day when Arabs and Americans, Latins and Scandinavians will be munching Ritz crackers as enthusiastically as they already drink Coke or brush their teeth with Colgate (p. 136).[6]

He then juxtaposes this with a quote from radical social critic Holly Sklar to the effect that the ultimate goal of transnational corporatism is creation of an utterly Eurocentric global monoculture as a basis for profit maximization and consequent underwriting of perpetual technological innovation:

Corporations not only advertise products, they promote lifestyles rooted in consumption, patterned largely after the United States....[They] look forward to a postnational age in which [Western] social, economic, and political values are transformed into universal values...a world economy in which all national economies beat to the rhythm of transnational corporate capitalism....The Western way is the good way, national culture is inferior (p. 136).[7]

Mander demonstrates conclusively that the technologies at issue are not merely the stuff of *Star Trek* fantasies but are already under development. Some are well on the way to "real world" manifestation. Lengthy quotes from such celebrated exponents of technotopianism as Herman Kahn (p. 144) and the late Gerard O'Neill (p. 145) illustrate the intended uses of such "advances."[8] To cap his presentation, he uses a passage which might have been drawn straight from the script of *Terminator*, showcasing the enthusiastic projections of Hans Moravec, a leading and highly-respected pioneer in the field of nanotechnics:

> Moravec calmly explains how in the next thirty years we will by-pass the present limits upon artificial intelligence and robotic mobility, to the point where we will be able to "download" all the content of our brains—which are now unfortunately stuck in decaying biological entities—into computers housed within mobile robots, thereby gaining "us" immortality, via these machines. The machines will "evolve" by their own design and, when given the knowledge of all the great thinkers on the planet, without the limitations and fragility of their flesh, will generate ideas and actions that will far exceed human achievement: "Such machines could carry on our cultural evolution, including their own construction and rapid self-improvement, without us, and without the genes that built us. When that happens, our DNA will find itself out of a job, having lost the evolutionary race to a new kind of competition....The new genetic takeover will be complete. Our culture will be able to evolve independently of human biology and its limitations, instead passing directly from generation to generation of ever more capable intelligent machinery" (p. 183).[9]

The overall exposition on the perils of proliferating techno-order, advanced with impeccable logic and anchored by the use of quotations, is marred only by occasional and relatively minor inaccuracies, e.g., observations that "the American and British military...first put [computers] to serious use...as guidance systems for missiles during World War II" (p. 68), and that U.S. nuclear testing in the

Marshall Islands occurred during the same war (p. 345). Relatedly, the author states that the U.S. used "machine guns" to slaughter native people "100 years ago," while completing its conquest of their homelands in "the lower forty-eight" states (p. 287). In actuality, neither the United States nor Great Britain possessed guided missiles during the Second World War, that dubious distinction being reserved to Germany, which developed no computers, in its creation of V-1 and V-2 weapons; World War II Allied computing capacity was devoted primarily to cryptography and nuclear physics.[10] Similarly, U.S. atomic weapons testing in the Marshalls did not begin until well after World War II, and true machine guns did not see application until World War I, fully a quarter-century after the 1890 Wounded Knee Massacre (the last episode of the so-called "Indian Wars" in North America).[11]

The Native Alternative?

The same sorts of problems with factual details appear when Mander takes up his second emphasis, the ongoing existence of land-based/nature-oriented indigenous cultures which he posits as containing the best and perhaps only valid conceptual and practical alternatives to the ecocide and species suicide inherent to finalization of Western technocracy.[12] For instance, the noted Anishinabe (Chippewa) activist Dennis Banks becomes "a fugitive Sioux Indian leader" (p. 242). The author also displays an odd and irritating habit of referring to *all* indigenous societies as "Indian"—"the Indian tribes" of the Philippines, for example (p. 353)— despite the fact that *no* native peoples outside the

146

Americas refer to themselves in this fashion.

Nonetheless, he provides a lengthy and largely accurate catalogue of the circumstances presently confronting native people in the U.S., and their resistance to it. Illustrations range from the dire effects of the 1973 Alaska Native Claims Settlement Act upon the circumpolar peoples of the Arctic North to the expropriation of Western Shoshone land in Nevada, the struggles of Native Hawaiians to regain control over some portion of their homeland, the forced relocation of more than 10,000 traditional Big Mountain Diné (Navajos), the usurpation of indigenous self-governance through the 1934 Indian Reorganization Act, and the more recent impact of the Supreme Court's "G-O Road Decision" voiding native rights to religious freedom.[13] This exposition on the United States is coupled to a survey of the situations—which he follows University of California geographer Bernard Nietschmann in terming "Fourth World Wars"—of native nations in Canada, Central and South America, the Pacific Basin, Africa, Asia and, to some extent, Europe.[14]

Such information is, like the analysis of techno-topianism, undeniably useful and important, and one wishes to like the book on this basis alone. Equally undeniably, however, most of the material has been covered elsewhere, earlier, and often better, by various American Indian writers and spokespersons. Some are mentioned, but few cited, in Mander's text. Moreover, the great bulk of what he offers with regard to native peoples is little more than a journalistic litany chronicling who's doing what to whom, where, and why. In this sense, it is a continuation of the author's substantiation of the negative effects of technocratic mentality rather than the promised explanation of the indigenous thinking. In this respect, aside from a couple of examples concerning "management of animal populations," the book does not come close—to borrow one of the author's pet phrases—to "living up to its advertising."

The reason for this becomes readily apparent when one considers the list of contemporary native "leaders and philosophers" Mander compiles on page 383—"the late Phillip Lame Deer [sic: he means Phillip Deer], Black Elk, Louis Bad Wound, Bill Wahpepah, and Dan Bomberry...Jeanette Armstrong, John Mohawk, Winona LaDuke, Dagmar Thorpe, Chris Peters, Oren Lyons, Leslie Silko, Vine Deloria, George Erasmus, N. Scott Momaday, Leonard Peltier, Leon Shenandoah, Alfonso Ortiz, Thomas Banyacya, Marie-Helen Laraque, Wilma Mankiller, and Paula Gunn Allen, to name a small number on this continent alone"—as having important things to tell non-Indians. This decidedly partial itemization of thinking Native Americans must be seen in the context that only three of them are quoted or cited at any point in the entire book. This stands in stark contrast to the author's extensive quotations/citations of Euroamericans (including, as was seen above, those with whom he professes the most fundamental disagreements).

Nor do the quotes selected from those on Mander's "Indian list" measure up substantively to those chosen to represent the thinking of their non-Indian counterparts. Poliklah activist Chris Peters is restricted to only a rhetorical flourish on the inability of the earth to sustain much more technocultural advancement (pp. 386-7). Acclaimed Seneca social philosopher John Mohawk is afforded space to advance the weighty notion that one must "listen with the heart" if one is to understand indigenous wisdom (p. 113). Onondaga faithkeeper Oren Lyons is interviewed to establish that the traditional government of the Haudenosaunee (Six Nations Iroquois Confederacy) still functions in what it considers to be a sovereign manner (pp. 240-45). Lyons is supported by a quote from Yamasee historian Donald Grinde on the influence of the Haudenosaunee on formation of the democratic ideals expressed by the U.S. Founding Fathers (p. 234). Elsewhere, Mander makes much of a pamphlet entitled *A Basic Call to Consciousness*, the edited transcript of a presentation made by the Haudenosaunee elders at a United Nations conference in 1977 (pp. 191-3).[15] And that's *it* for articulations of contemporary indigenous intellectualism.

It's not that these are the only native voices present in the volume. To the contrary, the author seems to have been at pains to assemble an impressive array of quotations—most of them lifted from books like Thomas R. Berger's superb *Village Journey* and Julian Burger's *Report from the Frontier*—from grassroots people in the Alaskan north country and elsewhere.[16] But, unmistakably, each of these statements assumes the form of "testimony." They are included not as intellectual contributions, but as documentation to the author's survey of damage and pain inflicted by the techno-order upon indigenous land and lives. Even quotations from activists such as Opegtah Matæmoh, a Menominee also known as Ingrid Washinawatok, are arrayed only to have them complain that "America never listens to American Indians" (p. 224). This is a far different matter than allowing them to explain for themselves what it is America hasn't heard and still isn't hearing.

When it comes time to wax philosophical, and to thus lend *meaning* to things, Mander inevitably turns not to native sources or "informants," but to an all but exclusively white, mostly male, oppositional intelligentsia of which he is a part. He designates this group as consisting of Jeremy Rifkin, as well as "Ernest Callenbach, Lester Brown, Wendell Berry, Thomas Berry, Wes Jackson, Anne Ehrlich, Paul Ehrlich, David Brower, Hazel Henderson, Gary Coats, Erik Dammann, Leopold Kohr, Kirkpatrick Sale, Joanna Macy, Carolyn Merchant, Delores LaChapelle, Riane Eisler, Ivan Illich, Peter Berg, Richard Register, Hunter Lovins, Amory Lovins, Gary Snyder, Langdon Winner, Francis Moore Lappé, Fritjof Capra, Stephanie Mills, Vandana Shiva, Elizabeth Dodson Gray, Charlene Spretnak, Arne Naess, Susan Griffin, Starhawk [a Euroamerican], Bill Devall, George Sessions, E.F. Schumacher, Malcolm Margolin, and Chellis Glendining" (p. 383). He might have added that notorious anthropological hoaxer, Carlos Castaneda, whose ersatz renderings of "native" philosophy are embraced more warmly and at much greater length by Mander than anything genuinely Native American (pp. 207-8).[17] In effect, real indigenous speakers are utilized throughout *In the Absence of the Sacred* as mere props, orchestrated by and large to accompany Mander's own "broader," more "universal" themes.

Cultural Imperialism

Of 305 bibliographical entries at the end of the book, only seventeen—three of them newspaper articles, two of them interviews, one an internal report, and another a memorandum—are identifiably written by American Indians.[18] Several others, such as Joseph Jorgenson's *Native Americans and Energy Development*, are anthologies assembled by Euroamerican editors, but containing one or more contributions by native researchers.[19] The remainder, more than 280 titles, mostly books and more than a hundred of them *about* indigenous peoples to one extent or another, are almost exclusively Euroamerican enterprises. Such a glaring skew simply *cannot* be attributed to a dearth of relevant and appropriate Native American material. Not one of the more than a dozen books by the acclaimed Lakota intellectual Vine Deloria, Jr., is so much as mentioned, for example.[20] This near-total eclipse of indigenous theory and scholarship, other than that which has been thoroughly "interpreted" by selected non-Indians, exists only because Mander wanted it that way.

One underlying message of *In the Absence of the Sacred* is clear enough. The traditional "mind/body split" by which Western intellectualism has always seen itself in relation to non-Westerners has been preserved in Mander's work. The "proper" role of native peoples is essentially physical (we experience, feel, suffer, and testify). The "natural" role of whites, on the other hand, is primarily cerebral. They think, explain, and philosophize, putting a "correct spin" on all phenomena, whether material or conceptual. Nonwestern knowledge is thereby "naturally" reduced to the status of being an element or component. Western élites—Mander and his carefully chosen coterie of "culturally transcendent" Euro–american thinkers no less than any other—are free (even obligated) to absorb these elements as their own "intellectual property." They go on to synthesize new (and therefore inherently "superior") vernaculars of societal/ecological reality. Thus they assume a self-reserved position of theoretical leadership, an effective monopoly on decision-making authority.[21] For Mander's group, this would be especially true in the event of anything resembling what they call the "paradigm shift" actually occurring.

Put another way, perceiving that the main body of their own tradition may be discarded in the near future—as surely it must be, given the technological precipice it has created for itself— Mander and his colleagues are busily projecting themselves as *the* group intrinsically best qualified to take charge of the replacement. The means to this end are the intellectual appropriation and continued Eurocentric domination of nonwestern traditions. In principle, the process is not appreciably different from that of previous eras of European cultural imperialism, as when the Crusaders gained eventual "Renaissance" and ascendancy for their culture by seizing, among other things, the Arabic concepts of zero, infinity, and the vaulted arch.[22] Hence, far from representing a bona fide attempt to negate the "white skin privilege" imbedded in Eurocentrism's undergirding attitudes, the thrust exhibited by Mander and kindred writers amounts to a sophisticated attempt to preserve its fundamentals in a rapidly changing and ostensibly nonwestern environment.

The technique is as subtle as it is perverse. The author rightly rejects the circular reasoning used to justify Eurocentric orthodoxy's insistent technotopian scientism: "It is true that the evolution of Western science and its proliferating technologies have brought us to our current dismal pass. *Therefore* only an ever greater abundance and refinement of science and technology can save us." This establishes him as a thoroughly "dissident" theoretician: one who can thus be trusted by the most oppressed. Simultaneously, however, precisely because of his stature as a dissident, he can replicate and extend much the same "logic" for his own purposes: It is true that the hegemonic tradition of Western intellectualism (of which scientism is only a part) has brought the entire planet to the brink of oblivion. *Therefore* only a continuation of this same hegemony (in the form of Mander's friends and himself) can fix things. Confronted with such a formulation, the author would probably acknowledge a "paradox" of sorts. But, for nonwestern peoples, the words of Peter Townshend ring much truer: "Meet the new boss, same as the old boss."[23]

A Hidden Agenda

Admittedly, all of this may appear overstated and tendentious. It could be argued that whatever Mander's oversights and omissions, they are more inadvertent or careless than deliberate and systematic. However flawed his final product, it is by no means malicious. Such a premise *might* be conceded, were it not for the obvious fashion in which Mander *chose*—there is simply no other word for it—to ignore certain dimensions of Native North

America he purports to examine. That these include many of the most visible and important figures, organizations, and events associated with Fourth World resistance on this continent over the past quarter-century speaks volumes to the idea that he might merely have "missed" a few things.[24] That he can be said to have pursued a readily discernible, and emphatically anti-indigenist, political agenda in leaving them unmentioned says even more. Unquestionably, he consciously sought to impose his own entirely alien notions of "legitimacy"—rather than those reflecting the integrity of native positions—upon struggles for indigenous rights. What he accomplished instead was a serious undermining of the integrity of his own positions, not only in relation to native peoples, but *vis-à-vis* technology as well.

The first hint of what is occurring comes when he fails, other than in a pair of passing references (pp. 307, 315), to remark upon the Black Hills Land Claim of the Lakota Nation. This is the longest—and certainly one of the hardest fought and best publicized—campaigns of its sort in North America.[25] Initially, an omission of such magnitude seems inexplicable in a narrative which ostensibly focuses on native/state conflicts, including many more obscure. An explanation starts to present itself, however, when the author repeats the performance during his world survey. Despite having touched upon such little known but geographically proximate indigenous liberation struggles as those of the Kurds in Iraq, Iran, Turkey, and Azerbaijan (p. 355), the Dinkas and other black nations of the Sudan (p. 366), and the Eritreans, Somalis, Tigrayans, and

Oromos in Ethiopia (pp. 366-7), he avoids mentioning a far more visible and "sensitive" corollary: the efforts of Palestinian Arabs to throw off the yoke of Israeli occupation in their Mideastern homeland.

These two glaring "oversights" are tied together by a third: the author's scrupulous refusal to make *any* reference to the American Indian Movement (AIM), probably *the* preeminent native resistance group in the U.S. since 1970. In order to address the Black Hills Land Claim in any depth, Mander would have *had* to have considered AIM, which has stood almost from its inception at the center of the battle for the Hills. In discussing AIM, it would have been necessary to have acknowledged the "Palestinian Question," at least insofar as AIM and the Palestine Liberation Organization (PLO) have long expressed a formal solidarity based in "united resistance to a common form of oppression."[26] Any one piece of the equation opens the door, so to speak, to each of the others. And, since it is the door to scrutiny of the Israeli state's posture concerning indigenous Arabs that Mander is most anxious to keep firmly closed, he has little alternative but to resort to a series of conspicuous silences, as if these several crucial topics were somehow irrelevant (or do not exist at all).

From here, the dominoes of ideologically necessitated deletion really begin to tumble. If the Black Hills case had to be ignored because of AIM's links to the PLO, then it was also necessary to evade mention of a number of other vital actions in which AIM was a key player: the 1972 Trail of Broken Treaties, 1973 Siege of Wounded Knee, 1978 Longest Walk, Black Hills International Survival

Gatherings, and the four-year occupation of Yellow Thunder Camp, just to name a few of the most widely publicized.[27] By the same token, the author could ill afford to bring up important organizations which have emerged as spin-offs from AIM. The International Indian Treaty Council, for example—a group which in its early years (1974-84) did more than any other to open international fora to indigenous participation—is noted only once, in passing (p. 285).[28] Another major entity coming out of AIM, Women of All Red Nations—which led the way in exposing the federal policy of involuntary sterilization directed against native women and which has figured crucially in documenting governmental/corporate uranium contamination of reservations—is not mentioned at all.[29]

Still less was Mander willing to attribute many of the ideas and positions he fields in his book to the various AIM leaders who first voiced or popularized them. The most obvious example comes when the author casually dismisses marxism as an alternative to capitalism in its effects upon indigenous societies (pp. 7, 373) without so much as an oblique reference to the seminal and quite influential indigenist critique of marxism published by Russell Means—complete with a cover photo and introduction comparing its import to Martin Luther King's 1963 "I Have a Dream" speech—in the well-circulated pages of *Mother Jones* magazine.[30] Similarly, while he applauds the fact that some elements of the Euroamerican environmental movement like Earth First!, the Rainforest Action Network, "Friends of the Earth, Earth Island Institute and others have [finally] allied themselves to [some] Indian causes in recent months" (p. 387). The author is careful to leave unmentioned the well-known and decisive effect the speeches, writings, and recordings of former AIM National Chair John Trudell have had in achieving precisely this positive result.[31]

This itemization of willful omissions could be continued at great length. Such distortions can hardly be termed "accidental." Mander did not "miss" or "forget to include" such things as are covered in this section. He *decided* to suppress them, and to do so with complete and ruthless consistency. Nor is why he did so particularly mysterious. There is a term defining the political persuasion he brought to bear in his tailoring of information. It is called "zionism." In its most predominant form, it is the assertion by a thoroughly Europeanized segment of the Jewish people of a self-proclaimed "inherent right" to the land of others.[32] Integral to zionist doctrine, quite similar in many ways to the sense of "Manifest Destiny" espoused by nineteenth century Euroamerica,[33] has always been the contention that criticism of its tenets or practice is by definition "anti-semitic," therefore "illegitimate," unworthy of exposure, and to be suppressed by any means available.[34] The author follows this prescription to the letter. He knew exactly what he was doing and why, at least in a substantial number of instances. His stifling of the native voice in favor of his own, and his ideological associates, was thus often conscious and intentional.

The Solution as Problem

What is perhaps most telling in Mander's insinuation of a zionist agenda is the implication that his support for and identification with the rights of indigenous peoples is, in the end, just as equivocal and conditional as any other Eurocentrist's. While he is quite prepared to denounce the subordination and dispossession of native peoples in contexts of which he disapproves (which is *almost* all of them), he is equally willing to endorse and defend identical policies in contexts of which he approves for "personal" reasons (e.g., Israeli treatment of Palestinians). Such qualified championing of indigenous self-determination reduces to a kind of vulgar opportunism, little different in principle from Ronald Reagan's loudly professed concern during the 1980s for the "national and human rights" of Sumu, Rama, and Miskito Indians in Sandinista Nicaragua while openly denying the same rights to native peoples within the United States.

Moreover, Mander's tacit zionist alignment qualifies—and thus flatly contradicts—the degree of his adherence to his own core perspective: that technoculture's massive alteration of nature has gone catastrophically wrong, can only get worse, and must therefore be opposed on all fronts. A main "proof" always advanced by apologists for Israel on the "Jewish right to occupancy" in Palestine is that the Israelis, unlike the Palestinians they've displaced, have "made the barren desert bloom" via a hydrological reworking of virtually the entire country.[35] This is no different in substance from the proud claims of Arizona land developers whose huge high-tech water diversion projects the author rightly decries as being suicidally destructive to the ecosphere. By standing mute concerning Israel's pronounced and accelerating transformation of its Mideastern habitat, he again demonstrates a willingness to accept such things, so long as they are undertaken by entities of which he otherwise approves.

Back in the 1960s, the Students for a Democratic Society (SDS) employed a slogan which contended that "if you're not part of the solution, you're part of the problem." Things have advanced a long distance since then, as In the Absence of the Sacred readily demonstrates. In handling this desperately important subject matter the way he has, seeking covertly to extend Western intellectual dominance across overtly nonwestern thought and action, Jerry Mander has done much to take a substantial portion of the solution to our current technocratic dilemma and convert it into an aspect of the problem itself. We—every one of us—had a right to expect far more, and far better, from this self-styled "alternative thinker." This book held the potential to yield a genuine breakthrough in popular consciousness regarding the possibility of a "Third Way" lying outside the capitalist/communist technological paradigm altogether. Instead, Mander has produced just another "dry white season," one more excursion into that all-pervasive will to dominate which emblemizes the Eurocentric mind. For this, we owe him no debt of gratitude.

Notes

1. Dee Brown, Bury My Heart at Wounded Knee: An Indian History of the American West (New York: Henry Holt Publishers, 1970).

2.   Kurt Vonnegut, Jr., *Hocus Pocus* (New York: G.P. Putnam's Sons, 1990, p. 324).

3.   Jerry Mander, *Four Arguments for the Elimination of Television* (New York: William Morrow/Quill Publishers, 1977).

4.   In addition to his own earlier work on the effects of television, Mander relies heavily on three other sources in making his current arguments: Marie Winn, *The Plug-In Drug* (New York: Viking Press, 1977); Marie Winn, *Unplugging the Plug-In Drug* (New York: Viking/Penguin Publisher, 1987); and Fred and Merrelyn Emery, *A Choice of Futures: To Enlighten or Inform?* (Canberra: Center for Continuing Education, Australian National University, 1975).

5.   Mander follows the articulations of Charles Pillar and Keith R. Yamamoto, in their *Gene Wars: Military Control Over the New Genetic Technologies* (New York: Beech Tree Books, 1988), while making his arguments in this connection.

6.   Mander acknowledges borrowing heavily from the thought of French philosopher/technocritic Jacques Ellul, especially the arguments advanced in his *Propaganda: The Formation of Men's Attitudes* (New York: Vintage/Random House Publishers, 1973); and *The Technological Society* (New York: Alfred A. Knopf Publishers, 1964).

7.   Quoted from Holly Sklar, ed., *Trilateralism: The Trilateral Commission and Elite Planning for World Management* (Boston: South End Press, 1980).

8.   See Herman Kahn, *World Economic Development* (New York: William Morrow/McQuill Publishers, 1979); and Gerald K. O'Neal, *The High Frontier* (New York: Bantam Books, 1976).

9.   Mander is referencing Hans Moravec, *Mind Children: The Future of Robot and Human Intelligence* (Cambridge: Harvard University Press, 1988), in this

passage.

10. On German missile development during World War II, and the absence of British or American counterpart technology, see Richard Anthony Young, *The Flying Bomb* (London: Ian Allan Publishers, 1978). On Allied use of computers in cryptography, see David Kahn, *The Codebreakers* (New York: Alfred A. Knopf Publishers, 1967); on their use in nuclear physics, see Richard G. Hewlett and Oscar E. Anderson, Jr., *The New World, 1939-1946, Vol. I: A History of the United States Atomic Energy Commission* (University Park, PA: Pennsylvania State University Press, 1962).

11. On nuclear testing in the Marshall Islands, see Alex Cockburn and James Ridgeway, "An Atoll, A Submarine and the U.S. Economy," in Michael Albert and David Dellinger, eds., *Beyond Survival: New Directions for the Disarmament Movement* (Boston: South End Press, 1983, pp. 155-86). On the development and use of machine guns, see F.W.A. Hobart, *Pictorial History of the Machine Gun* (London: Ian Allan Publisher, 1971); the weapon used at Wounded Knee was a Hotchkiss Gun, a Gatling Gun-like precursor of actual machine guns.

12. It should be noted that Mander follows Cree author George Manual—without attribution—in describing indigenous peoples as "Fourth World nations"; see George Manual and Michael Posluns, *The Fourth World: An Indian Reality* (New York: The Free Press, 1974). The nonindustrial reality posed by the term is as contrasted to the industrial-capitalist "First World," industrial-socialist "Second World," and industrializing-nonaligned "Third World" once described by Mao Tse-tung. Anishinabe activist Winona LaDuke has suggested that the Fourth World should actually be termed the "Host World" insofar as all of the other three are constructed squarely

atop it.

13. As will be dealt with more thoroughly later, attribution to native—as opposed to Euroamerican—sources is not Mander's strong suit. Abundant citation with regard to each of these examples may be found in Ward Churchill, *Struggle for the Land: Indigenous Resistance to Genocide, Ecocide and Expropriation in Contemporary North America* (Monroe, ME: Common Courage Press, 1992); M. Annette Jaimes, ed., *The State of Native America: Genocide, Colonization and Resistance* (Boston: South End Press, 1992); and Haunani-Kay Trask, *From a Native Daughter: Colonialism and Sovereignty in Hawai'i* (Monroe, ME: Common Courage Press, 1993).

14. Nietschmann deploys the term in a deceptively-titled essay, "The Third World War," *Cultural Survival Quarterly*, Vol. 11, No. 3, Fall 1987.

15. Editors (John Mohawk), *A Basic Call to Consciousness* (Rooseveltown, NY: *Akwesasne Notes*, 1978).

16. Thomas R. Berger, *Village Journey: The Report of the Alaska Native Review Commission* (New York: Hill and Wang Publishers, 1985); Julian Burger, *Report from the Frontier: The State of the World's Indigenous Peoples* (London: Zed Books, 1987).

17. Mander includes Castaneda's *The Teachings of Don Juan: A Yaqui Way of Knowledge* (Los Angeles: University of California Press, 1968) and *A Separate Reality: Further Conversations with Don Juan* (New York: Simon and Schuster, 1971) in his bibliography as "reputable" sources on indigenous thought. For a brief summary of the problems in this regard, see Ward Churchill, "Carlos Castaneda: The Greatest Hoax Since Piltdown Man," in M. Annette Jaimes, ed., *Fantasies of the Master Race: Literature, Cinema and the Colonization of American Indians* (Monroe, ME: Common Courage Press, 1991, pp. 43-64).

18. The following are those native-authored sources actually contained in Mander's bibliography. **Books and Pamphlets**: *A Basic Call to Consciousness, op. cit.*; Jeanette Armstrong, *Slash* (Penticton, B.C.: Theytus Books, 1985) and *The Native Creative Process* (Penticton, B.C.: Theytus Books, 1991); Art Davidson and the Association of Village Council Presidents, eds., *Does One Way of Life Have to Die So Another Can Live?* (Bethel, AL: Yupik Nation, 1974); Editors, *Denedeh: A Dene Celebration* (Yellowknife, NWT: Dene Nation, 1984); Jack D. Forbes, *Tribes and Masses: Explorations in Red, White and Black* (Davis, CA: D-Q University Press, 1978); Donald A. Grinde, Jr., *The Iroquois and the Founding of the American Nation* (San Francisco: American Indian Historical Society, 1977); John Fire Lame Deer and Richard Erdoes, *Lame Deer: Seeker of Visions* (New York: Simon and Schuster Publishers, 1972); N. Scott Momaday, *A House Made of Dawn* (New York: Harper & Row Publishers, 1985); Roxanne Dunbar Ortiz, *Roots of Resistance: Land Tenure in New Mexico, 1680-1980* (Los Angeles: UCLA Chicano Studies Research Publications and American Indian Studies Center, 1980); Dagmar Thorpe, *New Segobia: The Western Shoshone People and Land* (Lee, NV: Western Shoshone Sacred Lands Association, 1982); **Newspaper Articles**: Kahn-Tineta Horn, "The Akwesasne War: Why Can't the Mohawks Settle It Themselves?" (*Toronto Globe and Mail*, May 3, 1990); M. Helene Laraque, "Unity Grows After 500 Years" (*Native Press*, September 28, 1990) and "Toward the Next 500 Years" (*Native Press*, October 12, 1990); **Interviews**: Donald A. Grinde, Jr.; **Memoranda and Reports**: Robert T. Coulter and Steven Tullburg, *Report to the Kikmongwes* (Washington, D.C.: American Indian Law Resource Center, 1979); Chris Peters, "Native Thinking and Social Transformation" (Berkeley: Elmwood Institute, January 11, 1991).

19. Joseph Jorgenson, ed., *American Indians and Energy Development* (Cambridge, MA: Anthropology Resource Center, 1978).

20. The relevance of Deloria's work to Mander's project seems undeniable; see his *God Is Red* (New York: Delta Books, 1973) for a particularly clear example.

21. For further elaboration of this process, see Samir Amin, *Eurocentrism* (New York: Monthly Review Press, 1989).

22. For details, see Aziz S. Atiya, *Crusade, Commerce and Culture* (New York: John Wiley and Sons, Publishers, 1962).

23. Lyric from "Won't Get Fooled Again," by songwriter/guitarist Peter Townshend, recorded on the album *Who's Next* (Los Angeles: MCA Records, 1971).

24. He just happens, as examples, to overlook any mention whatsoever of such rather conspicuous figures in the contemporary North American struggle for indigenous liberation as Jimmie Durham, Janet McCloud, Russell, Bill, Lorelei, and Ted Means, Madonna Thunderhawk, John Trudell, and Phyllis Young.

25. The formal legislative and judicial aspects of the Black Hills Land Claim were initiated in 1921, nearly 25 years before its next closest competitor; see the special issue of *Wicazo Sa Review* (Vol. IV, No. 1, Spring 1988) devoted to the topic.

26. This has been very well publicized. During the 1982 Israeli assault upon the city of Beirut, for instance, AIM leader Russell Means was widely quoted as stating that "the Palestinians of North America offer sanctuary to the American Indians of the Middle East."

27. On these matters, see Peter Matthiessen, *In the Spirit of Crazy Horse* (New York: Viking Press, 1983).

28. The IITC and its work are covered in Rex Weyler, *Blood of the Land: The U.S. Government and*

Corporate War Against the American Indian Movement (New York: Everest House Publishers, 1982).

29. On WARN, see M. Annette Jaimes and Theresa Halsey, "American Indian Women: At the Center of Indigenous Resistance in North America," in *The State of Native America, op. cit.*, pp. 311-44.

30. Russell Means, "Fighting Words on the Future of Mother Earth," *Mother Jones*, January 1981; included under the title, "The Same Old Song," in Ward Churchill, ed., *Marxism and Native Americans* (Boston: South End Press, 1983, pp. 19-34).

31. For instance, John Trudell, *Living in Reality* (Minneapolis: Society of People Struggling to be Free, 1982). Trudell's several recordings—*Tribal Voice* (1982), *JT/JED* (1985), *Heart Jump Bouquet* (1986), *But This Isn't El Salvador* (1987), and *AKA: Graffiti Man* (1988, 1992)—have also been mainstay indigenous articulations of the very themes Mander pursues.

32. See International Organization for the Elimination of All Forms of Racial Discrimination, *Zionism and Racism: Proceedings of an International Symposium* (New Brunswick, NJ: North American Publishers, 1979).

33. See Reginald Horsman, *Racism and Manifest Destiny: The Origins of Racial Anglo-Saxonism* (Cambridge: Harvard University Press, 1981).

34. This is covered very well in Noam Chomsky, *The Fateful Triangle: Israel, Palestine and the United States* (Boston: South End Press, 1983). Also see Edward W. Said, *The Question of Palestine* (New York: Vintage Books, 2nd ed.,1992).

35. See Maxime Rodinson, *Israel: A Colonial-Settler State* (New York: Monad Press, 1973). Another good reading in this regard is Elia T. Zurayk, *The Palestinians in Israel: A Study in Internal Colonialism* (London: Routledge and Kegan Paul Publishers, 1979).

"P" is for Plagiarism

A Closer Look at Jack Weatherford's *Indian Givers*

> Of *course* Euroamerica is committed to ripping off Indians. I mean, it's a culture committed to ripping off everything, even itself.
>
> —Winona LaDuke, 1989

Plagiarism, the taking of a previous author's ideas, words, or writings without attribution, is undeniably one of the uglier and more uncomfortable of all the many criticisms a reviewer may advance. It plainly implies a degree of fundamental dishonesty, and perhaps maliciousness, on the part of the author thus charged, a matter which tends to erode (often needlessly) the sense of usefulness assigned by public perception to his or her published material. One therefore wishes to be extremely careful when extending such charges, all the more so when one holds a particular fondness for the book in which purloined concepts and content are suspected. Still, there are times when the appearance of plagiarism is so strong that the unfortunate topic simply must be raised, all desires to the contrary notwithstanding.

Take as a case in point Jack Weatherford's *Indian Givers: How the Indians of the Americas Transformed the World* (New York: Crown Publishers, 1988). Written in a highly lucid and accessible style designed for a general readership, it has increasingly become a standard text for survey courses—including my own—addressing the physical and intellectual attainments of precontact Native America. Covering areas such as American Indian medicine and pharmacology, agriculture and cuisine, governance and property relations, architecture and urban planning, commerce and social organization, it stands as a crushing rejoinder to the contentions of orthodox anthropologists and kindred academics that the hemisphere was sparsely populated by little more than "squalid stone age hunter-gatherers" wandering the landscape in "nomadic bands" until the European invasion acquainted them with the attributes of "civilization." In round-house fashion, he obliterates much of the contrived basis upon which the ideology of Western cultural supremacism is spawned, usually garbed in the attire of more conventional "scholarship." His book is thus of crucial importance, an ideal tool for debunking Eurocentrist mythologies in the classroom.

The problem is that *Indian Givers* has, since its release, been portrayed not only as the best available volume of its sort, but essentially as the *only* such work (while neither author nor publisher has quite come right out and said this, they have certainly done nothing to dispel the impression, which both are well aware has taken firm hold among teachers and other buyers). Consider now a second book, almost unknown in the United States but published by a small press in Penticton, British Columbia, two years earlier than Weatherford's. Written by the late Warren Lowes and produced by the Canadian Alliance in Solidarity with Native Peoples, it is entitled *Indian Giver: A Legacy of North American Native Peoples* (Theytus Books, 1986). As might be expected, the two publications share rather more than a passing similarity in titles.

Indeed, Weatherford appears in large part to have simply followed Lowes's script, item by item, albeit in a reorganized and greatly amplified fashion. The most immediately noticeable—and in some ways only—distinction between *Indian Giver* and *Indian Givers* is their respective lengths: Lowes's material runs a meager 114 pages, while Weatherford's comes to 272. Meanwhile, where Lowes offers a chapter entitled "Name Calling Made Popular," covering, among other things, the prevalence of Indian place names such as Chicago, Tallahassee, and Tennessee in contemporary North American society, Weatherford incorporates a section on the same matter (and using the same examples) in his chapter on "Architecture and Urban Planning." Where Lowes includes a chapter, "The Influences of Folk Democracy," centering to a considerable extent in the example of the Iroquois Six Nations Confederacy and its impact upon the thinking of both the framers of the U.S. Constitution and such European political theorists as Rousseau, Voltaire, and Marx, Weatherford covers precisely the same ground in chapters entitled "Liberty, Anarchism, and the Noble Savage" and "The Indian Founding Fathers." Lowes presents a chapter describing "The Gift of Better Health," Weatherford includes one dubbed "The Indian Healer." Lowes fields a chapter on "The Gift of Agriculture and Food," and Weatherford follows suit with chapters on "The Food Revolution," "Indian Agricultural Technology" and "The Culinary Revolution." In each case, many of the the illustrations deployed—in some instances down to the sequence and language with which they are introduced to the text—are virtually identical.

Before moving on, it would be well to take up suggestions, sure to be raised, that—however striking the parallels in title and content between the two books—all this might nonetheless be a matter of "coincidence" rather than an incident of plagiarism per se. The idea is that Lowes's earlier effort might have been so obscure that Weatherford remained unaware of it. Hence, the latter must be viewed as having just "happened" to take up the same concept for a book, approach it in almost the same way, and to occasionally say what was on his mind in exactly the same words as his predecessor/counterpart. Perhaps. Counterposed against such a possibility, however, is the fact that Weatherford *does* reference Lowes's work in his more recent, but much less directly related, *Native Roots: How the Indians Enriched America* (Crown Books, 1991), a project which was already in its initial stages when his 1988 book was released. Further, despite this conclusive evidence that Weatherford is acquainted with *Indian Giver*, and has been for some time, any acknowledgement to this effect remains absent from *Indian Givers* after several subsequent editions. The "theory of inadvertency," exceedingly thin in any event, becomes anorexic to the point of nothingness.

That Weatherford should have adopted such a posture seems inexplicable at a number of levels, given that his is by far the superior of the two titles.

Lowes's book reads more than anything like an extended outline or, at most, a preliminary draft of what was ultimately intended. Most probably it was a work in process—a series of extended notes, say, being collected *en route* to a more comprehensive manuscript—which was permanently interrupted by the death of the author, then posthumously assembled for publication with only light polishing by its editor(s). The result, of course, is a decidedly incomplete volume which yields an equally limited utility. Weatherford, then, can be said to have performed a necessary and not inconsiderable service by expanding Lowes's sketch to respectable proportions, as well as by developing logically related themes— e.g., the impact of American Indian resources in underwriting Europe's industrial revolution—left mostly dormant in the original book. His final product was (and is) therefore deserving of the widest possible attention in its own right, without resort to manipulation or pretension.

Attempting to apprehend the motivations which prompted Weatherford's needless but nonetheless abundantly evident determination to hide the fact that he extrapolated from an antecedent volume is thus an entirely speculative and somewhat mystifying endeavor. Maybe he believed the unlikely proposition that his sales would suffer if it were generally known that he had "borrowed" liberally from Lowes. Perhaps it was more a matter of ego and personal insecurity, the need to experience that peculiar assignment of intellectual stature, so pronounced in Euroamerican academic circles, which attends claims to being "first" in coming up with an idea or synthesis of ideas. Most likely, it was some melding of these themes. Whatever the case, the only thing Weatherford can truly be said to have accomplished with his attempted deception was the demonstration of his own lack of integrity and the depth of his disrespect, not only for an unoffending colleague whose work preceded his own, but for his readers and the native people who felt Lowes's writing was important and worthy of being committed to print in the first place.

"Renegades, Terrorists, and Revolutionaries"

The Government's Propaganda War Against the American Indian Movement

> The bigger the lie, the more likely it is to be believed.
>
> —Joseph Goebbels
> Nazi Propaganda Minister

During the 1970s, the U.S. government conducted what amounted to a counterinsurgency war against the American Indian Movement. The campaign was designed to "neutralize" that organization's ability to pursue an agenda of Indian treaty rights, land recovery, and national sovereignty in North America.[1] While many of the federal tactics took a directly physical form—assassinations, fabrication of evidence in criminal cases, and the like—a major propaganda effort was also integral to the government's strategy of repression. The motives for this lay not only in an official desire to deny AIM broad public support, but in a need to condition the citizenry to accept as "justified" the harsh and often extralegal nature of what authorities were otherwise doing to the group.

173

Opening Rounds

The first substantial anti-AIM propaganda operation appears to have begun during the spectacular "Trail of Broken Treaties" occupation of the Bureau of Indian Affairs (BIA) building in Washington, D.C., on the eve of the 1972 presidential election. The incumbent Nixon administration, eager to avoid the impression of a serious "Indian uprising" at such a critical moment, went far out of its way to prevent statements by the occupiers from surfacing in the media. Simultaneously, it spent more than $100,000 importing selected "representative Indian spokesmen" to discredit the AIM leadership. A star performer in this regard was Webster Two Hawks, president of the federally-sponsored National Tribal Chairmen's Association, who flamboyantly parroted the government line that AIM was composed of "renegades" and "irresponsible self-styled revolutionaries" who held no real standing in "Indian Country." Two Hawks's well-subsidized views were, of course, carried verbatim on national TV and splattered liberally across the front pages of the *Washington Post* and *New York Times*.[2]

It is worth noting that Two Hawks, Nixon's hand-picked "leader" of American Indians, barely had time to return home to the Rosebud Reservation in western South Dakota before being unseated as tribal chairman by AIM supporter Robert Burnette.[3] But by then federal media manipulators were at work against "the militants" even in this remote region. Solid evidence of this came on February 5, 1973, as AIM was organizing a demonstration at the Custer (S.D.) County Courthouse to protest the levying of mere manslaughter charges against a non-Indian who had brutally murdered a young Indian, Wesley Bad Heart Bull. On that date, an FBI agent impersonating an organizer called reporter Lyn Gladstone, causing a story stating the action had been cancelled to appear in the *Rapid City Journal*.[4] Consequently, when AIM members showed up as planned at the courthouse the next day, very few supporters joined them. Few supporters at the scene meant few witnesses, and so when AIM was promptly attacked by a specially-assembled force of riot police, "official spokesmen" were able to make it appear the other way around in the media.[5]

Wounded Knee

The ink was barely dry on the government's disinformation concerning "AIM violence" in Custer when federal forces laid siege to a group of organization members and supporters at Wounded Knee, on the nearby Pine Ridge Reservation. Contrary to the official line, immediately promulgated by the Justice Department and accepted by the press, that what was going on in the isolated hamlet was an "AIM occupation," the Indians had actually gone to Wounded Knee on the evening of February 27 in order to prepare for a press conference called for the following morning. Their purpose was to try and draw public attention to the corruption of Dick Wilson, the local tribal chairman, and the fact that federal authorities had blocked attempts by reservation residents to obtain even elementary due process in the matter. For instance, Wilson had been appointed by the BIA to preside over his own impeachment process, he had been funded to create

175

a *de facto* private army calling itself the "GOON squad" with which to suppress his opposition, and a 65-man SWAT team of U.S. marshals had been sent to further back him up.[6] Came the morning of February 28, the AIM group at Wounded Knee found itself completely surrounded by GOONs and marshals who were quickly reinforced by FBI, BIA police, non-Indian vigilante groups, and advisors from the army's élite 82nd Airborne Division.

Needless to say, the desired press conference never occurred. Instead, there began a 71-day confrontation during which numerous federal procedures were implemented by which to "regulate" (restrict) media access to those trapped inside the AIM perimeter. These rapidly manifested themselves in an outright barring of mainstream reporters from the scene of activity, and the issuance of threats of criminal prosecution to alternative press personnel who had essentially moved into Wounded Knee for the duration. "Press briefings" conducted by authorities were then substituted for direct coverage of what was happening. With this handy mechanism in place, the government was in a position to deliberately misrepresent reality in a number of ways. For example, when FBI agent Curtis Fitzpatrick was slightly wounded in the wrist by a spent rifle round on March 11, 1973, federal propagandists were able to arrange an extravaganza wherein reporters were allowed to witness his arrival at a nearby air force base in a military "med-evac" helicopter with his *head* swathed in bandages. Similarly, this eloquent (if utterly contrived) testament to "AIM violence" was still making the rounds nationally when federal "public relations officers" began announcing that individuals arrested for attempting to transport food and medical supplies into the AIM positions had actually been apprehended while smuggling "arms and ammunition." At one point, it was even announced that AIM was firing state-of-the-art M-60 machine guns at federal personnel despite the fact that the FBI was later revealed to have been fully aware that the Indians possessed no armaments other than an array of hunting rifles and shotguns.[7]

In addition to allowing AIM to be tarred with the brush of fiction, barring the media from Wounded Knee allowed the government to cover up many of its own actions. For instance, the burning of several buildings inside the hamlet—widely attributed to AIM "vandalism"—was actually caused by the profuse use of heavy-calibre military tracer ammunition and the repeated firing of magnesium flares directly at the wooden structures. Nor was any mainstream reporter in a position to observe exactly who initiated the massive firefights—federal forces fired more than 500,000 rounds into Wounded Knee during the siege—which frequently lit up the nights. Or, to take another example, when AIM member Buddy Lamont was killed at Wounded Knee on April 27, no mention was made of the fact that he had bled to death because FBI commander Joseph Trimbach deliberately delayed his being placed in an ambulance for 45 minutes.[8] Perhaps most importantly, a steadily increasing intimacy between the FBI and the GOONs—with the former providing the latter with automatic weapons and stores of ammunition, military communications gear and other material support, as well as intelligence information and virtual immunity from prosecution—was also obscured.

The "Reign of Terror"

During the three years following Wounded Knee, more than 300 AIM members and supporters were physically assaulted on Pine Ridge. Of these, at least 69 died, giving the reservation a political murder rate precisely comparable to that prevailing in Chile during the three years immediately following the 1973 Pinochet coup.[9] In virtually every instance, this "Third World" level of violence was plainly attributable to the GOONs, often on the basis of multiple eyewitness accounts. Yet the FBI—which held primary jurisdiction on the reservation, and which had thereon deployed the greatest concentration of agents to citizens in history—pled "lack of manpower" in solving or in most cases even investigating the homicides. Instead, despite the absence of casualties among the GOONs and police personnel, and the fact that the U.S. Commission on Civil Rights had formally concluded that the FBI and its GOON surrogate, rather than AIM, were fostering a "reign of terror" on Pine Ridge,[10] Bureau publicists maintained a national media drumbeat proclaiming it was *AIM* which was "violence-prone." This aspect of the government's disinformation campaign culminated during the spring of 1975 when Douglass Durham, an FBI infiltrator/*provocateur* who had worked himself into the position of AIM security chief, was allowed to testify as the sole witness before the Senate Committee on Internal Security. His uncorroborated, unsubstantiated, and in most cases utterly false testimony was then used as the basis for a widely disseminated official report branding AIM as a "revolutionary organization" committed to "the violent overthrow of the federal government."[11]

At this juncture, FBI strategists appear to have felt that the public had been sufficiently conditioned to accept a final stroke which would physically destroy AIM once and for all. Hence, on June 26, 1975, two agents—Ron Williams and Jack Coler— were sent to an AIM compound located on the Harry and Cecilia Jumping Bull property, near the reservation village of Oglala. Ostensibly, the agents were attempting to arrest a seventeen-year-old AIM member named Jimmy Eagle on the charge of stealing a pair of used cowboy boots. Given that some 150 FBI and BIA SWAT personnel were prepositioned in the immediate area as "back up," it seems that Coler's and Williams's real mission was to provoke an armed confrontation which would justify the use of overwhelming force to crush the AIM encampment. In the event, having precipitated a firefight, the agents were cut off from their intended support. They, along with an AIM member named Joe Stuntz Killsright, were killed. The rest of the Indians escaped.[12]

With their plan for a "quick kill" of AIM thus seriously off track, Bureau officials immediately rushed an additional 250 SWAT personnel to Pine Ridge. They also dispatched Tom Coll, a propaganda specialist, to "explain" why the FBI was suddenly conducting Vietnam-style search and destroy operations—complete with armored personnel carriers and attack helicopters—on an obscure South Dakota Indian reservation. The reason, according to Coll, was that the "terrorist American Indian Movement" had initiated "guerrilla warfare" on Pine Ridge. Agents Williams and Coler, he said, had been "lured into an ambush" where they were "attacked from a sophisticated bunker complex." After being wounded, he continued, they had been "dragged from their cars," "stripped," and "riddled with 15-20 bullets" apiece, the ammunition fired from "automatic weapons." In one account, they had also been "scalped." It had been "cold-blooded murder," said Coll, and agent Williams had been "executed" while lying on the ground "pleading with his killers to think of his wife and children."[13]

None of this was true, as Coll knew at the time he fed it to the media. Each agent had been hit only three times, and from long rather than close range. The fabled "bunkers" were actually old root cellars and animal shelters—common to any rural area— which had *not* been used as AIM positions during the firefight. There was no evidence that AIM had utilized automatic weapons. Neither agent had been stripped, scalped, or otherwise mutilated. Far from being "lured" to the firefight site, the agents had been sent there by their own superiors. Still, it was nearly a week before FBI director Clarence Kelley openly admitted these facts, and by then a wave of sensational headlines and TV "news" reports had firmly established a public sentiment supporting the Bureau in its massive campaign of kicking in the doors of reservation houses, conducting "air assaults" on the properties of known AIM supporters, and generally terrorizing the entire reservation population. Even a few of the GOONs are known to have protested what was going on at this point,[14] but under such circumstances the FBI was able to continue its invasion of Pine Ridge for three solid months without appreciable public outcry.

End Game Moves

It would probably be fair to say that the cap-stone of the federal propaganda war on AIM came a year later, in June of 1976, during the trial of Bob Robideau and Dino Butler in the deaths of Williams and Coler. In a bald attempt to influence the jury (and the public at large) against the defendants, the FBI suddenly announced that it had evidence that a force of "2,000 AIM warriors" known as "Dog Soldiers" and "trained in the Northwest" were about to arrive in South Dakota. Once there, they planned to "kill a cop a day...burn farmers...snipe at tour-ists...assassinate the governor...blow up the Bureau of Indian Affairs...blow up turbines at the Ft. Randall Dam...and destroy Mt. Rushmore National Monument," among other things. The "Dog Soldier Teletypes," as the FBI communiques quickly became known, also contended that this AIM activity was part of a multiracial venture in terrorism, planned jointly with a Denver-based Chicano group known as the Crusade for Justice, and Students for a Democratic Society (SDS; a long-defunct white radi-cal organization).[15] The information again brought on splashy headlines nationally, a situation which lasted until FBI director Kelley was cross-examined under oath by Butler/Robideau defense attorney William Kunstler. When asked whether there was a "shred of evidence" to support the allegations trum-peted in his Bureau's teletypes, Kelley responded: "I know of none."[16] The jury ultimately acquitted Butler and Robideau of the murder charges brought against them on the basis that they had killed the two FBI agents in self-defense. Nonetheless, the misimpression of AIM as a bunch of renegades, terrorists, and revolutionaries had once again been deliberately inculcated among the general public. Cumulatively, the combination of sustained physical hammering, judicial railroading, and persistent public misrepresentation had proven sufficient to enable the government to attain its objective of neutralizing most of AIM's political effectiveness.

Conclusion

As Malcolm X once put it, "If you're not careful, the newspapers will have you hating the people who are being oppressed, and loving the people who are doing the oppressing." Certain particularities notwithstanding, the experience of the American Indian Movement as a domestic target of federal propaganda is hardly unique. As Malcolm knew, entirely comparable disinformation campaigns were being conducted during the early '60s, not only against the Nation of Islam, but also against groups such as the Student Nonviolent Coordinating Committee, Socialist Workers Party, and the Fair Play for Cuba Committee. By the latter part of the decade, the list had been expanded to include organizations such as the Revolutionary Action Movement, Black Panther Party, Young Lords Party, Student Mobilization, and SDS. During the '70s, the Weather Underground, prison liberation movement and Black Liberation Army were targeted. More recently, we see the same tactics employed to varying extents against entities like the Palestine Solidarity Committee, Silo Plowshares, CISPES, and *Puertorriqueño Independentista* formations such as *los Macheteros* and the FALN. In this sense, the government's anti-AIM propaganda effort can serve as something of a textbook illustration of a much wider technique of political repression.

Notes

1. The term comes from a description of how success is measured in counterintelligence operations offered to Sanford J. Ungar by a high FBI official in 1974. The official is quoted in Ungar's *FBI: An Uncensored Look Behind the Walls* (Boston: Little, Brown Publishers, 1975).

2. The Trail of Broken Treaties and Webster Two Hawks's role—complete with clippings from the *Washington Post*—is best covered in Editors, *BIA, I'm Not Your Indian Any More* (Rooseveltown, NY: Akwesasne Notes, 1973). Also see Vine Deloria, Jr., *Behind the Trail of Broken Treaties* (New York: Delta Books, 1974).

3. Robert Burnette and John Koster, *The Road to Wounded Knee* (New York: Bantam Books, 1974).

4. Lyn Gladstone, "Custer Demonstration Canceled," *Rapid City Journal*, February 5, 1973.

5. The events at Custer are well covered in Editors, *Voices From Wounded Knee, 1973* (Rooseveltown, NY: Akwesasne Notes, 1974).

6. The reasoning behind the degree of federal support extended to the venal Wilson regime was initially rather mysterious. It later became apparent that a deal had been made wherein Wilson would be maintained in power at virtually any cost in exchange for his agreement to sign over title to the northeastern eighth of Pine Ridge to the government. The latter had secretly discovered the acreage in question to be rich in uranium and molybdenum; see J.P Gries, *Status of Mineral Resource Information on the Pine Ridge Indian Reservation* (Washington, D.C.: U.S. Department of Interior, BIA Report No. 12, 1976).

Wilson consummated the illegal transaction—which violates the consent provisions concerning Lakota land cessions contained in the still-binding 1868 Fort Laramie Treaty—during the summer of 1975.

7. For a detailed account of the siege of Wounded Knee, see Ward Churchill and Jim Vander Wall, *Agents of Repression: The FBI's Secret Wars Against the Black Panther Party and the American Indian Movement* (Boston: South End Press, 1988; esp. Chap. 5).

8. Frank Clearwater, a Cherokee from North Carolina, was also fatally wounded at Wounded Knee on April 17, 1973. After Clearwater's death, he was consciously defamed in the media by FBI propagandists who released false information that he was "not an Indian." See "Man killed at Wounded Knee no Indian says FBI," *Rapid City Journal*, April 19, 1973.

9. Looked at another way, according to the FBI's own *Uniform Crime Report* for 1976, the overall U.S. violent death rate was 9.7 per 100,000 during that year. Detroit, reputedly the "murder capital of the United States," had a violent death rate of 20.2 per 100,000 in 1974. Pine Ridge, on the other hand, maintained a violent death rate of 170 per 100,000 during the entire three-year period running from March 1, 1973 to March 1, 1976. For further information, see Bruce Johansen and Roberto Maestas, *Wasi'chu: The Continuing Indian Wars* (New York: Monthly Review Press, 1979).

10. U.S. Commission on Civil Rights, *Monitoring Events Relating to the Shooting of Two FBI Agents on the Pine Ridge Reservation* (Denver: Mountain States Regional Office, July 9, 1975) and *Events Surrounding Recent Murders on the Pine Ridge Reservation in South Dakota* (Denver: Mountain States Regional Office, March 31, 1976).

11. See U.S. Senate, Committee on the Judiciary, Subcommittee on Internal Security, *Revolutionary*

Organizations in the United States: The American Indian Movement (Washington, D.C.: 94th Cong., 2d Sess., U.S. Government Printing Office, 1975). It should be noted that Durham went directly from his Senate testimony to a lecture tour on the topic of "AIM terrorism" sponsored by the John Birch Society. The infiltrator had also been instrumental in orchestrating the publicity attending the sensational "Skyhorse/Mohawk Case" in California, beginning in 1974, in which two area AIM leaders were accused of perpetrating the "Manson-style" murder of Los Angeles cab driver George Aird. Paul "Skyhorse" Durant and Richard "Mohawk" Billings were eventually found innocent of the crime, but by then AIM had been graphically portrayed in the media as a bunch of mad dog killers for a sustained period.

12. Probably the best account of the events of June 26, 1975, may be found in Peter Matthiessen, *In the Spirit of Crazy Horse* (New York: Viking Press, [2nd ed., expanded] 1991).

13. See, for example, John Crewdson, "Two Men Die, Indian Slain," *New York Times*, June 27, 1975.

14. "Lakota council approves resolution asking FBI removal," *Rapid City Journal*, July 14, 1975.

15. The second Dog Soldier Teletype is reproduced in Ward Churchill and Jim Vander Wall, *The COINTEL-PRO Papers: Documents from the FBI's Secret Wars Against Dissent in the United States* (Boston: South End Press, 1990, pp. 277-80).

16. The Kelley-Kunstler exchange may be found in the Butler-Robideau trial transcript (CR-76-11, N. Dist., Iowa, 1976), Appendix A, p. 3.

The *Real* Revisionism

Notes on Stan Lyman's *Wounded Knee, 1973*

As Malcolm X once warned, if we're not careful, the establishment press will have us believing the oppressed are victimizing their oppressors.

—John Trudell, 1983

The memoirs of government functionaries are notoriously fraught with half-truth and distortion, outright fabrication and self-serving rationalization. Such is the case with *Wounded Knee, 1973: A Personal Account* (Lincoln: University of Nebraska Press, 1991), a reminiscence of the late Stanley D. Lyman. For those unfamiliar with the name, Lyman served as Bureau of Indian Affairs (BIA) Superintendent of the Pine Ridge Reservation during the sustained armed confrontation over the form, function, and extent of Indian rights to self-governance waged between local Oglala Lakota traditionalists and federal authorities, beginning with the "Siege of Wounded Knee" in 1973 and continuing until at least mid-1977. Also at issue in the Pine Ridge struggle was the question of whether the northwestern one-eighth of the impoverished reservation—an area the government was later discovered to have known contained a rich uranium deposit—would be transferred from Oglala to federal ownership.[1]

Although the book contains a few vignettes which broaden the historical record of this crucial period in U.S./Indian relations, its utility is overwhelmed by a vast number of factual omissions and inaccuracies. While the author himself may be to some extent forgiven (or at least understood) in this regard—he not only had a vested interest in fudging the truth to make his own side of the conflict look good, but may even have believed some portion of the false information he presents at the time he wrote it—the same cannot be said for Floyd O'Neil, June K. Lyman, and Susan McKay, the editorial team which prepared his diary for publication. At the very least, readers have a right to expect to be apprised through footnotes when gross and well-documented inaccuracies appear in an ostensibly non-fictional text. But at no point do the editors so much as attempt to fulfil their responsibilities in this regard.

Examples are far too numerous to detail here, and a relative handful will therefore have to suffice to make the point. To begin with, Lyman persistently refers to the Indian Reorganization Act (IRA) administration on Pine Ridge, with which he was aligned, as the sole "legitimate" body representing the interests of reservation residents; no mention is made, either in the text or by way of accompanying annotation, of the fact that the IRA was imposed by the BIA in 1936 over strong Oglala objections, or that the method used in obtaining this result was the stuffing of ballot boxes with "votes" cast by a sufficient number of dead people to "affirm" reorganization.[2] He also notes repeatedly that opposition efforts to impeach IRA President Dick Wilson failed in early 1973; unmentioned is the fact that the BIA appointed Wilson himself to oversee the impeachment proceedings, or that Wilson ordered the arrest and jailing of tribal council members likely to vote against him as a means of rigging the outcome.[3] Other glaring manipulations of the political process are dealt with in similar fashion, leaving the false impression that traditionalist attempts to gain some semblance of control over their government were profoundly "irrational" and "anti-democratic."[4]

In pursuing this theme, Lyman baldly dismisses as "groundless" the specific accusations—nepotism, financial malfeasance, and systematic use of physical intimidation among them—leveled by the opposition against the Wilson regime. The nepotism charge is simply ignored, despite the thoroughly-substantiated fact that Wilson had placed virtually his entire family (wife, brothers, sons, and several cousins) on the tribal payroll.[5] The author also asserts on several occasions that General Accounting Office (GAO) auditors "exonerated" the Wilsonites of misappropriating funds when in fact, as a well-publicized U.S. Civil Rights Commission study of conditions on Pine Ridge pointed out at the time, the GAO's 1974 final report on the matter reached an exactly opposite conclusion.[6]

It follows that Lyman would claim, as he does throughout his narrative, that a group he calls "Dick Wilson's goon squad"—an entity calling itself the **G**uardians **O**f the **O**glala **N**ation (GOON)—were merely "volunteers" devoted to the IRA system rather than a well-organized gang of hired thugs retained to terrorize opponents of it. Not a word is said about subsequent admissions by key GOON leaders that they were paid from federal monies allocated for other purposes,[7] or subsequent testimony by more rank-and-file members who'd been coerced, on pain of losing their jobs or worse, into moonlighting on Wilson's extralegal enforcement unit.[8] Still less is it acknowledged that about a third of the BIA police on Pine Ridge—the very entity Lyman insists the traditionalists should have called upon to protect them from "alleged violence" the Wilsonites were directing against them—were themselves doubling as GOONs, or that this roster included the reservation's two ranking BIA police officials, Delmar Eastman and Duane Brewer.[8]

Instead, the question of reservation violence during this crucial period is handled as a rather crude exercise in victim-blaming. On balance, this seems designed not only to mask what was really happening on Pine Ridge, but to justify the massive use of federal force to crush opposition to the status quo. For instance, at three points Lyman suggests the March 25, 1973, suicide of Leo Wilcox, a clinically unbalanced Wilson supporter, was an "assassination" by the American Indian Movement (AIM), an organization called onto the reservation by tribal elders to support the traditionalists. In reality, the notion that Wilcox was murdered by AIM or anyone else was refuted, even at the time, by no less than R.D. Hurd, a federal prosecutor who excelled at taking even the thinnest cases against AIM members to trial. Meanwhile, the author remains silent about events such as the March 1 firebombing of the home of anti-Wilson journalists Aaron and Betty DeSersa, an incident which left the house in ruins and Mrs. DeSersa badly burned.[9]

The *Real* Revisionism

In the same vein, Lyman makes much—although he confesses to never having seen such a document—of a supposed "death list" compiled by AIM at Wounded Knee, naming selected IRA officials and GOONS for "liquidation." Left entirely unaddressed is the obvious fact that no individual allegedly named on this list, beginning with Wilson and Lyman himself, was ever assaulted—much less killed—by AIM "terrorists." Even more conspicuously unstated is the fact that the Wilsonites themselves are known to have compiled a "hit list" during Wounded Knee, complete with photos of most of their targets.[10] During the ensuing three years, AIM and the grassroots Oglalas suffered at least 342 serious physical assaults at the hands of the goons, more than sixty of them fatal (see "AIM Casualties on Pine Ridge, 1973-1976," following this essay).

Uncited, even in the bibliography, are four official investigative reports prepared by the Commission on Civil Rights, each of which found that an outright "reign of terror" was occurring on Pine Ridge, *not* through the actions of AIM "insurgents,"[11] but as a result of Wilson's methods of curtailing dissent.[12] It is worth noting in this connection that the Civil Rights Commission also observed a strong appearance that federal entities such as the FBI and Lyman's own BIA office were actively colluding in this lethal and utterly illegal process of political repression.[13]

Not only is balancing and corrective annotation to Lyman's wildly skewed account omitted from the main text, but from the editors' introduction as well. To the contrary, they elect to reinforce the author's disinformation as if it were the essence of veracity, trotting out the Wilcox "issue" one more time, even advancing an absurd contention that AIM was a "bona fide national security threat" claiming "300,000 members" in 1973 (a tally amounting to nearly a third of all Indians in the United States in that year).[14] There is much which needs to be understood about the counterinsurgency campaign conducted on Pine Ridge during the '70s, but this volume offers no valid insights at all. Indeed, the editors' handling prevents *Wounded Knee, 1973* from being a potentially useful contribution to the literature, making it instead an excursion into propaganda of the most insidious type. In the form it was released, the book would be much more appropriately associated with such unabashedly right-wing publishers as Arlington House than a reputedly scholarly and objective press like that representing the University of Nebraska.

Notes

1. This concerns the so-called Sheep Mountain Gunnery Range, "borrowed" by the U.S. as a training field for aerial gunners during World War II and never returned, although it remained Lakota property in an at least nominal sense. After uranium was discovered there during a top secret 1970 satellite-mapping exercise conducted jointly by NASA and the National Uranium Resource Evaluation Institute (NURE), the government appears to have concocted an elaborate—if legally invalid—scheme to obtain "clear title" to the parcel. Increasing agitation on the part of Oglala traditionals to recover this land during 1971 and 1972 threatened to foil the plan, and thus—unbeknownst to the victims—became a major

contributing factor to the form and intensity of federal repression visited upon Pine Ridge "Indian militants" over the subsequent three years. Once the resistance was considered broken, the desired land transfer was in fact concluded. On the uranium specifically, see J.P. Gries, *Status of Mineral Resource Information on the Pine Ridge Indian Reservation, S.D.* (Washington, D.C.: U.S. Department of Interior, BIA Report No. 12, 1976). For details of the land transfer, see "Memorandum of Agreement Between the Oglala Sioux Tribe of South Dakota and the National Park Service of the Department of Interior to Facilitate Establishment, Development, Administration and Public Use of the Oglala Tribal Lands, Badlands National Monument (January 2, 1976)," in Master Plan, Badlands National Monument (Denver: Rocky Mountain Region, National Park Service, U.S. Department of Interior, 1978). Lyman, of course, mentions none of this. Nor do the editors. Overall, see Jacqueline Huber, et al., *The Gunnery Range Report* (Pine Ridge, SD: Oglala Sioux Tribe, Office of the President, 1981).

2. In general, see Thomas Biolsi, *Organizing the Lakota: The Political Economy of the New Deal on the Pine Ridge and Rosebud Reservations* (Tucson: University of Arizona Press, 1992).

3. This is well covered in Editors, *Voices from Wounded Knee, 1973* (Rooseveltown, NY: *Akwesasne Notes*, 1974, pp. 17-26).

4. For example, immediately after the impeachment "failed," Wilson issued a ban against meetings of more than three people anywhere on the reservation without his personal okay. He also attempted to enjoin enrolled tribal members such as Russell Means from "setting foot on Pine Ridge." A 65-member SOG ("Special Operations Group") composed of SWAT-trained and combat-equipped—M-60 machine

guns, M-16 rifles, M-79 grenade launchers, etc.—
U.S. marshals had already been deployed to help en-
force such unlawful edicts. See Robert Burnette and
John Koster, *The Road to Wounded Knee* (New York:
Bantam Books, 1974).

5. The GAO found, according to the *New York Times*
(April 22, 1975), that Wilson had raised his own
salary from $5,500 to $15,000 per year between
1972 and 1973. He had also named his wife to run
the Oglala Head Start Program at a salary of $18,000
annually, and had hired his brother, Jim, to head up
the tribal planning office at an annual salary of
$25,000 (plus another $15,000 per year in tribal
"consulting fees"). Another brother, George, was
retained to "manage tribal affairs" at a rate of
$20,000 per year. Wilson's son, "Manny," had been
placed on the payroll of the "Tribal Rangers" (GOONs)
at an undisclosed rate, as had several cousins and
nephews. This was during a period when the average
annual income of an Oglala resident on the reservation was less than $1,000 and one of its three coun-
ties—Shannon—was the poorest in the United
States; see Cheryl McCall, "Life on Pine Ridge Bleak,"
Colorado Daily, May 16, 1975. When confronted with
all this, Wilson himself had responded defiantly that
"there's no law against nepotism"; quoted in *Voices
from Wounded Knee, op. cit.*, p. 34.

6. William Muldrow and Shirley Hill Witt, *Report on
Investigation: Oglala Sioux Tribe. General Election,
1974* (Denver: Rocky Mountain Regional Office, U.S.
Commission on Civil Rights, 1974).

7. The GAO established that the GOONs had been
established on the basis of a $67,000 BIA block
grant dispensed for purposes of forming a "Tribal
Ranger Group" in 1972, and that there was a "clear
appearance" that it was maintained during 1973 and
1974 through misappropriation of some $347,000 in

federal highway improvement funds provided to the Wilson regime. See U.S. Commission on Civil Rights, *Hearing Held Before the U.S. Commission on Civil Rights: American Indian Issues in South Dakota, Hearing Held in Rapid City, South Dakota, July 27-28, 1978* (Washington, D.C.: U.S. Government Printing Office, 1978).

8. See, for example, the analysis of a 125-page interview given by former BIA Police/GOON leader Duane Brewer quoted extensively by Ward Churchill in "Death Squads in the United States: Confessions of a Government Terrorist," *Yale Journal of Law and Liberation*, No. 3, Fall 1992, pp. 83-99.

9. *The Road to Wounded Knee, op. cit.*, p. 228.

10. "Death Squads in the United States," *op. cit.*

11. The characterization of AIM activists as "insurgents" rather than as "militants," "radicals" or "extremists"—the usual vernacular employed by the FBI to describe political targets—comes from the Bureau's own documents. Hence, the FBI's operations against AIM on Pine Ridge can be classified as comprising an outright counterinsurgency (military) campaign rather than falling within the rubric of the counterintelligence activities more typically directed by the Bureau against "objectionable" political groups. As illustration, see the document reproduced at p. 264 of Ward Churchill and Jim Vander Wall, *The COINTELPRO Papers: Documents from the FBI's Secret Wars Against Dissent in the United States* (Boston: South End Press, 1990).

12. In addition to *Report of Investigation* (*op. cit.*) and *American Indian Issues in South Dakota* (*op. cit.*), see William Muldrow and Shirley Hill Witt, *Monitoring of Events Related to the Shootings of Two FBI Agents on the Pine Ridge Reservation* (Denver: Mountain States Regional Office, U.S. Commission on Civil Rights, September 1975); and *Events Surrounding Recent*

Murders on the Pine Ridge Reservation in South Dakota (Denver: Mountain States Regional Office, U.S. Commission on Civil Rights, March 31, 1976).

13. This is a theme consistently repeated in all Civil Rights Commission investigative reports on the matter. Commission investigator William Muldrow also testified to this effect during the 1976 murder trial of AIM members Bob Robideau and Darrell "Dino" Butler in Cedar Rapids, Iowa.

14. AIM's own estimate of its membership during this period was that there were as many as 350 "hard core" members—barely over one percent of the editors' ridiculous tally—and another thousand or so others actively involved in one capacity or another. The FBI's estimates conform rather closely to those of AIM itself.

AIM Casualties on Pine Ridge, 1973-1976

with Jim Vander Wall

In our books, *Agents of Repression* (South End Press, 1988) and *The COINTELPRO Papers* (South End Press, 1990) we have used the figure 69 as the minimum number of AIM members and supporters murdered on the Pine Ridge Reservation from mid-1973 through mid-1976. This has provoked claims on the parts of various FBI apologists that we "exaggerate" the gravity of the situation. Our first response to such critics is that it ultimately matters little in terms of the implications at issue whether the number of AIM casualties was in the upper forties—as the Bureau itself has admitted—or the upper sixties, as we contend. Our second response is the following itemized list of casualties, including the names of the victims, the dates and causes of their deaths (where known), and, so far as is possible, the status of FBI investigations (if any) into their murders. Our third response is that, as we've said all along, even this itemization is undoubtedly incomplete. We therefore request any individuals having knowledge of murders other than those listed—or who are aware of the names of any of the individuals killed while packing supplies into Wounded Knee—to contact us with this information.

04/17/73   *Frank Clearwater*—AIM member killed by heavy machine gun round at Wounded Knee. No investigation.

04/23/73   *Between eight and twelve individuals* (names unknown) packing supplies into Wounded Knee were intercepted by GOONs and vigilantes. None were ever heard from again. Former Rosebud Tribal President Robert Burnette and U.S. Justice Department Solicitor General Kent Frizzell conducted unsuccessful search for mass grave after Wounded Knee siege. No further investigation.

04/27/73   *Buddy Lamont*—AIM member hit by M-16 fire at Wounded Knee. Bled to death while pinned down by fire. No investigation.

06/19/73   *Clarence Cross*—AIM supporter shot to death in ambush by GOONs. Although assailants were identified by eyewitnesses, brother Vernal Cross—wounded in ambush—was briefly charged with crime. No further investigation.

07/14/73   *Priscilla White Plume*—AIM supporter killed at Manderson by GOONs. No investigation.

07/30/73   *Julius Bad Heart Bull*—AIM supporter killed at Oglala by "person or persons unknown." No investigation.

09/22/73   *Melvin Spider*—AIM member killed at Porcupine, South Dakota. No investigation.

09/23/73   *Philip Black Elk*—AIM supporter killed

when his house exploded. No investigation.

10/05/73   *Aloysius Long Soldier*—AIM member killed at Kyle, S.D. by GOONs. No investigation.

10/10/73   *Phillip Little Crow*—AIM supporter beaten to death by GOONs at Pine Ridge. No investigation.

10/17/73   *Pedro Bissonette*—Oglala Sioux Civil Rights Organization (OSCRO) organizer and AIM supporter assassinated by BIA Police/GOONs. Body removed from Pine Ridge jurisdiction prior to autopsy by government contract coroner. No further investigation.

11/20/73   *Allison Fast Horse*—AIM supporter shot to death near Pine Ridge by "unknown assailants." No investigation.

01/17/74   *Edward Means, Jr.*—AIM member found dead in Pine Ridge alley, beaten. No investigation.

02/18/74   *Edward Standing Soldier*—AIM member killed near Pine Ridge by "party or parties unknown." No investigation.

02/27/74   *Lorinda Red Paint*—AIM supporter killed at Oglala by "unknown assailants." No investigation.

04/19/74   *Roxeine Roark*—AIM supporter killed at Porcupine by "unknown assailants." Investigation opened, still "pending."

09/07/74   *Dennis LeCompte*—AIM member killed at Pine Ridge by GOONs. No investigation.

09/11/74   *Jackson Washington Cutt*—AIM member killed at Parmalee by "unknown individuals." Investigation still "ongoing."

09/16/74   *Robert Reddy*—AIM member killed at Kyle by gunshot. No investigation.

11/16/74   *Delphine Crow Dog*—sister of AIM spiritual leader Leonard Crow Dog. Beaten by BIA police and left lying in a field. Died from "exposure." No investigation.

11/30/74   *Elaine Wagner*—AIM supporter killed at Pine Ridge by "person or persons unknown." No investigation.

12/25/74   *Floyd S. Binias*—AIM supporter killed at Pine Ridge by GOONs. No investigation.

12/28/74   *Yvette Lorraine Lone Hill*—AIM supporter killed at Kyle by "unknown party or parties." No investigation.

01/05/75   *Leon L. Swift Bird*—AIM member killed at Pine Ridge by GOONs. Investigation still "ongoing."

03/01/75   *Martin Montileaux*—killed in a Scenic, S.D. bar. AIM leader Richard Marshall later framed for his murder. Russell Means also charged and acquitted.

03/20/75   *Stacy Cottier*—shot to death in an ambush at Manderson. No investigation.

03/21/75   *Edith Eagle Hawk and her two children*—AIM supporter killed in automobile accident after being run off the road by a white vigilante, Albert

Coomes. Coomes was also killed in the accident. GOON Mark Clifford identified as having also been in Coomes car, escaped. Investigation closed without questioning of Clifford.

03/27/75   *Jeanette Bissonette*—AIM supporter killed by sniper in Pine Ridge. Unsuccessful attempt to link AIM members to murder; no other investigation.

03/30/75   *Richard Eagle*—grandson of AIM supporter Gladys Bissonette killed while playing with loaded gun kept in the house as protection from GOON attacks.

04/04/75   *Hilda R. Good Buffalo*—AIM supporter stabbed to death at Pine Ridge by GOONs. No investigation.

04/04/75   *Jancita Eagle Deer*—AIM member beaten and run over with automobile. Last seen in the company of FBI *agent provocateur* Douglass Durham. No investigation.

05/20/75   *Ben Sitting Up*—AIM member killed at Wanblee by "unknown assailants." No investigation.

06/01/75   *Kenneth Little*—AIM supporter killed at Pine Ridge by GOONs. Investigation still "pending."

06/15/75   *Leah Spotted Elk*—AIM supporter killed at Pine Ridge by GOONs. No investigation.

06/26/75   *Joseph Stuntz Killsright*—AIM member killed by FBI sniper during Oglala firefight. No investigation.

07/12/75   *James Brings Yellow*—heart attack caused by FBI air assault on his home. No investigation.

07/25/75   *Andrew Paul Stewart*—nephew of AIM spiritual leader, Leonard Crow Dog, killed by GOONs on Pine Ridge. No investigation.

08/25/75   *Randy Hunter*—AIM supporter killed at Kyle by "party or parties unknown." Investigation still "ongoing."

09/09/75   *Howard Blue Bird*—AIM supporter killed at Pine Ridge by GOONs. No investigation.

09/10/75   *Jim Little*—AIM supporter stomped to death by GOONs in Oglala. No investigation.

10/26/75   *Olivia Binias*—AIM supporter killed in Porcupine by "person or persons unknown." Investigation still "open."

10/26/75   *Janice Black Bear*—AIM supporter killed at Manderson by GOONs. No investigation.

10/27/75   *Michelle Tobacco*—AIM supporter killed at Pine Ridge by "unknown assailants." Investigation still "ongoing."

12/06/75   *Carl Plenty Arrows, Sr.*—AIM supporter killed at Pine Ridge by "unknown persons." No investigation.

12/06/75   *Frank LaPointe*—AIM supporter killed at Pine Ridge by GOONs. No investigation.

02/??/76   *Anna Mae Pictou Aquash*—AIM organizer assassinated on Pine Ridge. FBI involved in attempt to conceal cause of death. Ongoing attempt to establish "AIM involvement" in murder. Key FBI personnel never deposed. Coroner never deposed.

01/05/76   *Lydia Cut Grass*—AIM member killed at Wounded Knee by GOONs. No investigation.

01/30/76   *Byron DeSersa*—OSCRO organizer and AIM supporter assassinated by GOONs in Wanblee. Arrests by local authorities result in two GOONs—Dale Janis and Charlie Winters—serving two years of five-year state sentences for "manslaughter." Charges dropped against two GOON leaders, Manny Wilson and Chuck Richards, on the basis of "self-defense" despite DeSersa having been unarmed when shot to death.

02/06/76   *Lena R. Slow Bear*—AIM supporter killed at Oglala by GOONs. No investigation.

03/01/76   *Hobart Horse*—AIM member beaten, shot, and repeatedly run over with automobile at Sharp's Corners. No investigation.

03/26/76   *Cleveland Reddest*—AIM member killed at Kyle by "person or persons unknown." No investigation.

04/28/76   *Betty Jo DuBray*—AIM supporter beaten to death at Martin, S.D. No investigation.

05/06/76   *Marvin Two Two*—AIM supporter shot

to death at Pine Ridge. No investigation.

05/09/76   *Julia Pretty Hips*—AIM supporter killed at Pine Ridge by "unknown assailants." No investigation.

05/24/76   *Sam Afraid of Bear*—AIM supporter shot to death at Pine Ridge. Investigation "ongoing."

06/04/76   *Kevin Hill*—AIM supporter killed at Oglala by "party or parties unknown." Investigation still "open."

07/03/76   *Betty Means*—AIM member killed at Pine Ridge by GOONs. No investigation.

07/31/76   *Sandra Wounded Foot*—AIM supporter killed at Sharp's Corners by "unknown assailants." No investigation.

It should be noted that, using the preliminary figure of only 61 homicides of AIM members and supporters during the same period, researchers Bruce Johansen and Roberto Maestas, in their book *Wasi'chu: The Continuing Indian Wars* (New York: Monthly Review Press, 1979, pp. 83-4), arrived at the following analysis of its implications: "Using only documented political deaths, the yearly murder rate on Pine Ridge Reservation between March 1, 1973, and March 1, 1976, was 170 per 100,000. By comparison, Detroit, the reputed 'murder capital of the United States,' had a rate of 20.2 per 100,000 in 1974. The U.S. average was 9.7 per 100,000....An estimated 20,000 persons were murdered in the United States during 1974. In a nation of 200 million persons, a murder rate comparable with that of Pine Ridge between 1973 and 1976 would have left

AIM Casualties on Pine Ridge, 1973-76

340,000 persons dead for political reasons alone in one year; 1.32 million in three....The political murder rate at Pine Ridge between March 1, 1973, and March 1, 1976, was almost equivalent to that in Chile during the three years after a military coup supported by the United states deposed and killed President Salvador Allende....Based on Chile's population of 10 million, the estimated fifty thousand persons killed in three years of political repression in Chile (1973-1976) roughly paralleled the murder rate at Pine Ridge."

Note: The authors would like to express appreciation to Candy Hamilton, Bruce Ellison, and Ken Tilson for their various assistance in assembling this detailed chronology.

Indians Are Us?

Reflections on the "Men's Movement"

We are living at an important and fruitful
moment, now, for it is clear to men that the
images of adult manhood given by the popular
culture are worn out; a man can no longer
depend on them. By the time a man is thirty-
five he knows that the images of the right man,
the tough man, the true man he received in high
school do not work in life. Such a man is open
to new visions of what a man is supposed to be.

—Robert Bly, 1990

We have met the enemy and he is us.

—Pogo

There are few things in this world I can conceive
as being more instantly ludicrous than a prosper-
ously middle-aged lump of pudgy Euroamerican
verse-monger, an apparition looking uncannily like
some weird cross between the Mall-O-Milk
Marshmallow Man and Pillsbury's Doughboy, suited
up in a grotesque mismatch combining pleated
Scottish tweeds with a stripped Brooks Brothers
shirt and Southwest Indian print vest, peering
myopically along his nose through coke-bottle steel-
rim specs while holding forth in stilted and somewhat nasal tonalities on the essential virtues of viril-

ity, of masculinity, of being or becoming a "warrior." The intrinsic absurdity of such a scene is, moreover, compounded by a factor of five when it is witnessed by an audience—all male, virtually all white, and on the whole obviously well accustomed to enjoying a certain pleasant standard of material comfort— which sits as if spellbound, rapt in its attention to every nuance of the speaker, altogether fawning in its collective nods and murmurs of devout agreement with each detail of his discourse.

At first glance, the image might seem to be the most vicious sort of parody, a satire offered in the worst of taste, perhaps a hallucinatory fragment of a cartoon or skit offered by the likes of *National Lampoon* or *Saturday Night Live*. Certainly, in a reasonable universe we would be entitled (perhaps required) to assume that no group of allegedly functional adults would take such a farce seriously, never mind line up to pay money for the privilege of participating in it. Yet, as we know, or should by now, the universe we are forced to inhabit has been transformed long since—notably by the very group so prominent in its representation among those constituting our warrior/mystic/wordsmith's assemblage—into something in which reasonable behavior and comportment play only the smallest of parts. And so the whole travesty is advanced with the utmost seriousness, at least by its proponents and a growing body of adherents who subsidize and otherwise support them.

The founder and reigning Grand Pooh-Bah of that variant of the "New Age" usually referred to as the "Men's Movement" is Robert Bly, a rather owlish butterball of a minor poet who seems to have set out at fifty-something to finally garner unto himself some smidgin of the macho self-esteem his physique and life-of-letters had conspired to deny him up to that point.[1] Writerly even in this pursuit, however, Bly has contented himself mainly with devising a vague theory of "masculinism" designed or at least intended to counter prevailing feminist dogma concerning "The Patriarchy," rising interest in "multicultural" interpretations of how things work, and an accompanying sense among middle-to-upper-middle-class males that they are "losing influence" in contemporary society.[2]

A strange brew consisting of roughly equal parts Arthurian, Norse, and Celtic legend, occasional adaptations of fairy tales by the brothers Grimm, a scattering of his own and assorted dead white males' verse and prose, a dash of environmentalism, and, for spice, bits and pieces of Judaic, Islamic, East Asian, and American Indian spiritualism, Bly's message of "male liberation" has been delivered via an unending series of increasingly well-paid podium performances beginning in the mid-80s. Presented in a manner falling somewhere between mystic parable and pop psychology, Bly's lectures are frequently tedious, often pedantic, pathetically pretentious in both content and elocution. Still, they find a powerful emotional resonance among those attracted to the central themes announced in his interviews and advertising circulars, especially when his verbiage focuses upon the ideas of "reclaiming the primitive within us...attaining freedom through use of appropriate ritual...[and] the rights of all men to transcend cultural boundaries in redeeming their warrior souls."[3]

By 1990, the master had perfected his pitch to the point of committing it to print in a turgid but rapidly-selling tome entitled *Iron John*.[4] He had also established something like a franchise system, training cadres in various localities to provide "male empowerment rituals" for a fee (a "Wild Man Weekend" goes at $250 a pop; individual ceremonies are usually pro-rated). Meanwhile, the rising popularity and consequent profit potential of Bly's endeavor had spawned a number of imitators—Patrick M. Arnold, Asa Baber, Tom Daly, Robert Moore, Douglas Gillette, R.J. Stewart, Kenneth Wetcher, Art Barker, F.W. McCaughtry, John Matthews, and Christopher Harding among them—literary and otherwise.[5] Three years later, the Men's Movement has become pervasive enough to be viewed as a tangible and growing social force rather than merely as a peculiar fringe group; active chapters are listed in 43 of the 50 major U.S. cities (plus four in Canada) in the movement's "selected" address list; 25 periodicals are listed in the same directory.[6]

An Interlude with Columbus in Colorado

> The ability of a male to shout and be fierce does not imply domination, treating people as if they were objects, demanding land or empire, holding on to the Cold War—the whole model of machismo....The Wild Man here amounts to an invisible presence, the companionship of the ancestors and the great artists among the dead....The native Americans believe in that healthful male power.
>
> —Robert Bly
> 1990

Indians Are Us?

At first glance, none of this may seem particularly threatening. Indeed, the sheer silliness inherent to Bly's routine at many levels is painfully obvious, a matter driven home to me one morning last spring when, out looking for some early sage, I came upon a group of young Euroamerican males cavorting about stark naked in a meadow near Lyons, Colorado. Several had wildflowers braided into their hair. Some were attempting a chant I failed to recognize. I noticed an early growth of poison oak near where I was standing, but determined it was probably best not to disrupt whatever rite was being conducted with anything so mundane as a warning about the presence of discomforting types of plant life. As discreetly as possible, I turned around and headed the other way, both puzzled and somewhat amused by what I'd witnessed.

A few days later, I encountered one of the participants, whom I knew slightly, and who kept scratching at his left thigh. Seizing the opportunity, I inquired as to what it was they'd been doing. He responded that since he and the others had attended a workshop conducted by Robert Bly earlier in the year, they'd become active in the Men's Movement and "made a commitment to recover the Druidic rituals which are part of our heritage" (the man, who is an anthropology student at the University of Colorado, is of Slavic descent, making Druidism about as distant from his own cultural tradition as Sufism or Zen Buddhism). Interest piqued, I asked where they'd learned the ritual form involved and its meaning. He replied that, while they'd attempted to research the matter, "it turns out there's not really a lot known about exactly how

211

the Druids conducted their rituals."

"It's mostly guesswork," he went on. "We're just kind of making it up as we go along." When I asked why, if that were the case, they described their ritual as being Druidic, he shrugged. "It just sort of feels good, I guess," he said. "We're trying to get in touch with something primal in ourselves."

Harmless? Maybe. But then again, maybe not. The Druids, after all, have reputedly been dead and gone for millennia. They are thus immune to whatever culturally destructive effects might attend such blatant appropriation, trivialization, and deformation of their sacred rites by non-Druidic feel-gooders. Before departing the meadow, however, I had noticed a couple of the men gamboling about in the grass were adorned with facepaint and feathers. So I queried my respondent as to whether in the view of his group such things comprised a part of Druid ritual life.

"Well, no," he confessed. "A couple of the guys are really into American Indian stuff. Actually, we all are. Wallace Black Elk is our teacher.[7] We run sweats on the weekends, and most of us have been on the hill [insider slang for the undertaking of a Vision Quest]. I myself carry a Sacred Pipe and am studying herbal healing, Lakota Way. Three of us went to the Sun Dance at Crow Dog's place last summer. We've made vows, and are planning to dance when we're ready."[8] Intermingled with these remarks, he extended glowing bits of commentary on his and the others' abiding interest in a diversity of cultural/spiritual elements ranging from Balinese mask-making to Andean flute music, from Japanese scent/time orientation to the deities of the

Indians Are Us?

Assyrians, Polynesian water gods, and the clitoral circumcision of Somali women.

I thought about protesting that spiritual traditions cannot be used as some sort of Whitman's Sampler of ceremonial form, mixed and matched—here a little Druid, there a touch of Nordic mythology followed by a regimen of Hindu vegetarianism, a mishmash of American Indian rituals somewhere else—at the whim of people who are part of none of them. I knew I should say that to play at ritual potluck is to debase all spiritual traditions, voiding their internal coherence and leaving nothing usably sacrosanct as a cultural anchor for the peoples who conceived and developed them, and who have consequently organized their societies around them. But, then, in consideration of who it was I was talking to, I abruptly ended the conversation instead. I doubted he would have understood what I was trying to explain to him. More importantly, I had the distinct impression he wouldn't have cared, even if he had. Such observations on my part would most likely have only set loose "the warrior in him," a flow of verbal diarrhea in which he asserted his and his peers' "inalienable right" to take anything they found of value in the intellectual property of others, converting it to whatever use suited their purposes at the moment. I was a bit tired, having just come from a meeting with a white environmental group where I'd attempted unsuccessfully to explain how their support of native land rights might bear some positive relationship to their announced ecological concerns, and felt it just wasn't my night to deal with the ghost of Christopher Columbus for a second time, head on.

That's an excuse, to be sure. Probably, I failed in my duty. Perhaps, regardless of the odds against success, I should have tried reasoning with him. More likely, I should've done what my ancestors should have done to Columbus himself when the "Great Discoverer" first brought his embryo of the Men's Movement to this hemisphere. But the amount of prison time assigned these days to that sort of appropriate response to aggression is daunting, to say the least. And I really do lack the wall-space to properly display his tanned hide after skinning him alive. So I did nothing more than walk out of the coffee shop in which we'd been seated, leaving him to wonder what it was that had gotten me upset. Not that he's likely to have gotten the message. The result of my inaction is that, so far as I know, the man is still out there cruising the cerebral seas in search of "spiritual landscapes" to explore and pillage. Worse, he's still sending his booty back to his buddies in hopes of their casting some "new synthesis of paganism"—read, "advancement of civilization as we know it"—in which they will be able to continue their occupancy of a presumed position at the center of the universe.

Indians Are Us?

> We must get out of ourselves, or, more accurately, the selves we have been conned into believing are "us." We must break out of the cage of artificial "self" in which we have been entrapped as "men" by today's society. We must get in touch with our true selves, recapturing the Wild Man, the animal, the primitive warrior being which exists in the core of every man. We

must rediscover the meaning of maleness, the art of being male, the way of the warrior priest. In doing so, we free ourselves from the alienating tyranny of being what it is we're told we are, or what it is we should be. We free ourselves to redefine the meaning of "man," to be who and what we can be, and what it is we ultimately must be. I speak here, of course, of genuine liberation from society's false expectations and thus from the false selves these expectations have instilled in each and every one of us here in this room. Let the Wild Man loose, I say! Free our warrior spirit!

—Robert Bly
1991

In retrospect, it seems entirely predictable that, amidst Robert Bly's welter of babble concerning the value of assorted strains of imagined primitivism and warrior spirit, a substantial segment of his following—and he himself in the workshops he offers on "practical ritual"—would end up gravitating most heavily toward things Indian. After all, Native Americans and our ceremonial life constitute living, ongoing entities. We are therefore far more accessible in terms of both time and space than the Druids or the old Norse Odinists. Further, our traditions offer the distinct advantage of seeming satisfyingly exotic to the average Euroamerican yuppie male, even while not forcing them to clank about in the suits of chain mail and heavy steel armor which would be required if they were to opt to act out their leader's hyperliterate Arthurian fantasies. I mean, really....Jousting, anyone? A warrior-type fella could get seriously hurt that way.[9]

A main sticking point, of course, rests precisely

in the fact that the cultures indigenous to America *are* living, ongoing entities. Unlike the Druids or the ancient Greek man-cults who thronged around Hector and Achilles, Native American societies *can* and *do* suffer the socioculturally debilitating effects of spiritual trivialization and appropriation at the hands of the massively larger Euro-immigrant population which has come to dominate literally every other aspect of our existence. As Margo Thunderbird, an activist of the Shinnecock Nation, has put it: "They came for our land, for what grew or could be grown on it, for the resources in it, and for our clean air and pure water. They stole these things from us, and in the taking they also stole our free ways and the best of our leaders, killed in battle or assassinated. And now, after all that, they've come for the very last of our possessions; now they want our pride, our history, our spiritual traditions. They want to rewrite and remake these things, to claim them for themselves. The lies and thefts just never end."[10] Or, as the Oneida scholar Pam Colorado frames the matter:

> The process is ultimately intended to supplant Indians, even in areas of their own culture and spirituality. In the end, non-Indians will have complete power to define what is and what is not Indian, even for Indians. We are talking here about a complete ideological/conceptual subordination of Indian people in addition to the total physical subordination they already experience. When this happens, the last vestiges of real Indian society and Indian rights will disappear. Non-Indians will then claim to "own" our heritage and ideas as thoroughly as they now claim to own our land and resources.[11]

From this perspective, the American Indian Movement passed a resolution at its 1984 Southwest Leadership Conference condemning the laissez-faire use of native ceremonies and/or ceremonial objects by anyone not sanctioned by traditional indigenous spiritual leaders.[12] The AIM position also echoed an earlier resolution taken by the Traditional Elders Circle in 1980, condemning even Indians who engage in "use of [our] spiritual ceremonies with non-Indian people for profit."[13] Another such condemnation had been issued during the First American Indian Tribunal at D-Q University in 1982.[14] As of this writing—June 1993—the Lakota Nation as a whole is preparing to enact a similar resolution denouncing non-Lakotas who presume to "adopt" their rituals, and censoring those Lakotas who have chosen to facilitate such cultural appropriation (see "Declaration of War Against Exploiters of Lakota Spirituality," following this essay). Several other indigenous nations and national organizations have already taken comparable positions, or are preparing to (see "Alert Concerning the Abuse and Exploitation of American Indian Sacred Traditions").

This may seem an exaggerated and overly harsh response to what the Spokane/Coeur d'Alene writer Sherman Alexie has laughingly dismissed as being little more than a "Society for Confused White Men."[15] But the hard edges of Euroamerican hubris and assertion of proprietary interest in native assets which has always marked Indian/white relations are abundantly manifested in the organizational literature of the Men's Movement itself. Of even greater concern is the fact that the sort of appropriation evidenced in these periodicals is no longer restricted simply to claiming "ownership" of Indian ceremonies and spiritual objects, as in a passage in a recent issue of the *Men's Council Journal* explaining that "sweats, drumming, dancing, [and] four direction-calling [are] once-indigenous now-ours rituals."[16] Rather, participants have increasingly assumed a stance of expropriating native identity altogether, as when, in the same journal, it is repeatedly asserted that "we...are all Lakota" and that members of the Men's Movement are now displacing actual Lakotas from their "previous" role as "warrior protectors" (of what is left unclear).[17]

The indigenous response to such presumption was perhaps best expressed by AIM leader Russell Means, himself an Oglala Lakota, when he recently stated that "This is the ultimate degradation of our people, even worse than what's been done to us by Hollywood and the publishing industry, or the sports teams who portray us as mascots and pets. What these people are doing is like Adolf Eichmann claiming during his trial that, at heart, he was really a zionist, or members of the Aryan Nations in Idaho claiming to be 'True Jews'."[18] Elsewhere, Means has observed that:

> What's at issue here is the same old question that Europeans have always posed with regard to American Indians, whether what's ours isn't somehow theirs. And, of course, they've always answered the question in the affirmative....We are resisting this because spirituality is the basis of our culture. If our culture is dissolved [via the expedients of spiritual appropriation/expropriation], Indian people as such will cease to exist. By definition, the causing of any culture to cease to exist is an act of genocide.[19]

Indians Are Us?

Noted Hunkpapa Lakota author Vine Deloria, Jr., agrees in principle, finding that as a result of the presumption of groups like the Men's Movement, as well as academic anthropology, "the realities of Indian belief and existence have become so misunderstood and distorted at this point that when a real Indian stands up and speaks the truth at any given moment, he or she is not only unlikely to be believed, but will probably be publicly contradicted and 'corrected' by the citation of some non-Indian and totally inaccurate 'expert'."[20]

> Moreover, young Indians in [cities and] universities are now being trained to view themselves and their cultures in the terms prescribed by such experts *rather than* in the traditional terms of the tribal elders. The process automatically sets the members of Indian communities at odds with one another, while outsiders run around picking up the pieces for themselves. In this way [groups like the Men's Movement] are perfecting a system of self-validation in which all semblance of honesty and accuracy are lost. This is...absolutely devastating to Indian societies.[21]

Even Sherman Alexie, while choosing to treat the Men's Movement phenomenon with scorn and ridicule rather than open hostility, is compelled to acknowledge that there is a serious problem with the direction taken by Bly's disciples. "Peyote is not just an excuse to get high," Alexie points out. "A Vision Quest cannot be completed in a convention room rented for that purpose....[T]he sweat lodge is a church, not a free clinic or something....A warrior does not have to scream to release the animal that is supposed to reside inside every man. A warrior does not necessarily have an animal inside him at all. If there happens to be an animal, it can be a parakeet or a mouse just as easily as it can be a bear or a wolf. When a white man adopts an animal, he [seems inevitably to choose] the largest animal possible. Whether this is because of possible phallic connotations or a kind of spiritual steroid abuse is debatable, [but] I can imagine a friend of mine, John, who is white, telling me that his spirit animal is the Tyrannosaurus Rex."[22]

> The men's movement seems designed to appropriate and mutate so many aspects of native traditions. I worry about the possibilities: men's movement chain stores specializing in portable sweat lodges; the "Indians 'R' Us" commodification of ritual and artifact; white men who continue to show up at powwows in full regalia and dance.[23]

Plainly, despite sharp differences in their respective temperaments and resultant stylistic approaches to dealing with problems, Alexie and many other Indians share Russell Means's overall conclusion that the "culture vultures" of the Men's Movement are "not innocent or innocuous...cute, groovy, hip, enlightened, or any of the rest of the things they want to project themselves as being. No, what they're about is cultural genocide. And genocide is genocide, no matter how you want to 'qualify' it. So some of us are starting to react to these folks accordingly."[24]

View from a Foreign Shore

> Western man's connection to the Wild Man has
> been disturbed for centuries now, and a lot of
> fear has been built up [but] Wild Man is part of
> a company or a community in a man's psyche.
> The Wild Man lives in complicated interchanges
> with other interior beings. A whole community
> of beings is what is called a grown
> man....Moreover, when we develop the inner
> Wild Man, he keeps track of the wild animals
> inside us, and warns when they are liable to
> become extinct. The Wild One in you is the one
> which is willing to leave the busy life, and able
> to be called away.
>
> —Robert Bly, 1990

In many ways, the salient questions which present themselves with regard to the Men's Movement center on motivation. Why, in this day and age, would any group of well-educated and self-proclaimedly sensitive men, the vast majority of whom may be expected to exhibit genuine outrage at my earlier comparison of them to Columbus, elect to engage in activities which can be plausibly categorized as culturally genocidal? Assuming initial ignorance in this regard, why do they choose to persist in these activities, often escalating their behavior after its implications have been explained by its victims repeatedly and in no uncertain terms? And, perhaps most of all, why would such extraordinarily privileged individuals as those who've flocked to Robert Bly—a group marked by nothing so much as the kind of ego-driven self-absorption required to insist upon its "right" to impose itself on a tiny minority even to the point of culturally exterminating it—opt to do so in a manner which makes them appear not only repugnant, but utterly ridiculous to anyone outside their ranks?

Sometimes it is necessary to step away from a given setting in order to better understand it. For me, the answers to these seemingly inexplicable questions were to a large extent clarified during a recent (unpaid) political speaking tour of Germany, during which I was repeatedly confronted by the spectacle of Indian "hobbyists," all of them men resplendently attired in quillwork and bangles, beaded moccasins, chokers, amulets, medicine bags, and so on.[25] Some of them sported feathers and buckskin shirts or jackets; a few wore their blond hair braided with rawhide in what they imagined to be high plains style (in reality, they looked much more like Vikings than Cheyennes or Shoshones). When queried, many professed to have handcrafted much of their own regalia.[26] A number also made mention of having fashioned their own pipestone pipes, or to have been presented with one, usually after making a hefty monetary contribution, by one of a gaggle of Indian or pretended-Indian hucksters.[27]

Among those falling into this classification, belonging to what Christian Feest has branded the "Faculty of Medicine" currently plying a lucrative "Greater Europa Medicine Man Circuit,"[28] are Wallace Black Elk, "Brooke Medicine Eagle" (a bogus Cherokee; real name unknown), "John Redtail Freesoul" (a purported Cheyenne-Arapaho; real name unknown), Archie Fire Lamedeer (Northern Cheyenne), "Dhyani Ywahoo" (supposedly a 27th-generation member of the nonexistent

222

"Etowah" band of the Eastern Cherokees; real name unknown), "Eagle Walking Turtle" (Gary McClain, an alleged Choctaw), "Eagle Man" (Ed McGaa, Oglala Lakota), "Beautiful Painted Arrow" (a supposed Shoshone; real name unknown).[29] Although the success of such people "is completely independent of traditional knowledge, just so long as they can impress a public impressed by the books of Carlos Castaneda,"[30] most of the hobbyists I talked to noted they'd "received instruction" from one or more of these "Indian spiritual teachers" and had now adopted various deformed fragments of Native American ritual life as being both authentic and their own.

Everyone felt they been "trained" to run sweats. Most had been provided similar tutelage in conducting Medicine Wheel Ceremonies and Vision Quests. Several were pursuing what they thought were Navajo crystal-healing techniques, and/or herbal healing (where they figured to gather herbs not native to their habitat was left unaddressed). Two mentioned they'd participated in a "sun dance" conducted several years ago in the Black Forest by an unspecified "Lakota medicine man" (they displayed chest scars verifying that they had indeed done something of the sort), and said they were now considering launching their own version on an annual basis. Half-a-dozen more inquired as to whether I could provide them entrée to the Sun Dances conducted each summer on stateside reservations (of special interest are those of the "Sioux").[31] One poor soul, a Swiss national as it turned out, proudly observed that he'd somehow managed to survive living in an Alpine tipi for the past several years.[32] All of them maintained that at this point they actually consider themselves to *be* Indians, at least "in spirit."[33]

These "Indians of Europe," as Feest has termed them, were uniformly quite candid as to why they felt this way.[34] Bluntly put—and the majority were precisely this harsh in their own articulations—they absolutely *hate* the idea of being Europeans, especially Germans. Abundant mention was made of their collective revulsion to the European heritage of colonization and genocide, particularly the ravages of nazism. Some went deeper, addressing what they felt to be the intrinsically unacceptable character of European civilization's relationship to the natural order in its entirety. Their response, as a group, was to try and disassociate themselves from what it was/is they object to by announcing their personal identities in terms as diametrically opposed to it as they could conceive. "Becoming" American Indians in their own minds apparently fulfilled this deepseated need in the most gratifying fashion.[35]

Yet, when I delved deeper, virtually all of them ultimately admitted they were little more than weekend warriors, or "cultural transvestites," to borrow another of Feest's descriptors.[36] They typically engage in their Indianist preoccupations only during their off hours while maintaining regular jobs—mainly quite responsible and well-paying positions, at that— squarely within the very system of Germanic business-as-usual they claimed so heatedly to have disavowed, root and branch. The most candid respondents were even willing to admit, when pushed, that were it not for the income accruing from their daily roles as "Good Germans," they'd

not be able to afford their hobby of imagining themselves as being something else...or to pay the fees
charged by imported Native American "spirit leaders" to validate this impression. Further, without
exception, when I inquired as to what they might be
doing to challenge and transform the fundamental
nature of the German culture, society, and state
they profess to detest so deeply, they observed that
they had become "spiritual people" and are therefore
"apolitical." Queries concerning whether they might
be willing to engage in activities to physically defend
the rights and territories of indigenous peoples in
North America drew much the same reply.

The upshot of German hobbyism, then, is that,
far from constituting the sort of radical divorce from
Germanic context its adherents assert, part-time
impersonation of American Indians represents a
means through which they can psychologically reconcile themselves to it. By pretending to be what
they are not—and in fact can never be, because the
objects of their fantasies have never existed in real
life—the hobbyists are freed to be what they are (but
deny), and to "feel good about themselves" in the
process.[37] And, since this sophistry allows them to
contend in all apparent seriousness that they are
somehow entirely separate from the oppressive status quo upon which they depend, and which their
"real world" occupations do so much to make possible, they thereby absolve themselves of any obligation whatsoever to materially confront it (and thence
themselves). Voila! "Wildmen" and "primitives" carrying out the most refined functions of the German
corporate state; "warriors" relieved of the necessity
of doing battle other than in the most metaphorical

of senses, and then always (and only) in service to the very structures and traditions they claim—and may even have convinced themselves to *believe* at some level or another—their perverse posturing negates.[38]

The Dynamics of Denial

> Contemporary business life allows competitive relationships only, in which the major emotions are anxiety, tension, loneliness, rivalry and fear....Zeus energy has been steadily disintegrating decade after decade in the United States. Popular culture has been determined to destroy respect for it, beginning with the "Maggie and Jiggs" and "Dagwood and Blondie" comics of the 1920s and 1930s, in which the man is always weak and foolish...The recovery of some form of [powerful rituals of male] initiation is essential to the culture. The United States has undergone an unmistakable decline since 1950, and I believe if we do not find [these kinds of male ritual] the decline will continue.
>
> —Robert Bly
> 1990

Obviously, the liberatory potential of all this for actual American Indians is considerably less than zero. Instead, hobbyism is a decidedly parasitical enterprise, devoted exclusively to the emotional edification of individuals integrally and instrumentally involved in perpetuating and perfecting the system of global domination from which the genocidal colonization of Native America stemmed and by which it is continued. Equally obviously, there is a strikingly close, if somewhat antecedent, correspondence between German hobbyism on the one hand, and the North American Men's Movement on the other. The class and ethnic compositions are virtually identical, as are the resulting social functions, internal dynamics, and external impacts.[39] So close is the match, not only demographically, but motivationally and behaviorally, that Robert Bly himself has scheduled a tour of Germany during the summer of 1993 to bring the Old World's Teutonic sector into his burgeoning fold.[40]

Perhaps the only significant difference between the Men's Movement at home and hobbyism abroad is just that: the hobbyists at least are "over there," but the Men's Movement is right here, where we live. Hobbyism in Germany may contribute to what both Adolf Hitler and George Bush called the "New World Order," and thus yield a negative but somewhat indirect effect upon native people in North America, but the Men's Movement is quite *directly* connected to the ever more efficient imposition of that order upon Indian lands and lives in the U.S. and Canada. The mining engineer who joins the Men's Movement and thereafter spends his weekends "communing with nature in the manner of an Indian" does so—in precisely the same fashion as his German colleagues—in order to exempt himself from either literal or emotional responsibility for the fact that, to be who he is and live at the standard he does, he will spend the rest of his week making wholesale destruction of the environment an operant reality. Not infrequently, the land being strip-mined under his supervision belongs to the very Indians whose spiritual traditions he appropriates and reifies in the process of "finding inner peace" (i.e., empowering himself to do what he does).[41]

By the same token, the corporate lawyer, the Wall Street broker, and the commercial banker who accompany the engineer into a sweat lodge do so because, intellectually, they understand quite well that, without them, his vocation would be impossible. The same can be said for the government bureaucrat, the corporate executive, and the marketing consultant who keep Sacred Pipes on the walls of their respective offices. All of them are engaged, to a greater or lesser degree—although, if asked, most will adamantly reject the slightest hint that they are involved at all—in the systematic destruction of the residue of territory upon which prospects of native life itself are balanced. The charade by which they cloak themselves in the identity of their victims is their best and ultimately most compulsive hedge against the psychic consequences of acknowledging who and what they really are.[42]

Self-evidently, then, New Age-style rhetoric to the contrary notwithstanding, this pattern of emotional/psychological avoidance imbedded in the ritual role-playing of Indians by a relatively privileged stratum of Euroamerican men represents no alternative to the status quo. To the contrary, it has become a steadily more crucial ingredient in an emergent complex of psychosocial mechanisms allowing North American business-as-usual to sustain, stabilize, and reenergize itself. Put another way, had the Men's Movement not come into being, compliments of Robert Bly and his clones, it would have been necessary—just as the nazis found it useful to do in their day—for North America's governmental-corporate élite to have created it on their own.[43] On second thought, it's not altogether clear they didn't.[44]

Alternatives

> The ancient societies believed that a boy becomes a man only through ritual and effort—only through the "active intervention of the older men." It's becoming clear to us that manhood doesn't happen by itself; it doesn't just happen because we eat Wheaties. The active intervention of the older men means the older men welcome the younger man into the ancient, mythologized, instinctive male world.
>
> —Robert Bly, 1990

With all this said, it still must be admitted that there is a scent of undeniably real human desperation—an all but obsessive desire to find some avenue of alternative cultural expression different from that sketched above—clinging to the Men's Movement and its New Age and hobbyist equivalents. The palpable anguish this entails allows for, or requires, a somewhat more sympathetic construction of the motives prodding a segment of the movement's membership, and an illative obligation on the part of anyone not themselves experiencing it to respond in a firm, but helpful rather than antagonistic, manner.

Perhaps more accurately, it should be said that the sense of despair at issue evidences itself not so much in the ranks of the Men's Movement and related phenomena themselves, but within the milieu from which these manifestations have arisen: white, mostly urban, affluent or affluently reared, well-schooled, young (or youngish) people of both genders who, in one or another dimension, are thoroughly dis-eased by the socioeconomic order into which they were born and their seemingly predestined roles within it.[45] Many of them openly seek, some through serious attempts at political resistance, a viable option with which they may not only alter their own individual fates, but transform the overall systemic realities they correctly perceive as having generated these fates in the first place.[46] Yet, as a whole, they seem sincerely baffled by the prospect of having to define for themselves the central aspect of this alternative.

They cannot put a name to it, and so they perpetually spin their wheels, waging continuous theoretical and sometimes practical battles against each "hierarchical" and "patriarchal" fragment of the whole they oppose: capitalism and fascism, colonialism, neocolonialism and imperialism, racism and sexism, agism, consumerism, the entire vast plethora of "isms" and "ologies" making up the "modern" (or "post-modern") society they inhabit.[47] Frustrated and stymied in their efforts to come up with a new or different conceptualization by which to guide their oppositional project, many of the most alienated—and therefore most committed to achieving fundamental social change—eventually opt for the intellectual/emotional reassurance of prepackaged "radical solutions." Typically, these assume the form of yet another battery of "isms" based in all the same core assumptions as the system being opposed. This is especially true of that galaxy of doctrinal tendencies falling within the general rubric of "marxism"—bernsteinian revisionism, council communism, marxism-leninism, stalinism, maoism, etc.—but it is also an actuality pervading most variants of feminism, environmentalism, and anarchism/anti-authoritarianism as well.[48]

Others, burned out by an endless diet of increasingly sterile polemical chatter and symbolic political action, defect from the resistance altogether, deforming what German New Left theorist Rudi Dutschke[49] once advocated as "a long march through the institutions" into an outright embrace of the false and reactionary "security" found in statism and bureaucratic corporatism (this is a tendency exemplified in the U.S. by such 1960s radical figures as Tom Hayden, Jerry Rubin, Eldridge Cleaver, David Horowitz, and Rennie Davis).[50] A mainstay occupation of this coterie has been academia, wherein they typically maintain an increasingly irrelevant and detached "critical" discourse, calculated mainly to negate whatever transformative value or utility might be lodged in the concrete oppositional political engagement they formerly pursued.[51]

Some members of each group—formula radicals and sell-outs—end up glossing over the psychic void left by their default in arriving at a genuinely alternative vision, immersing themselves either in some formalized religion (Catholicism, for example, or, somewhat less frequently, denominations of Islam or Buddhism), or the polyglot "spiritualism" offered by the New Age/Men's Movement/Hobbyism syndrome.[52] This futile cycle is now in its third successive generation of repetition among European and Euroamerican activists since the so-called "new student movement" was born only thirty years ago. At one level or another, almost all of those currently involved, and quite a large proportion of those who once were, are figuratively screaming for a workable means of breaking the cycle, some way of foundationing themselves for a sustained and successful effort to effect societal change rather than the series of dead-ends they've encountered up till now. Yet a functional alternative exists, and has always existed.

The German Tour Revisited

This was brought home to me most dramatically during my earlier-mentioned speaking tour of Germany, a trip geared to include not only my own presentations, but those of M. Annette Jaimes, Bob Robideau, and Paulette D'Auteuil as well.[53] The question most frequently asked by those who turned out to hear us speak on the struggle for liberation in Native North America was "What can we do to help?" Quite uniformly, the answer provided by all four of us to this query was that, strategically, the most important assistance the people in the audience could render American Indians would be to win their own struggle for liberation in Germany. In effect, we reiterated time after time, this would eliminate the German corporate state as a linchpin of the global politico-economic order in which the United States (along with its Canadian satellite) serves as the hub.

"You must understand," we stated each time the question arose, "that we really mean it when we say we are all related. Consequently, we see the mechanisms of our oppression as being equally interrelated. Given this perspective, we cannot help but see a victory for you as being simultaneously a victory for us, and vice versa; that a weakening of your enemy here in Germany necessarily weakens ours there, in North America; that your liberation is inseparably linked to our own, and that you should see ours as advancing yours. Perhaps, then, the question should be reversed: what is it that we can best do to help *you* succeed?"

As an expression of solidarity, these sentiments were on every occasion roundly applauded. Invariably, however, they also produced a set of rejoinders intended to qualify the implications of what we'd said to the point of negation. The usual drift of these responses was that the German and American Indian situations and resulting struggles are entirely different, and thus not to be compared in the manner we'd attempted. This is true, those making this point argued, because Indians are colonized peoples while the Germans were colonizers. We Indians, they went on, must therefore fight to free our occupied and underdeveloped landbase(s) while the German opposition, effectively landless, struggles to rearrange social and economic relations within an advanced industrial society. Most importantly, they concluded, native people in America hold the advantage of possessing cultures separate and distinct from that which we oppose, while the German opposition, by contrast, must contend with the circumstance of being essentially "cultureless" and disoriented.[54]

After every presentation, we were forced to take strong exception to such notions. "As long-term participants in the national liberation struggle of American Indians," we said, "we have been forced into knowing the nature of colonialism very well. Along with you, we understand that the colonization we experience finds its origin in the matrix of European culture. But, apparently unlike you, we also understand that in order for Europe to do what it has done to us—in fact, for Europe to become 'Europe' at all—it first had to do the same thing to all of you. In other words, to become a colonizing culture, Europe had first to colonize *itself*.[55] To the extent that this is true, we find it fair to say that if our struggle must be explicitly anticolonial in its form, content, and aspirations, yours must be even more so. You have, after all, been colonized far longer than we, and therefore much more completely. In fact, your colonization has by now been consolidated to such an extent that—with certain notable exceptions, like the Irish and Euskadi (Basque) nationalists—you no longer even see yourselves as having been colonized.[56] The result is that you've become self-colonizing, conditioned to be so self-identified with your own oppression that you've lost your ability to see it for what it is, much less to resist it in any coherent way.

"You seem to feel that you are either completely disconnected from your own heritage of having been conquered and colonized, or that you can and should disconnect yourselves from it as a means of destroying that which oppresses you. We believe, on the other hand, that your internalization of this self-hating outlook is exactly what your oppressors want most to see you do. Such a posture on your part simply perfects and completes the structure of your domination. It is inherently self-defeating because in denying yourselves the meaning of your own history and traditions, you leave yourselves with neither an established point-of-departure from which to launch your own struggle for liberation, nor any set of goals and objectives to guide that struggle other than abstractions. You are thereby left effectively anchorless and rudderless, adrift on a stormy sea. You have lost your maps and compass, so you have no idea where you are or where to turn for help. Worst of all, you sense that the ship on which you find yourselves trapped is rapidly sinking. We can imagine no more terrifying situation to be in, and, as relatives, we would like to throw you a life preserver.

"So here it is," we went on. "It takes the form of an insight offered by our elders: 'To understand where you are, you must know where you've been, and you must know where you are to understand where you are going.'[57] For us, you see, the past, present, and future are all equally important parts of the same indivisible whole. And we believe this is as true for you as it is for us. In other words, you must set yourselves to reclaiming your own indigenous past. You must come to know it in its own terms—the terms of its internal values and understandings, and the way these were applied to living in this world—not the terms imposed upon it by the order which set out to destroy it. You must learn to put your knowledge of this heritage to use as a lens through which you can clarify your present circumstance, to "know where you are," so to speak. And, from this, you can begin to chart the course of your struggle into the future. Put still another way, you, no less than us, must forge the conceptual tools that will allow you to carefully and consciously orient your struggle to regaining what it is that has been taken from you rather than presuming a unique ability to invent it all anew. You must begin with the decolonization of your own minds, with a restoration of your understanding of who you are, where you come from, what it is that has been done to you to take you to the place in which you now find yourselves. Then, and *only* then, it seems to us, will you be able to free yourselves from your present dilemma.

"*Look* at us, and really *hear* what we're saying," we demanded. "We are not unique in being indigenous people. *Everyone* is indigenous somewhere. *You* are indigenous here. You, no more than we, are landless; your land is occupied by an alien force, just like ours. You, just like us, have an overriding obligation to liberate your homeland. You, no less than we, have models in your own traditions upon which to base your alternatives to the social, political, and economic structures now imposed upon you. It is your responsibility to put yourselves in direct communication with these traditions, just as it is our responsibility to remain in contact with ours. We cannot fulfil this responsibility for you any more than you can fulfil ours for us.

"You say that the knowledge we speak of was taken from you too long ago, at the time of Charlemagne, more than a thousand years ago. Because of this, you say, the gulf of time separating then from now is too great, that what was taken then is now lost and gone. We know better. We know, and so do you, that right up into the 1700s your 'European' colonizers were still busily burning 'witches' at the stake. We know, and you know too, that these women were the leaders of your own indigenous cultures.[58] The span of time separating you from a still-flourishing practice of your native ways is thus not so great as you would have us— and yourselves—believe. It's been 200 years, no more. And we also know that there are still those among your people who retain the knowledge of your past, knowledge handed down from one generation to the next, century after century. We can give you directions to some of them if you like, but we think you know they are there.[59] You *can* begin to draw appropriate lessons and instruction from these faith-keepers, if you want to.

"We have said that 'for the world to live, Europe must die.'[60] We meant it when we said it, and we still do. But do not be confused. The statement was never intended to exclude you or consign you, as people, to oblivion.We believe the idea underlying that statement holds just as true for you as it does for anyone else. You *do* have a choice, because you are *not* who you've been convinced to believe you are. Or, at least not necessarily. You are not necessarily a part of the colonizing, predatory reality of 'Europe.' You are not even necessarily 'Germans,' with all that that implies. You are, or can be, who your ancestors were and who the faith-keepers of your cultures remain: Angles, Saxons, Huns, Goths, Visigoths. The choice is yours, but in order for it to have meaning you must meet the responsibilities which come with it."

Objections and Responses

Such reasoning provoked considerable consternation among listeners. "But," more than one exclaimed with unpretended horror, "*think* of who you're speaking to! These are very dangerous ideas you are advocating. You are in Germany, among people raised to see themselves as Germans, and yet, at least in part, you are telling us we should do exactly what the nazis did! We Germans, at least those of us who are consciously anti-fascist and anti-racist, renounce such excavations of our heritage precisely because of our country's own recent experiences with them. We *know* where Hitler's politics of 'blood and soil' led not just us but the world. We *know* the outcome of Himmler's reassertion of 'Germanic paganism.' Right now, we are being forced to confront a resurgence of nazism in this country. Surely you can't be arguing that we should *join* in the resurrection of all that."

"Of course not!" we retorted. "We, as American Indians, have at least as much reason to hate nazism as any people on earth. Not much of anything done by the nazis to people here had not already been done to us, for centuries, and some of the things the nazis did during their twelve years in power are *still* being done to us today. Much of what has been done to us in North America was done, and continues to be done, on the basis of philosophical rationalizations indistinguishable from those used by the nazis to justify their policies. If you want to look at it that way, you could say that anti-nazism is part of the absolute bedrock upon which our struggle is based. So, don't even *hint* that any part of our perspective is somehow 'pro-nazi.'

"We are aware that this is a highly emotional issue for you. But try and bear in mind that the world isn't one-dimensional. Everything is multidimensional, possessed of positive as well as negative polarities. It should be obvious that the nazis didn't represent or crystallize your indigenous traditions. Instead, they perverted your heritage for their own purposes, using your ancestral traditions against themselves in a fashion meant to supplant and destroy them. The European predator has always done this, whenever it was not simply trying to suppress the indigenous host upon which it feeds. Perhaps the nazis were the most overt, and in some ways the most successful, in doing this in recent times. And for that reason some of us view them as being a sort of culmination of all that is European. But, the point is, they very deliberately tapped the negative rather than the positive potential of what we are discussing.

"Now, polarities aside," we continued, "the magnitude of favorable response accorded by the mass of Germans to the themes taken up by the nazis during the 1930s illustrates perfectly the importance of the question we are raising.[61] There is unquestionably a tremendous yearning among all peoples, including your own—and you yourselves, for that matter—for a sense of connectedness to their roots. This yearning, although often sublimated, translates quite readily into transformative power whenever (and however) it is effectively addressed.[62] Hence, part of what we are arguing is that you must consciously establish the positive polarity of your heritage as a counter to the negative impulse created by the nazis. If you don't, it's likely we're going to witness German officials walking around in black death's head uniforms all over again. The signs are there, you must admit.[63] And you must also admit there's a certain logic involved, since you yourselves seem bent upon abandoning the power of your indigenous traditions to nazism. Suffice it to say we'd not give *our* traditions over to the uncontested use of nazis. Maybe you shouldn't either."

Such remarks usually engendered commentary about how the audience had "never viewed the matter in this light," followed by questions as to how a positive expression of German indigenism might be fostered. "Actually," we said, "it seems to us you're already doing this. It's all in how you look at things and how you go about explaining them to others. Try this: You have currently, as a collective response to perceived problems of centralization within the German left, atomized into what you call *Autonomen.* These we understand to be a panorama of autonomous affinity groups bound together in certain lines of thought and action by a definable range of issues and aspirations.[64] Correct? So, instead of trying to explain this development to yourselves and everyone else as some "new and revolutionary tendency"—which it certainly is not—how about conceiving of it as an effort to recreate the kinds of social organization and political consensus marking your ancient 'tribal' cultures (adapted of course to the contemporary context)?

"Making such an effort to connect what you are doing to what was done quite successfully by your ancestors, and using that connection as a mode through which to prefigure what you wish to accomplish in the future, would serve to (re)contextualize your efforts in a way you've never before attempted. It would allow you to obtain a sense of your own cultural continuity which, at present, appears to be conspicuously absent in your struggle. It would allow you to experience the sense of empowerment which comes with reaching into your own history at the deepest level and altering outcomes you've quite correctly decided are unacceptable. This is as opposed to your trying to invent some entirely different history for yourselves. We predict a project of this sort, if approached carefully and with considerable flexibility from the outset, would revitalize your struggle in ways which will astound you.

"Here's another possibility: You are at the moment seriously engaged in efforts to redefine power relations between men and women, and in finding ways to actualize these redefined relationships. Instead of trying to reinvent the wheel in this respect, why not see it as an attempt to reconstitute in the modern setting the kind of gender balance that prevailed among your ancestors? Surely this makes as much sense as attempting to fabricate a whole new set of relations. And, quite possibly, it would enable you to explain your intentions in this regard to a whole range of people who are frankly skeptical right now, in a manner which would attract them rather than repelling them.

"Again: You are primarily an urban-based movement in which 'squatting' plays a very prominent role.[65] Why not frame this in terms of liberating your space in very much the same way we approach the liberation of our land? The particulars are very different, but the principle involved would seem to us to be quite similar. And it looks likely to us that thinking of squatting in this way would tend to lead you right back toward your traditional relationship

241

to land/space. This seems even more probable when squatting is considered in combination with the experiments in collectivism and communalism which are its integral aspects. A lot of translation is required to make these connections, but that too is exactly the point. Translation between the concrete and the theoretical is *always* necessary in the formation of praxis. What we're recommending is no different from any other approach in this respect. The question is whether these translations will serve to link political activity to reassertion of indigenous traditions, or to force an even further disjuncture in that regard. That's true in any setting, whether it's yours or ours. As we said, there are choices to be made.

"These are merely a few preliminary possibilities we've been able to observe during the short time we've been here," we concluded. "We're sure there are many others. What's important, however, is that we can and must all begin wherever we find ourselves. Start with what already exists in terms of resistance, link this resistance directly to your own native traditions, and build from there. The sequence is a bit different, but that's basically what we in the American Indian Movement have had to do. And we can testify that the process works. You end up with a truly organic and internally sustainable framework within which to engage in liberatory struggle. Plainly, this is something very different from Adolf Hitler's conducting of 'blood rituals' on the playing fields of Nuremberg,[66] or Heinrich Himmler's convening of some kind of 'Mystic Order of the SS' in a castle at Wewelsburg,[67] just as it's something very different from tripped-out hippies prancing about in the grass every spring pretending they're 'rediscovering' the literal ceremonial forms of the ancient Celts, or a bunch of yuppies spending their off-hours playing at being American Indians. All of these are facets of the negative polarity you so rightly reject. We are arguing, not that you should drop your rejection of the negative, but that you should its positive alternative. Let's not confuse the two. And let's not throw the baby out with the bath water. Okay?"

Applications to North America

It is not necessary for crows to become eagles.

—Sitting Bull
1888

Much of what has been said with regard to Germany can be transposed for application in North America, albeit there can be no suggestion that Euroamericans are in any way indigenous to this land (cutesy bumper stickers reading "Colorado Native" and displayed by blond suburbanites do nothing to change this). What is meant is that the imperative of reconnecting themselves to their own traditional roots pertains as much, and in some ways more, to this dislocated segment of the European population as it does to their cousins who have remained in the Old World. By extension, the same point can be made with regard to the descendants of those groups of European invaders who washed up on the beach in other quarters of the planet these past five hundred years: in various locales of South and Central America, for instance, and in Australia, New Zealand, South Africa, and much of Polynesia and Micronesia. In effect, the rule would apply wherever settler state colonialism has come into existence.[68]

Likely, it will be far more difficult for those caught up in Europe's far-flung diaspora to accomplish this than it may be for those still within the confines of their native geography. The latter plainly enjoy a much greater proximity to the sources of their indigenous traditions, while the former have undergone several generations of continuous indoctrination to see themselves as "new peoples" forging entirely new cultures.[69] The sheer impossibility of this last has inflicted upon those among the Euro-diaspora with an additional dimension of identity confusion largely absent among even the most conspicuously deculturated elements of the subcontinent itself. Rather than serving as a deterrent, however, this circumstance should be understood as heightening the urgency assigned the reconstructive task facing Euroamericans and others, elsewhere, who find themselves in similar situations.

By and large, the Germans have at least come to understand, and to accept, what nazism was and is. This has allowed the best among them to seek to distance themselves from it by undertaking whatever political action is required to destroy it once and for all.[70] Their posture in this respect provides them a necessary foundation for resumption of cultural/spiritual traditions among themselves which constitute a direct and fully-internalized antidote to the nazi impulse. In effecting this reconnection to their own indigenous heritage, the German dissidents will at last be able to see nazism—that logical culmination of so much of the predatory synthesis which is "Europe"—as being, not something born of their own traditions, but as something as alien and antithetical to those traditions as it was/is to the traditions of any other people in the world. In this way, by reintegrating themselves with their indigenous selves, they simultaneously reintegrate themselves with the rest of humanity itself.

In North America, by contrast, no such cognition can be said to have taken hold, even among the most politically-developed sectors of the Euroamerican population. Instead, denial remains the norm. Otherwise progressive whites still seek at all costs to evade even the most obvious correlations between their own history in the New World and that of the nazis in the Old. A favorite intellectual parlor game remains the debate over whether genocide is "really" an "appropriate" term to describe the physical eradication of some 98 percent of the continent's native population between 1500 and 1900.[71] "Concern" is usually expressed that comparisons between the U.S. government's assertion of its "Manifest Destiny" to expropriate through armed force about 97.5 percent of all native land, and the nazis' subsequent effort to implement what they called "*Lebensraumpolitik*"—the expropriation through conquest of territory belonging to the Poles, Slavs, and other "inferior" peoples only a generation later—might be "misleading" or "oversimplified."[72]

The logical contortions through which Euroamericans persist in putting themselves in this process of avoiding reality are sometimes truly amazing. A salient example is that of James Axtell, a white "revisionist" historian quite prone to announcing his "sympathies" with Indians, has repeatedly gone on record arguing in the most vociferous fashion that it is both "unfair" and "contrary to sound historiography" to compare European invaders and settlers in the Americas to nazis. His reasoning? Because, he says, the former were, "after all, human beings. They were husbands, fathers, brothers, uncles, sons and lovers. And we must try to reach back in time to understand them as such."[73] Exactly what he thinks the nazis were, if not human beings fulfilling identical roles in their society, is left unstated. For that matter, Axtell fails to address how he ever arrived at the novel conclusion that either the nazis or European invaders and Euroamerican settlers in the New World consisted only of men.

A more sophisticated ploy consists of a ready concession on the part of white activists/theorists that what was done to America's indigenous peoples was "tragic,"even while raising carefully loaded questions suggesting that things are working out "for the best" in any event.[74] "Didn't Indians fight wars with one another?" the question goes, implying that the native practice of engaging in rough intergroup skirmishing—a matter more akin to full-contact sports like football, hockey, and rugby than anything else—somehow equates to Europe's wars of conquest and annihilation, and that traditional indigenous societies therefore stand to gain as much from Euroamerican conceptions of pacifism as anyone else.[75] (You bet, boss. Left to our own devices, we'd undoubtedly have exterminated ourselves. Praise the lord that y'all came along to save us from ourselves.)

Marxian organizations like the Revolutionary Communist Party USA express deep concern that native people's economies might have been so unrefined that we were commonly forced to eat our own excrement to survive, a premise clearly implying that Euroamerica's industrial devastation of our homelands has ultimately worked to our advantage, ensuring our "material security" whether we're gracious enough to admit it or not.[76] (Thanks, boss. We were tired of eating shit anyway. Glad you came and taught us to farm.[77]) The "cutting edge" ecologists of Earth First! have conjured up queries as to whether Indians weren't "the continent's first environmental pillagers"—they claim we beat all the woolly mammoths to death with sticks, among other things—meaning we were always sorely in need of Euroamerica's much more advanced views on preserving the natural order.[78]

White male anarchists fret over possible "authoritarian" aspects of our societies—"You had *leaders*, didn't you? That's hierarchy!"[79] — while their feminist sisters worry that our societies may have been "sexist" in their functioning.[80] (Oh no, boss. We too managed to think our way through to a position in which women did the heavy lifting and men bore the children. Besides, hadn't you heard? We were all "queer," in the old days, so your concerns about our being patriarchal have always been unwarranted.[81]) Even the animal rights movement chimes in from time to time, discomfited that we were traditionally so unkind to "non-human members of our sacred natural order" as to eat their flesh.[82] (Hey, no sweat, boss. We'll jump right on your no-meat bandwagon. But don't forget the sacred Cherokee Clan of the Carrot. You'll have to reciprocate our gesture of solidarity by not eating any more fruits and vegetables either. Or had you forgotten that plants are non-human members of the natural order as well? Have a nice fast, buckaroo.)

Not until such apologist and ultimately white supremacist attitudes begin to be dispelled within at least that sector of Euroamerican society which claims to represent an alternative to U.S./Canadian business-as-usual can there be hope of *any* genuinely positive social transformation in North America. And only in acknowledging the real rather than invented nature of their history, as the German opposition has done long since, can they begin to come to grips with such things.[83] From there, they too will be able to position themselves— psychologically, intellectually, and eventually in practical terms—to step outside that history, not in a manner which continues it by presuming to appropriate the histories and cultural identities of its victims, but in ways allowing them to recapture its antecedent meanings and values. Restated, Euroamericans, like their European counterparts, will then be able to start reconnecting themselves to their indigenous traditions and identities in ways which instill pride rather than guilt, empowering themselves to join in the negation of the construct of "Europe" which has temporarily suppressed their cultures as well as ours.

At base, the same principle applies here that pertains "over there." As our delegation put it repeatedly to the Germans in our closing remarks, "The indigenous peoples of the Americas can, have, and will continue to join hands with the indigenous peoples of this land, just as we do with those of any other. We are reaching out to you by our very act of being here, and of saying what we are saying to you. We have faith in you, a faith that you will be able to rejoin the family of humanity as peoples interacting respectfully and harmoniously—on the basis of your own ancestral ways—with the traditions of all other peoples. We are at this time expressing a faith in you that you perhaps lack in yourselves. But, and make no mistake about this, we *cannot* and *will not* join hands with those who default on this responsibility, who instead insist upon wielding an imagined right to stand as part of Europe's synthetic and predatory tradition, the tradition of colonization, genocide, racism, and ecocide. The choice, as we've said over and over again, is yours to make. It cannot be made for you. You alone must make your choice and act on it, just as we have had to make and act upon ours."

In North America, it will be evident that affirmative choices along these lines have begun to emerge among self-proclaimed progressives, not when figures like Robert Bly are simply dismissed as being ridiculous kooks, or condoned as harmless irrelevancies,[84] but when they come to be treated by "their own" as signifying the kind of menace they actually entail. Only when white males themselves start to display the sort of profound outrage at the activities of groups like the Men's Movement as is manifested by its victims—when they rather than we begin to shut down the movement's meetings, burn its sweat lodges, impound and return the sacred objects it desecrates, and otherwise make its functioning impossible—will we be able to say with confidence that Euroamerica has finally accepted that Indians are Indians, not toys to be played with by whoever can afford the price of the game. Only then will we be able to say that the "Indians 'R' Us" brand of cultural appropriation and genocide has passed, or at least is passing, and that Euroamericans are finally coming to terms with who they've been and, much more importantly, who and what it is they can become. Then, finally, these immigrants can at last be accepted among us upon our shores, fulfilling the speculation of the Dwamish leader Seattle in 1854: "We may be brothers after all." As he said then, "We shall see."[85]

Notes

1. Bly's political dimension began to take form with publication of his interview "What Men Really Want" in *New Age*, May 1982. For an overview of his verse, see Robert Bly, *Selected Poems* (New York: Harper & Row Publishers, 1986). Earlier collections include *Silence in the Snowy Fields* (Middletown, CT: Wesleyan University Press, 1962), *This Body Is Made from Camphor and Gopherwood* (New York: Harper & Row Publishers, 1977), *This Tree Will Be Here for a Thousand Years* (New York: Harper & Row Publishers, 1979), *News of the Universe* (San Francisco: Sierra Club Books, 1981), *The Man in the Black Coat Turns* (New York: Doubleday Publishers, 1981), and *Loving a Woman in Two Worlds* (New York: Doubleday Publishers, 1985).

2. See Susieday, "Male Liberation," *Z Magazine*, June 1993, pp. 10-12. The author cites a recent *Newsweek* poll indicating that some 48 percent of Euroamerican males believe they are being "victimized" by a "loss of influence" in U.S. society. She

points out that, by this, they appear to mean that they've been rendered marginally less empowered to dominate everyone else than they were three decades ago. Their response is increasingly to overcome this perceived victimization by finding ways and means, often through cooptation of the liberatory methods developed by those they're accustomed to dominating, of reestablishing their "proper authority."

3. Statements by Robert Bly during workshop session at the University of Colorado/Boulder, 1992.

4. Robert Bly, *Iron John: A Book About Men* (Reading, MA: Addison-Wesley Publishing, 1990). The title is taken from the fairy tale "The Story of Iron John" by Jakob and Wilhelm Grimm, of which Bly provides his own translation from the German.

5. As examples, see Patrick M. Arnold, *Wildmen, Warriors and Kings: Masculine Spirituality and the Bible* (New York: Crossroad Publishers, 1991); Robert Moore and Douglas Gillette, *King, Warrior, Magician, Lover: Rediscovering the Archetypes of Masculine Nature* (New York: Harper & Row Publishers, 1990); R.J. Stewart, *Celebrating the Male Mysteries* (Bath, UK: Arcania Publications, 1991); and Kenneth Wetcher, Art Barker, and F.W. McCaughtry, *Save the Males: Why Men Are Mistreated, Misdiagnosed, and Misunderstood* (Washington, D.C.: Pia Press, 1991). Anthologies include John Matthews's *Choirs of the God: Revisioning Masculinity* (London: Harper Mandala Books, 1991); and Christopher Harding's *Wingspan: Inside the Men's Movement* (New York: St. Martin's Press, 1992). Or, in another medium, try Robert Moore, *Rediscovering Men's Potentials* (Wilmette, IL: Chiron, 1988; set of four cassette tapes).

6. Consider, for example, *Shaman's Drum* (produced in Willits, CA), described as a "glossy quarterly 'journal of experiential shamanism,' native medicineways,

transpersonal healing, ecstatic spirituality, and care-taking of the earth. Includes regional calendars, resource directory, information on drums."

7.   Wallace Black Elk, an Oglala Lakota, is a former apprentice to Sicangu (Brûlé) Lakota spiritual leader Leonard Crow Dog and was a member of the American Indian Movement during the period of the Wounded Knee siege (*circa* 1972-76). Subsequently, he became associated with the late "Sun Bear" (Vincent LaDuke), an Anishinabe who served as something of a prototype for plastic medicine men, and discovered the profit potential of peddling ersatz Indian spirituality to New Agers. Despite the fact that he is *not*, as he claims, the grand-nephew of the Black Elk made famous by John Neihardt (*Black Elk Speaks* [Lincoln: University of Nebraska Press, 1963]) and Joseph Epes Brown (*The Sacred Pipe* [Norman: University of Oklahoma Press, 1953])—it's an entirely different family—"Grampa Wallace" has become a favorite icon of the Men's Movement. In fact, the movement has made him, at age 71, something of a best-selling author; see Wallace Black Elk and William S. Lyon, *Black Elk: The Sacred Ways of the Lakota* (San Francisco: Harper Books, 1991).

8.   The Sun Dance is the central ceremony of Lakota ritual life; the geographical reference is to "Crow Dog's Paradise," near Grass Mountain, on the Rosebud Reservation in South Dakota.

9.   Another obvious alternative to "American Indianism" might be for the Men's Movement to turn toward certain warrior-oriented strains of Buddhism or even Shintoism. But then, Bly and the boys would be compelled to compete directly—both financially and theologically—with much more longstanding and refined institutions of spiritual appropriation like the Naropa Institute. Enterprises preoccupied with the various denominations of Islam are similarly well-

rooted in North America.

10. Statement made at the Socialist Scholars Conference, New York, 1988.

11. Letter to the author, November 14, 1985.

12. The AIM resolution specifically identified several native people—the Sun Bear, Wallace Black Elk, and the late Grace Spotted Eagle (Oglala Lakota) among them—as being primary offenders. Also named were non-Indians, including Cyfus McDonald, "Osheana Fast Wolf," and "Brooke Medicine Eagle" (spelled "Medicine Ego" in the document), and one non-Indian organization, Vision Quest, Inc. For the complete text, see Ward Churchill, *Fantasies of the Master Race: Literature, Cinema and the Colonization of American Indians* (Monroe, ME: Common Courage Press, 1992, pp. 226-8).

13. The resolution was signed by Tom Yellowtail (Crow), Larry Anderson (Navajo), Izadore Thom (Lummi), Thomas Banyacya (Hopi), Walter Denny (Chippewa-Cree), Austin Two Moons (Northern Cheyenne), Tadadaho (Haudenasaunee), Frank Fools Crow (Oglala Lakota), Frank Cardinal (Cree), and Peter O'Chiese (Anishinabe), all well-respected traditional spiritual leaders within their respective nations. For the complete text, see *ibid.*, pp. 223-5.

14. For complete text, see *Oyate Wicaho*, Vol. 2, No. 3, November 1982.

15. Sherman Alexie, "White Men Can't Drum: In Going Native for Its Totems, the Men's Movement Misses the Beat," *New York Times Magazine*, October 4, 1992. For a Men's Movement perspective on the importance of drumming, and the association of their usage (in their minds) with African and American Indian rituals, see George A. Parks, "The Voice of the Drum," in *Wingspan* (*op. cit.*, pp. 206-13).

16. Paul Reitman, "*Clearcut*: Ritual Gone Wrong," *The Men's Council Journal*, No. 16, February 1993, p. 17.

17. Paul Shippee, "Among the Dog Eaters," *The Men's Council Journal*, No. 16, February 1993, pp. 7-8.

18. Telephone conversation, June 7, 1993. Means's comparisons to Eichmann and the Aryan Nation are not merely hyperbolic. Adolf Eichmann, SS "Jewish liaison" and transportation coordinator for the Holocaust, actually asserted on numerous occasions that he felt himself to be a zionist; see Hannah Arendt, *Eichmann in Jerusalem: A Report on the Banality of Evil* (New York: Viking Press, 1963, p. 40). On the 'True Jew" dogma of "Identity Christianity," religious creed of the rabidly antisemitic Idaho-based Aryan Nations, see Leonard Zeskind, *The Christian Identity Movement: A Theological Justification for Racist and Anti-Semitic Violence* (New York: Division of Church and Society of the National Council of Churches of Christ in the U.S.A., 1986).

19. Means's characterization of the process corresponds quite well with the observations of many experts on cultural genocide. Consider, for example, the statement made by Mark Davis and Robert Zannis in their book, *The Genocide Machine in Canada: The Pacification of the North* (Montréal: Black Rose Books, 1973, p. 137): "If people suddenly lose their 'prime symbol' [such as the sanctity of spiritual tradition], the basis of their culture, their lives lose meaning. They become disoriented, with no hope. A social disorganization often follows such a loss, they are often unable to ensure their own survival....The loss and human suffering of those whose culture has been healthy and is suddenly attacked and disintegrated is incalculable."

20. Statement made at the 1982 Western Social Science Association Conference; quoted in *Fantasies of the Master Race*, *op. cit.*, p. 190.

21. *Ibid.*, pp. 190-1.

22. "White Men Can't Drum," *op. cit.*

23. *Ibid.* The final example refers to an anecdote with which Alexie opens his article: "Last year on the local television news, I watched a short feature on a meeting of the Confused White Men chapter in Spokane, Wash. They were all wearing war bonnets and beating drums, more or less. A few of the drums looked as if they might have come from Kmart, and one or two of the men just beat their chests. 'It's not just the drum,' the leader of the group said, 'it's the idea of the drum.' I was amazed at the lack of rhythm and laughed, even though I knew I supported a stereotype. But it's true: White men can't drum. They fail to understand that a drum is more than a heartbeat. Sometimes it is the sound of thunder, and many times it just means some Indians want to dance."

24. Quoted in *Fantasies of the Master Race, op. cit.*, p. 194. It should be noted that Means's sentiments correspond perfectly with those expressed by Gerald Wilkinson, head of the politically much more conservative National Indian Youth Council, in a letter endorsing an action planned by Colorado AIM to halt the sale of ceremonies to non-Indians in that state by Sun Bear in 1983: "The National Indian Youth Council fully supports your efforts to denounce, embarrass, disrupt, or otherwise run out of Colorado, [Sun Bear's] Medicine Wheel Gathering....For too long the Bear Tribe Medicine Society has been considered repugnant but harmless to Indian people. We believe they not only line their pockets but do great damage to us all. Anything you can do to them will not be enough." Clearly, opposition to the misuse and appropriation of spiritual traditions is a transcendently unifying factor in Indian Country.

25. For an excellent overview of the German hobbyist tradition from its inception in the early twentieth century, see Hugh Honour, *The New Golden Land:*

European Images of the Indian from the Discovery to the Present Time (New York: Pantheon Books, 1975).

26. Interestingly, at least some hobbyist replica objects—all of them produced by men who would otherwise view such things as "women's work,"—are of such high quality that they have been exhibited in a number of ethnographic museums throughout Europe.

27. This seems to be something of a tradition on "The Continent." As examples, "William Augustus Bowles, an American Tory dressed up as an Indian, managed to pass in the upper crust of London's society in 1791 as 'commander-in-chief of the Creek and Cherokee' nations....A person calling himself Big Chief White Horse Eagle, whose somewhat fictional autobiography was written by a German admirer (Schmidt-Pauli 1931), found it profitable to travel Europe in the 1920s and 1930s, adopting unsuspecting museum directors and chairmen of anthropology departments into his tribe....None of them, however, could match the most flamboyant fake Indian to visit Europe....This party, named Capo Cervo Bianco (Chief White Elk), arrived in Italy during the 1920s, claiming to be on his way to the League of Nations to represent the Iroquois of upstate New York. He was received by Mussolini and for a time managed to live richly out of his believers' purses [until he was] exposed as an Italo-American by the name of Edgardo Laplant"; see Christian F. Feest, "Europe's Indians," in James A. Clifton, ed., *The Invented Indian: Cultural Fictions & Government Policies* (New Brunswick, NJ: Transaction Publishers, 1990, pp. 322-3). The reference is to Edgar von Schmidt-Pauli, *We Indians: The Passion of a Great Race by Big Chief White Horse Eagle* (London, 1931).

28. "Europe's Indians," *op. cit.*, p. 323.

29. "Freesoul" claims to be the "sacred pipe carrier" of something called the "Redtail Hawk Medicine

256

Society...established by Natan Lupan and James Blue Wolf...in 1974...fulfill[ing a] Hopi prophecy that new clans and societies shall emerge as part of a larger revival and purification of the Red Road"; see John Redtail Freesoul, *Breath of the Invisible: The Way of the Pipe* (Wheaton, IL: Theosophical Publishing House, 1986, pp. 104-5). For a heavy dose of the sort of metaphysical gibberish passed off as "traditional Cherokee religion" by "Ywahoo" and her Sunray Meditation Foundation, see her *Voices of Our Ancestors* (Boston: Shambala Press, 1987). For analysis of "Eagle Man" McGaa's bilge, see the essay concerning his *Mother Earth Spirituality* (San Francisco: Harper Books, 1990) in this volume.

30. "Europe's Indians," *op. cit.*, p. 323. For detailed exposure of Carlos Castaneda as a fraud, see Richard De Mille, *Castaneda's Journey: The Power and the Allegory* (Santa Barbara, CA: Capra Press, 1976). In his recent essay "Of Wild Men and Warriors," however, Men's Movement practitioner Christopher X. Burant posits *Tales of Power* by "C.M. Castaneda" as one of his major sources (*Wingspan, op. cit.*, p. 176).

31. The Sun Dance is both culturally and geographically specific, and thus totally misplaced in the Black Forest among Germans. By extension, of course, this makes the series of Sun Dances conducted by Leonard Crow Dog in the Big Mountain area of the Navajo Nation, in Arizona, over the past few years equally misplaced and sacrilegious. A culturally specific ceremony is no more a "Pan-Indian" phenomenon than it is transcultural in any other sense.

32. Tipis were never designed to serve as mountain dwellings, which is why no American Indian people has ever used them for that purpose.

33. For a classic and somewhat earlier example of this sort of adoption of an outright "Indian identity" by a German, see the book by Adolf Gutohrlein, who

called himself "Adolf Hungry Wolf," *The Good Medicine* (New York: Warner Paperback Library, 1973). Also see the volume he coauthored with his Blackfeet wife, Beverly, *Shadows of the Buffalo* (New York: William Morrow Publishers, 1983).

34. "Europe's Indians," *op. cit.*, pp. 313-32). For a broader view on this and related matters, see the selections from several analysts assembled by Feest as *Indians and Europe: An Interdisciplinary Collection of Essays* (Aachen: Rader Verlag, 1987).

35. The roots of this perspective extend deep within the European consciousness, having been first articulated in clear form at least as early as the 1703 publication of a book by the Baron de Lahontan (Louis-Armand Lom d'Arce) entitled *New Voyages to North-America* (Chicago: A.C. McClurg & Co., 1905).

36. "Europe's Indians," *op. cit.*, p. 327.

37. Concerning the fantasy dimension of hobbyist projections about "Indianness," Dutch analyst Ton Lemaire probably put it best (in Feest's translation): "On closer look, these 'Indians' turn out to be a population inhabiting the European mind, not the American landscape, a fictional assemblage fabricated over the past five centuries to serve specific cultural and emotional needs of its inventors"; *De Indiaan In Ons Bewustzijn: De Ontmoeting van de Oude met de Nieuwe Wereld* (Baarn: Ambo S.V., 1986).

38. Implications attending use of the term "Wildman" in the European context, from which Robert Bly borrowed the concept, sheds a certain light on the U.S. Men's Movement's deployment of the term. From there, the real attitudes of both groups regarding American Indians stand partially revealed. See Susi Colin, "The Wild Man and the Indian in Early 16th Century Illustration," in *Indians and Europe, op. cit.*, pp. 5-36.

39. Absent the appropriative fetishism regarding

American Indian spiritual life marking the Men's Movement, there is a remarkable similarity between its composition and sentiments and those of another group of "Indian lovers" whose activities spawned disastrous consequences for native people during the nineteenth century. See Francis Paul Prucha, *Americanizing the American Indian: Writings of the "Friends of the Indian," 1800-1900* (Lincoln: University of Nebraska Press, 1973).

40. There was some talk among German activists, while I was in Germany during May 1993, of disrupting Bly's planned tour in July.

41. For analysis of the extent and implications of such activities on U.S. and Canadian reservation lands, see Ward Churchill, *Struggle for the Land: Indigenous Resistance to Genocide, Ecocide and Expropriation in Contemporary North America* (Monroe, ME: Common Courage Press, 1992).

42. This represents an interesting inversion of the psychosis, in which the oppressed seeks to assume the identity of the oppressor, analyzed by Frantz Fanon in his *Black Skin, White Masks: The Experiences of a Black Man in a White World* (New York: Grove Press, 1967). Perhaps an in-depth study of the Men's Movement should be correspondingly entitled *White Skin, Red Masks.*

43. In terms of content, this comparison of nazi mysticism to that of the Men's Movement is not superficial. Aside from preoccupations with a fantastic vision of "Indianness"—Hitler's favorite author was Karl May, writer of a lengthy series of potboilers on the topic—nazi "spirituality" focused upon the mythos of the Holy Grail; see Nicholas Goodrick-Clark, *The Occult Roots of Nazism: Secret Aryan Cults and Their Influence on Nazi Ideology* (New York: New York University Press, 1992). Bly and the bunch have mixed up very much the same stew; see Robert

Cornett, "Still Questing for the Holy Grail," in *Wingspan, op. cit.*, pp. 137-42. Indeed, the movement pushes Emma Jung's and Marie-Louise von Franz's neo-nazi tract on the topic, *The Grail Legend* (London: Hodder and Stoughton Publisher, 1960), as "essential reading." Another movement mainstay is John Matthews' *The Grail Quest for the Eternal* (New York: Crossroads Publishing, 1981).

44. The Central Intelligence Agency, to name one governmental entity with an established track record of fabricating "social movements" which are anything but what they appear, has undertaken far more whacked out projects in the past; see John Marks, *The Search for the Manchurian Candidate: The CIA and Mind Control* (New York: W.W. Norton Publishers, 1979).

45. This is hardly a recent phenomenon, having been widely remarked in the literature by the mid-1960s. The semantic construction "dis-ease" comes from British psychiatrist R.D. Laing's *The Politics of Experience* (New York: Ballantine Books, 1967).

46. Tapping into the malaise afflicting precisely this social stratum was the impetus behind the so-called "New Left" during the 1960s. For alternative approaches to organizing strategies in this sector, both of which failed, see Kirkpatrick Sale, *SDS* (New York: Random House Publishers, 1973), and Abbie Hoffman, *The Woodstock Nation* (New York: Vintage Books, 1969).

47. Occasionally, unsuccessful attempts are made to effect a synthesis addressing the whole. See, for example, Michael Albert, Leslie Cagan, Noam Chomsky, Robin Hahnel, Mel King, Lydia Sargent, and Holly Sklar, *Liberating Theory* (Boston: South End Press, 1986).

48. For indigenous critique of marxism as being part and parcel of Eurocentrism, see Ward Churchill, ed., *Marxism and Native Americans* (Boston: South End

Press, 1983).

49. Rudi Dutschke was a crucially important leader of the German SDS (*Sozialistischer Deutscher Studentenbund*) during the first major wave of student confrontation with state authority during the late 1960s. On March 11, 1968, he was shot in the head at close range by a would-be neo-nazi assassin. The wounds severely and permanently impaired Dutschke's physical abilities and eventually, in 1980, resulted in his death. A seminal New Left theorist on anti-authoritarianism, the great bulk of his writing has, unfortunately, yet to be published in English translation. For the single exception I know of, see his essay "On Anti-Authoritarianism," in Carl Ogelsby, ed., *The New Left Reader* (New York: Grove Press, 1969, pp. 243-53).

50. As concerns American SDS (Students for a Democratic Society) founder Tom Hayden, he is now a very wealthy and increasingly liberal member of the California state legislature. Former SDS and YIPPIE! leader Jerry Rubin is now a stock consultant and operator of a singles club in Manhattan. Eldridge Cleaver, former Minister of Information of the Black Panther Party and a founder of the Black Liberation Army, now earns his living trumpeting right-wing propaganda, as does David Horowitz, former editor of the radical *Ramparts* magazine. Rennie Davis, former SDS organizer and leader of the Student Mobilization to End the War in Vietnam, became an insurance salesperson and real estate speculator. Hayden, Rubin, and Davis, defendants in the "Chicago 8" (Seditious) Conspiracy Trial, were considered at the time to be the "benchmark" Euroamerican radicals of their generation. The German SDS has surpassed all this: its first president, Helmut Schmidt, actually went on to become chancellor of West Germany during the 1980s.

51. For a partial analysis of this phenomenon in the U.S., see Russell Jacoby, *The Last Intellectuals: American Culture in the Age of Academe* (New York: Basic Books, 1987).

52. Eldridge Cleaver, for instance, first became a "born again" Christian, and then converted to Mormonism. In 1971, Rennie Davis became a groupie of the then-adolescent guru Maharaj Ji.

53. M. Annette Jaimes (Juaneño/Yaqui) is editor of *The State of Native America: Genocide, Colonization, and Resistance* (Boston: South End Press, 1992). Bob Robideau, long-time AIM activist, was a codefendant of Leonard Peltier and former National Director of the Peltier Defense Committee. Paulette D'Auteuil is a Euroamerican anti-imperialist activist and former member of the Prairie Fire Organizing Committee.

54. The same recording is played in a seemingly endless loop in the United States. If I had a dollar for every white student or activist who has approached me over the past decade bemoaning the fact that he or she has "no culture," I'd need no other income next year. If American Indians as a whole received such payment, we could probably buy back North America and be done with it (just kidding, folks).

55. I personally date the advent of Europe from the coronation of Charlemagne as Holy Roman Emperor in A.D. 800, and the subsequent systematic subordination of indigenous Teutonic peoples to central authority. In his book, *The Birth of Europe* (Philadelphia/New York: Evans-Lippencott Publishers, 1966), Robert Lopez treats this as a "prelude," and dates the advent about two centuries later. In some ways, an even better case can be made that "Europe" in any true sense did not emerge until the mid-to-late fifteenth century, with the final Ottoman conquest of Byzantium (Constantinople), defeat of the Moors in Iberia, and the first Columbian

voyage. In any event the conquest and colonization of the disparate populations of the subcontinent must be viewed as an integral and requisite dimension of Europe's coming into being.

56. For interesting insights on the 800-year—and counting—Irish national liberation struggle against English colonization, see Ciarán de Baróid, *Ballymurphy and the Irish War* (London: Pluto Press, 1990). On the Euskadi, see Pedro Ibarra Guëll, *La evolución estratégica de ETA* (Donstia, 1987).

57. Although I doubt this is a "definitive" attribution, I first heard the matter put this way by the late Creek spiritual leader Phillip Deer in 1982.

58. As Carolyn Merchant observes in her book, *The Death of Nature: Women, Ecology, and the Scientific Revolution* (San Francisco: Harper & Row Publishers, 1980, pp. 134, 140): "Based on a fully articulated doctrine emerging at the end of the fifteenth century in the antifeminist tract *Malleus Maleficarum* (1486), or "Hammer of the Witches," by the German Dominicans Heinrich Institor and Jacob Sprenger, and in a series of art works by Hans Baldung Grien and Albert Dürer, witch trials for the next two hundred years threatened the lives of women all over Europe, especially in the lands of the Holy Roman Empire....The view of nature associated with witchcraft was personal animism. The world of the witches was antihierarchical and everywhere infused with spirits. Every natural object, every animal, every tree contained a spirit...." Sound familiar? These women who were being burned alive, were thus murdered precisely because they served as primary repositories of the European subcontinent's indigenous codes of knowledge and corresponding "pagan" ritual.

59. The Cherokee artist Jimmie Durham tells a story of related interest. In 1986, after delivering an invited lecture at Oxford, he was asked whether he'd like to

visit a group of people "who are actually indigenous to these islands." Somewhat skeptically, he accepted the invitation and was driven to a nearby village where the inhabitants continued to perform rites utilizing a variety of objects, including a pair of reindeer antlers of a species extinct since the last Ice Age (roughly 15,000 years ago). It turns out the people were of direct lineal Pictic descent and still practiced their traditional ceremonies, handed down their traditional stories, and so forth. The British government, getting wind of this, subsequently impounded the antlers as being "too important for purposes of science" to be left in possession of the owners. The dispossessed Picts were then provided a plastic replica of their sacred item, "so as not to disturb their religious life."

60. From Russell Means, "Fighting Words on the Future of Mother Earth," *Mother Jones*, February 1981.

61. See Wilhelm Reich, *The Mass Psychology of Fascism* (New York: Farrar, Straus & Giroux Publishers, 1970). Also see George L. Mosse, *Nazi Culture: Intellectual, Cultural, and Social Life in the Third Reich* (New York: Schocken Books, 1966).

62. An excellent early study of these dynamics may be found in Hermann Rauschning, *The Revolution of Nihilism: Warning to the West* (New York: Longmans, Green & Co., 1939). More recently, see Fritz Stern, *The Politics of Cultural Despair: A Study in the Rise of Germanic Ideology* (Berkeley: University of California Press, 1961), and Robert A. Poos, *National Socialism and the Religion of Nature* (London/Sydney: Croom Helm Publishers, 1986).

63. During the two weeks I was in the newly reunified Germany, five refugees—all people of color—were murdered by neo-nazi firebombings. Another forty were injured in the same manner. The German legislature repealed Article 16 of the Constitution, an

important anti-nazi clause guaranteeing political asylum to all legitimate applicants, thus opening the door to mass deportation of non-whites. The legislature also severely restricted women's rights to abortions, while continuing its moves toward repeal of a constitutional prohibition against German troops operating anywhere beyond the national borders. Meanwhile, the government locked the Roma-Cinti Gypsies *out* of the former Neuengemme concentration camp where their ancestors had been locked *in*, en route to the extermination center at Auschwitz. This was/is part of an official effort to drive all Gypsies out of Germany (again); 120 million deutschmarks have been authorized for payment to Poland to convince it to accept an unlimited number of Roma deportees, while another 30 million each have been earmarked as payments to Rumania and Macedonia for the same purpose (yet another such deal is being cut with Slovakia). Overtly nazi-oriented organizations are calling for the reacquisition of Silesia and parts of Prussia—eastern territories lost to Poland at the end of World War II—and are striking responsive chords in some quarters.

64. The *Autonomen*, which may be the defining characteristic of the German opposition movement today, are proliferative and essentially anarchistic in their perspective.

65. Our entire group was rather stunned by the sheer number of "squats"—usually abandoned commercial or apartment buildings in which a large number of people can live comfortably—in Germany. Some, like the Haffenstrasse in Hamburg and Keiffenstrasse in Dusseldorf—each comprised of an entire block or more of buildings—have been occupied for more than a decade and serve not only as residences, but bases for political organizing and countercultural activities.

66. See Hamilton T. Burden, *The Nuremberg Party*

Rallies, 1923-39 (New York: Praeger Publishers, 1967).

67. On Wewelsburg castle, see Heinz Höhne, *The Order of the Death's Head: The Story of Hitler's SS* (New York: Howard-McCann Publishers, 1969, pp. 151-3). For photographs, see the section entitled "Dark Rites of the Mystic Order" in Editors, *The SS* (Alexandra, VA: Time-Life Books, 1988, pp. 38-49). The scenes of Wewelsburg should be compared to those described in Isabel Wyatt's *From Round Table to Grail Castle* (Sussex, UK: Lanthorn Press, 1979), a work highly recommended by leaders of the U.S. Men's Movement today.

68. For analysis of the settler state phenomenon, see J. Sakai, *Settlers: The Mythology of the White Proletariat* (Chicago: Morningstar Press, 1983). Also see Ronald Weitzer, *Transforming Settler States: Communal Conflict and Internal Security in Northern Ireland and Zimbabwe* (Berkeley: University of California Press, 1992).

69. This bizarre concept cuts across all political lines in settler state settings. In the United States, to take what is probably the most pronounced example, reactionary ideologues have always advanced the thesis that American society comprises a racial/cultural "melting pot" which has produced a wholly new people, even while enforcing racial codes indicating the exact opposite. Their opposition, on the other hand, has consistently offered much the same spurious argument. Radical Chicanos, for instance, habitually assert that they represent "la Raza," a culturally-mixed "new race" developed in Mexico and composed of "equal parts Spanish and Indio blood." Setting aside the question of what, exactly, a "Spaniard" might be in genetic terms—the main "stock" would seem to be composed of Visigoths, who are "Germanic"—the contention is at best absurd.

During the three centuries following the conquest of Mexico, approximately 200,000 immigrants arrived there from Iberia. Of these, about one-third were Moors, and another one-third were Jewish "conversos" (both groups were being systematically "exported" from Spain at the time, as an expedient to ridding Iberia of "racial contaminants"). This leaves fewer than 70,000 actual "Spaniards," by whatever biological definition, to be genetically balanced against nearly 140,000 "other" immigrants, and some thirty *million* Indians native to Mexico. Moreover, the settlers brought with them an estimated 250,000 black chattel slaves, virtually all of whom eventually intermarried. Now, how all this computes to leaving a "half-Spanish, half-Indio" Chicano population as an aftermath is anybody's guess. Objectively, the genetic heritage of la Raza is far more African—black and Moorish—than European, and at least as much Jewish (semitic) as Spanish.

70. The worst among them, of course, understands the nature of nazism and therefore embraces it, while the "mainstream"—including the bulk of the government and state bureaucracy—accepts it as being their "destiny."

71. For a classic articulation of this pervasive theme, see J.H. Elliott, "The Rediscovery of America," *New York Review of Books*, June 24, 1993: "Stannard takes the easy way out by turning his book into a high-pitched catalogue of European crimes, diminishing in the process the message he wants to convey. In particular, his emotive vocabulary seems self-defeating. 'Holocaust,' 'genocide,' even 'racism,' carry with them powerful contemporary freight....'Genocide,' as used of the Nazi treatment of the Jews, implies not only mass extermination, but a clear intention on the part of a higher authority [and] it debases the word to write, as Stannard writes, of 'the genocidal

encomienda system,' or to apply it to the extinction of a horrifyingly large proportion of the indigenous population through the spread of European diseases." Elliott is critiquing David E. Stannard's superb *American Holocaust: Columbus and the Conquest of the New World* (London/New York: Oxford University Press, 1992), in which official intentionality—including intentionality with regard to inculcation of disease as a means of extermination—is amply demonstrated.

72. Even Frank Parella, whose graduate thesis *Lebensraum and Manifest Destiny: A Comparative Study in the Justification of Expansion* (Washington, D.C.: Georgetown University, 1950) was seminal in opening up such comparisons, ultimately resorted to feeble "philosophical distinctions" in order to separate the two processes in his concluding section.

73. James Axtell, presentation at the American Historical Association Annual Conference, Washington, D.C., December 1992. For full elaboration of such inane apologetics, see this "preeminent American historian's" *Beyond 1492: Encounters in Colonial America* (London/New York: Oxford University Press, 1992).

74. See, for example, Robert Roybal's observation in his *1492 and All That: Political Manipulations of History* (Washington, D.C.: Ethics and Public Policy Center, 1992): "Whatever evils the Spanish introduced [to the "New World" of the Aztecs]—and they were many and varied—they at least cracked the age-old shell of a culture admirable in many ways but pervaded by repugnant atrocities and petrification." Leaving aside the matter of Aztec "atrocities"—which mostly add up to time-honored but dubious Euroamerican mythology—the idea of applying terms like "age-old" or "petrified" to this culture, which had existed for barely 500 years at the time of the Spanish conquest, speaks for itself. Roybal hadn't a clue what he was prattling on about.

75. For a good overview of traditional American Indian concepts and modes of warfare, see Tom Holm, "Patriots and Pawns: State Use of American Indians in the Military and the Process of Nativization in the United States," in *The State of Native America, op. cit.*, pp. 345-70.

76. Revolutionary Communist Party USA, "Searching for the Second Harvest," in *Marxism and Native Americans, op. cit.*, pp. 35-58. It is illuminating to note that the RCP, which professes to be totally at odds with the perspectives held by the Euroamerican status quo, lifted its assertion that ancient Indians consumed a "second harvest" of their own excrement verbatim from a hypothesis recently developed by a pair of the most "bourgeois" anthropologists imaginable, as summarized in that "citadel of establishment propaganda," the *New York Times*, on August 12, 1980. A better illustration of the confluence of interest and outlook regarding native people in Euroamerica, between what the RCP habitually (and accurately) describes as "fascism," and the party itself, would be difficult to find. In any event, for a good survey of the real level of material attainment evident in the precolumbian Western Hemisphere, see M. Annette Jaimes, "Re-Visioning Native America: An Indigenist View of Primitivism and Industrialism," *Social Justice*, Vol. 19, No. 2, Summer 1992, pp. 5-34.

77. In reality, about two-thirds of all vegetal foodstuffs commonly consumed by all of humanity today were under cultivation in the Americas—and nowhere else in the world—at the time the European invasion began. Indians were thus the consummate farmers on the planet in 1492. Plainly, then, we taught Europe the arts of diversified agriculture, not the other way around (as Eurocentric mythology insists). For further information, see Jack Weatherford,

Indian Givers: How the Indians of the Americas Transformed the World (New York: Crown Publishers, 1988).

78. For example: George Wuerthner, "An Ecological View of the Indian," *Earth First!*, Vol. 7, No. 7, August 1987. This rather idiotic argument is closely related to that of the quasi-official Smithsonian Institution, adopted *in toto* by the RCP, that native people traditionally engaged in such environmentally devastating practices as "jumpkilling" masses of bison—that is to say, driving entire herds off cliffs—in order to make use of a single animal ("Searching for the Second Harvest, *op. cit.*, p. 45).

79. In the most recent issue of *Anarchy* (No. 37, Summer 1993, p. 74), for instance, editor Jason McQuinn patronizingly dismisses American Indian writer M. Annette Jaimes's argument that certain extreme anarchist arguments against social hierarchy are "anti-natural" (since nature itself functions in terms of multitudinous interactive hierarchies) as being "authoritarian" and by a person "not overly concerned with freedom." In the process he neatly (if unwittingly) replicates Eurocentrism's fundamental flaw, separating human—"*social* and *institutional*" (his emphasis)—undertakings from nature altogether. Yup. White boys certainly do have all the answers...to everything.

80. For a solid rejoinder to such "worries" on the part of Euroamerican feminists, see M. Annette Jaimes and Theresa Halsey, "American Indian Women: At the Center of Indigenous Resistance in Contemporary North America," in *The State of Native America, op. cit.*, pp. 311-44.

81. For a foremost articulation of the absurd notion that all or even most Indians were traditionally homosexual or at least bisexual—which has made its author a sudden celebrity among white radical feminists and

recipient of the proceeds deriving from having a mini-bestseller on her hands as a result—see Paula Gunn Allen, *The Sacred Hoop: Recovering the Feminine in Native American Traditions* (Boston: Beacon Press, 1986, p. 256): "[L]esbianism and homosexuality were probably commonplace. Indeed, same-sex relationships may have been the norm for primary pair bonding...the primary personal unit tended to include members of one's own sex rather than members of the opposite sex." For a counterpart male proclamation, see Walter L. Williams, *The Spirit and the Flesh: Sexual Diversity in American Indian Culture* (Boston: Beacon Press, 1986). Both writers waltz right by the fact that if homosexuals were considered special, and therefore sacred, in traditional native societies—a matter upon which they each remark accurately and approvingly—then homosexuality could not by definition have been "commonplace" since that is a status diametrically opposed to that of being "special." Both Allen and Williams are simply playing to the fantasies of gay rights activists, using Indians as props in the customary manner of Euroamerica.

82. The language is taken from a note sent to me on June 7, 1993, by an airhead calling himself "Sky" Hiatt. It was enclosed along with a copy of Peter Singer's *Animal Liberation* (New York: *New York Review of Books*, 1975). Actually, the Euroamerican "animal liberation" movement is no joking matter to native people, as white activists—most of whom have never lifted a finger in defense of indigenous rights of any sort, and some of whom have openly opposed them—have come close to destroying what remains of traditional Inuit and Indian subsistence economies in Alaska and Canada; see Jerry Mander, *In the Absence of the Sacred: The Failure of Technology & the Survival of the Indian Nations* (San Francisco: Sierra Club Books, 1991, pp. 287, 296, 387).

83. This premise is simply a cultural paraphrase of the standard psychotherapeutic tenet that a patient cannot begin to be cured of pathology until s/he first genuinely acknowledges that he/she is afflicted with it.

84. This is, of course, already happening. Witness the observation of Lance Morrow in the August 19, 1991 issue of *Time* magazine, for example: "Bly may not be alive to certain absurdities in the men's movement...a silly, self-conscious attempt at manly authenticity, almost a satire of the hairy-chested.... As a spiritual showman (shaman), Bly seeks to produce certain effects. He is good at them. He [therefore] could not begin to see the men's movement, and his place within it, as a depthless happening in the goofy circus of America."

85. Quoted in Virginia Irving Armstrong, ed., *I Have Spoken: American History Through the Voices of the Indians* (Chicago: The Swallow Press, 1971, p. 79).

Declaration of War Against Exploiters of Lakota Spirituality

(Ratified by the Dakota, Lakota and Nakota Nations, June 1993)

WHEREAS we are the conveners of an ongoing series of comprehensive forums on the abuse and exploitation of Lakota spirituality; and

WHEREAS we represent the recognized traditional spiritual leaders, traditional elders, and grass-roots advocates of the Lakota people; and

WHEREAS for too long we have suffered the unspeakable indignity of having our most precious Lakota ceremonies and spiritual practices desecrated, mocked, and abused by non-Indian "wannabes," hucksters, cultists, commercial profiteers, and self-styled "New Age Shamans" and their followers; and

WHEREAS our precious Sacred Pipe is being desecrated through the sale of pipestone pipes at flea markets, powwows, and "New Age" retail stores; and

INDIANS ARE US?

WHEREAS pseudo-religious corporations have been formed to charge people money for admission to phony "sweat lodges" and "vision quest" programs; and

WHEREAS sacrilegious "sun dances" for non-Indians are being conducted by charlatans and cult leaders who promote abominable and obscene imitations of sacred Lakota Sun Dance rites; and

WHEREAS non-Indians have organized themselves into "tribes," assigning themselves make-believe "Indian names" to facilitate their wholesale expropriation and commercialization of our Lakota traditions; and

WHEREAS academic disciplines have sprung up at colleges and universities institutionalizing the sacrilegious imitation of our spiritual practices by students and instructors under the guise of educational programs in "shamanism"; and

WHEREAS non-Indian charlatans and "wannabes" are selling books that promote the systematic colonization of our Lakota spirituality; and

WHEREAS the television and film industry continues to saturate the entertainment media with vulgar, sensationalist, and grossly distorted representations of Lakota spirituality and culture which reinforce the public's negative stereotyping of Indian people and which gravely impair the self-esteem of our children; and

WHEREAS individuals and groups involved in the "New Age Movement," the "Men's Movement," in [other] "neo-pagan" cults, and in "shamanism" workshops all have exploited the spiritual traditions of our Lakota people by imitating our ceremonial ways and by mixing such imitation rituals with non-Indian occult practices in an offensive and harmful pseudo-religious hodgepodge; and

WHEREAS the absurd public posturing of this scandalous assortment of pseudo-Indian charlatans, "wannabes," commercial profiteers, cultists, and "New Age Shamans" comprises a momentous obstacle in the struggle of traditional Lakota people for an adequate public appraisal of the legitimate political, legal, and spiritual needs of real Lakota people; and

WHEREAS this exponential exploitation of our Lakota spiritual traditions requires that we take immediate action to defend our most precious Lakota spirituality from further contamination, desecration, and abuse;

THEREFORE WE RESOLVE AS FOLLOWS:

1. We hereby and henceforth declare war against all persons who persist in exploiting, abusing, and misrepresenting the sacred traditions and

spiritual practices of our Lakota, Dakota, and Nakota people.

2. We call upon all Lakota, Dakota, and Nakota brothers and sisters from reservations, reserves, and traditional communities in the United States and Canada to actively and vocally oppose this alarming take-over and systematic destruction of our sacred traditions.

3. We urge our people to coordinate with their tribal members living in urban areas to identify instances in which our sacred traditions are being abused, and then to resist this abuse, utilizing whatever specific tactics are necessary and sufficient—for example, demonstrations, boycotts, press conferences, and acts of direct intervention.

4. We especially urge all our Lakota, Dakota, and Nakota people to take action to prevent our people from contributing to and enabling abuse of our sacred ceremonies and spiritual practices by outsiders; for, as we all know, there are certain ones among our own people who are prostituting our spiritual ways for their own selfish gain, with no regard for the spiritual well-being of the people as a whole.

5. We assert a posture of zero-tolerance for any "white man's shaman" who rises from within our own communities to "authorize" the expropriation of our ceremonial ways by non-Indians; all such "plastic medicine men" are enemies of the

Declaration of War

Lakota, Dakota, and Nakota people.

6. We urge traditional people, tribal leaders, and governing councils of all other Indian nations, as well as the national Indian organizations, to join us in calling for an immediate end to the rampant exploitation of our respective American Indian sacred traditions by issuing statements denouncing such abuse; for it is not the Lakota, Dakota, and Nakota people alone whose spiritual practices are being systematically violated by non-Indians.

7. We urge all our Indian brothers and sisters to act decisively and boldly in our present campaign to end the destruction of our sacred traditions, keeping in mind our highest duty as Indian people: to preserve the purity of our precious traditions for our future generations, so that our children and our children's children will survive and prosper in the sacred manner intended for each of our respective peoples by our Creator.

Alert Concerning the Abuse and Exploitation of American Indian Sacred Traditions

(Spring 1993)

Center for the SPIRIT (**S**upport and **P**rotection of **I**ndian **R**eligions and **I**ndigenous **T**raditions) is a nonprofit organization of American Indian people dedicated to the preservation and revitalization of American Indian spiritual practices and religious traditions. Headquartered in the San Francisco Bay Area, we have begun to systematically address the momentous problem of "New Age" exploitation and expropriation of the sacred traditions of American Indian [nations]—a problem which has proliferated alarmingly in the Bay Area and throughout California in recent years. We are issuing this bulletin...in our continuing effort to raise public awareness about this new and insidious assault on American Indian religious freedom.

Traditional ceremonies and spiritual practices like the Lakota Sacred Pipe Ceremony, the Vision Quest, the Sun Dance, and the Sweat Lodge Ceremony, are precious gifts given to Indian people by our Creator. These sacred ways have enabled us as Indian people to survive—miraculously—the onslaught of five centuries of continuous effort by non-Indians and their government to exterminate us by extinguishing all traces of our traditional ways of life. Today, these precious sacred traditions continue to afford American Indian people of all [nations] the strength and vitality we need in the struggles we face every day; they also offer us our best hope for a stable and vibrant future. These sacred traditions are an enduring and indispensable "life raft" without which we would be quickly overwhelmed by the adversities that still threaten our survival. Because our sacred traditions are so precious to us, we cannot allow them to be desecrated and abused.

Therefore, we urge all supporters of American Indian people to join us in calling for an immediate end to the cynical, sacrilegious spectacle of non-Indian "wannabes," would-be gurus of the "New Age," and "plastic medicine men" shamelessly exploiting and mocking our sacred traditions by performing bastardized imitations of our ceremonies. They are promoters of "spiritual genocide" against Indian people; and while some of them may be guilty "merely" of complicity in "genocide with good intentions," others have become aggressive in insisting on their "right" to profiteer by exploiting and prostituting American Indian sacred traditions.

It is appropriate and indeed imperative that all supporters of American Indian religious freedom address the onslaught of "New Age" exploitation and hucksterism as a significant component of the "final phase of genocide" to which American Indian people are currently exposed. For five centuries, we as

Alert Concerning Sacred Indian Traditions

Indian people have suffered a holocaust that non-Indians and their government have inflicted upon us. Historically, we have been deprived of our homelands, our natural resources, our health, our prosperity, our children, our Native languages, our self-determination, our liberty and our lives. And now, we are in danger of having our sacred spiritual ways stolen from us—the essence of our identity and the key to our survival. We must raise a united voice of protest against those who would steal our spiritual traditions: YOU CANNOT HAVE THEM. NOT TODAY. NOT TOMORROW. NEVER.

We ask all those who care about Indian people in our struggle for justice and peace to help us put an end to spiritual genocide. We urge you to protest against "plastic medicine men" and hucksters wherever they appear in public; to lend them no degree of credibility; and to warn your friends who, through ignorance or naïveté, are in danger of being swindled by these con artists.

Editor's Note: The thematics and much of the terminology in this alert are taken directly from Ward Churchill's "Spiritual Hucksterism: The Rise of the Plastic Medicine Men," in his *Fantasies of the Master Race: Literature, Cinema and the Colonization of American Indians* (Monroe, ME: Common Courage Press, 1992, pp. 215-22). That essay also appeared in *Z Magazine* in December 1990.

Do It Yourself "Indianism"

The Case of Ed McGaa's *Mother Earth Spirituality*

> If a ceremony works, or can be made to work for
> our purposes, we use it.
>
> —Men's Movement organizer, 1992

When I was a little boy, my mother, bless her heart, used to buy me books like Ben Hunt's *Indian Crafts and Lore* in a forlorn effort to keep me somewhat "in touch" with the indigenous aspect of my heritage. Hence, early on, I was exposed to such boy scoutish "homages" to things Indian as using uncooked macaroni to simulate the bone employed in making chokers and breastplates, making "peace pipes" out of wooden dowels, and pasting carefully colored bits of graph paper to tee-shirts in an effort to create the appearance of a beaded "Indian costume." It was, mom's best intentions notwithstanding, the stuff of John Ford movies, "Koshari" dancers, and little white kids dressed in paint and turkey feathers during the nation's annual pre-Thanksgiving classroom "sensitivity" exercises, an unconscionably arrogant trivialization and degradation by the dominant society of everything meaningful in native material culture.

Of course, there were always more than a few

283

straight-off-the-nickel-looking Indians willing—for a fee—to say the exact opposite. They'd shuffle in with their crewcuts and VFW medallions, carrying "tom-toms" and wearing their "genuine" Cherokee "war bonnets," announce that they were the "hereditary chiefs" of some real or invented native people, mumble a few "traditional chants" as a benediction, and then solemnly thank the assembled Euroamericans for the "respect and understanding" they demonstrated by having become Indian hobbyists. With that, they'd pocket the $50 or so they'd thus "earned," and head for the nearest bar to prepare for the next day's appearance at the local museum. There, they'd tearfully bless the curator for his complicity in expropriating and displaying everything of physical significance, including the bones of their ancestors, for non-Indian edification. The rubric employed at museums and burial mounds was usually "intercultural communication." The rate charged for such endorsements and "authentications" was typically a bit higher than that charged for addressing hobby groups.

At a certain point in my life, all this became a matter of great confusion and anxiety for me. How could I—or anyone else—reconcile the craven image presented by these beings with the ideals of fierce and undeviating native pride embodied in the historical resistance of Tecumseh and Osceola, Crazy Horse and Satanta, Sitting Bull and Mangus Colorado, Victorio and Dull Knife, Satank, Geronimo, Gall, and so many others? Surely, the legacy of such struggles and suffering could not reasonably be said to have transformed itself into the transparently accommodationist posturing of those individuals wandering the "Friends of the Indian" lecture and performance circuits, or whooping it up in Walt Disney productions like *Tonka*. How to make sense of this non sequiter? Indeed, could sense actually *be* made of such a seeming paradox?

It was not until my mid-20s, after I'd been to Vietnam and subsequently become part of the American Indian Movement, that I was able to figure it out. The answer resides in the fact that, for every indigenous nation on the continent, the point of first contact with Euroamericans marks the end of their own homogeneous histories and traditions. Instead, when confronted with white imperial pretensions, each nation quickly came to manifest at least two mutually exclusive histories and traditions. On the one hand is the reality of native patriotism signified by those who fought back against overwhelming odds to defend their people's rights and ways of life. On the other is an equally important, if much less discussed, history of those who weren't up to the task, who obediently, and often for petty reasons of perceived self-interest, joined hands with the invaders to destroy their people's ability to resist colonization. Both histories are real and both are ongoing. The question is merely who is part of which heritage.

Viewed in this way, apprehending the meaning of that "Indian" behavior which once perplexed me is not particularly difficult. Those who participate in a song and dance routine for the pleasure of their conquerors, who say upon command what their conquerors wish to hear, are simply part of that time-honored, if not especially honorable, tradition called "hanging around the fort" (in more contemporary parlance, it's called "selling out"). In the old days, they made a habit of staying rather close to the nearest army post, all the better to be in position to sign instruments conveying "legal title" over other Indians' land to the United States. In exchange for such "services," they were officially designated as "leaders of their people" by various government commissions, usually receiving a bit of sugar to sweeten their coffee as "compensation." A little later, when the land was mostly gone, they began to trade blankets, beadwork, medicine bags—their younger sisters, if need be—for half-pints of rotgut whiskey. In their shame and degradation, they actively assisted in the destruction of those who refused to go along: it was an Oglala, after all, who held the arms of Crazy Horse while he was bayonetted by a soldier; a Hunkpapa led the Indian police unit which murdered Sitting Bull; a Chiricahua helped the army track down Geronimo. Unfortunately, there is no shortage of comparable examples occurring in Indian Country even as these words are written.

Things have, to be sure, "progressed" over the years. Today, not only the land and resources have long since been taken (or brokered away), but also the art and artifacts which formed the fetishes of my youth. Increasingly, the non-Indian commerce in that which belongs to Indians has come to center in our last definable asset, our conceptual property, the spiritual practices and understandings which hold together the final residue of humanity which was once Native America. When these are gone—or hopelessly prostituted—there will truly be nothing left with which we may sustain ourselves. Yet, as al-

Do It Yourself "Indianism"

ways, there are those of Indian lineage who step forward, eagerly offering up that which was never theirs to sell. Already we endure a raft of hucksters, emblematically represented by "Sun Bear" (Vincent LaDuke), an erstwhile Chippewa "holy man" and founder of something called the "Bear Tribe," who has made a lucrative career penning New Age texts and peddling ersatz "Indian ceremonies" to an endless gaggle of white groupies.

Now comes Ed McGaa, an Oglala Lakota attorney calling himself "Eagle Man," who has gone Sun Bear one better, publishing *Mother Earth Spirituality: Native Paths to Healing Ourselves and Our World* (Harper-Collins Publishers, 1991), a Ben Hunt-style "how to" manual on his people's ritual life: by the numbers, now, this is how to do a Sun Dance; one-two-three-four, here's the way to build a sweat lodge (see the "Sweat Lodge Check List" starting at page 223); turn to chapter nine for instruction on how to do a vision quest; read chapters six and eight for a thin "explanatory" veneer concerning what it all means; page 135 begins the lesson on how to construct a sacred pipe (all non-Indians are qualified to be pipe carriers, even if all Lakotas are not); for investment of the $15 cover price and the time it takes to read this hokey little tome, anyone can purport to have the "inside scoop" on native religion, even becoming a "medicine man" in his or her "own right" (Eagle Man himself said so, said so).

On top of all their other contemporary problems, the Lakotas may now expect to shortly be engulfed by a wave of newly-enlightened hippies demanding their "inherent right" to be included in the rituals of their choice or, worse, joining that eternal chorus of pompous Euroamerican academics asserting their "qualifications" to "teach" Indians the "true" meaning of their spiritual traditions ("we are all related, so we are all the same, which means we are entitled to anything of yours we want"). Nor is there some magic barrier restricting these sorry effects to McGaa's own people, a circumstance readily corroborated by the recently-acquired and growing penchant of groups like the "Rainbow Tribe" to dabble in everything from the Aztec Calendar to Navajo crystal healing ceremonies. Perhaps we should all anticipate that some Mormonized Hopi will soon publish a volume titled *Kiva Classics*, simultaneously breaching the shield of confidentiality with which the traditional priesthood has protected itself for many generations, and bastardizing their worldview beyond any possible redemption.

Ed McGaa knows full well he is peddling a lie, that it takes a lifetime of training to become a genuine Lakota spiritual leader (which he is not), that the ceremonies he describes are at best meaningless when divorced from their proper conceptual context, and that the integrity of Lakota cultural existence is to a large extent contingent upon the people's retention of control over their spiritual knowledge. He has transgressed against Lakota rights and survival in every bit as serious a fashion as those hang-around-the-forts who once professed to legitimate the U.S. expropriation of the Black Hills, the only slight redemption being that most of the information he presents is too sloppy and inaccurate to be as damaging as might otherwise be the case. One can only hope that the author of this culturally genocidal travesty didn't repeat the error of his predecessors by selling himself too cheaply. But that might be expecting a bit much from someone of his evident sensibilities. In any event, now that he's made his money, in whatever amount, it's high time he came to be treated like the sell-out he is. There must be enough *real* Indians left to accomplish *that*. And from there, perhaps we can begin to recover some of what we've lost these past couple of centuries rather than continuing to give up the pittance of ourselves we have left.

Naming Our Destiny

Toward a Language of American Indian Liberation

> Until the last decade of the treaty-making period, terms familiar to modern international diplomacy were used in the Indian treaties....Many provisions show the international status of Indian tribes, through clauses relating to war, boundaries, passports, extradition, and foreign relations.
>
> —Felix S. Cohen
> *Handbook on Federal Indian Law*

"What's your tribe?" This familiar query, typically coming after introductory greetings between American Indians, or extended by non-Indians when introduced to Indians, is hardly as innocuous as it may seem on its face. Nor is the usual reply, offered reflexively and consisting of only a few words: "I'm a member of the Kiowa Tribe," or "the Mohawk Tribe," the "Lummi Tribe," or any of several hundred comparable designations popularly, anthropologically, and often legally recognized as describing the status of the many distinct peoples indigenous to North America. Although both the question and its response(s) may appear harmless enough, merely a cordial or even "sensitive" intercultural speech-pattern which has become well accepted through customary usage, they are actually charged with a high

291

degree of political content, all of it implicitly negative in terms of native rights and dignity. Indeed, the vernacular of "tribalism" is one which goes a long way toward foreclosing on the potential for positive changes in the socioeconomic and political situation of American Indians occurring in the future.

The principles at issue are both fundamental and straightforward. How one is perceived by others does much to determine the nature of the respect—or lack of it—they are likely to accord you. By the same measure, how one sees oneself is a crucial element—the predicating element, in fact—by which one ultimately defines the type and extent of respect (and attendant rights) one asserts as one's due. If one is generally viewed by others as being "shiftless," s/he will be treated quite differently than an individual who is considered to be "motivated." To the extent that one adopts or accepts this externally-imposed designation of shiftlessness as an accurate depiction of oneself, it will be validated, the accompanying treatment one is accorded permanently locked in place as being both necessary and appropriate. Only when one's self-concept is at odds with the views of others does the foundation exist for one to challenge and resist one's classification and the treatment which results from it. Moreover, the degree to which one rejects a given categorization correlates rather precisely to the kind and depth of challenge and resistance one is likely to offer, and, correspondingly, the probability that one will be able to force changes in external perceptions and the circumstances that derive from them.

Such matters are, of course, as relevant to the dynamics of interactive group processes as they are to the realm of interpersonal relations: how a group is seen by others, and how it sees itself, are factors that in many ways define the conditions under which the group will live, and the options it will be able to exercise in affecting these conditions. It is, for example, one thing to see oneself as being part of a social or political movement, quite another to be lumped in as a member of a mere "gang." Or, to take another illustration, there is a very different connotation to being described as a "law enforcement officer" on the one hand, and being branded as part of "a mob of common thugs" on the other (albeit, in practice, it's often hard to tell the difference between the conduct of the two groups). Hence, it seems self-evident that how individuals and groups are labeled or named—and, perhaps more importantly, how they name themselves—is vital to the circumstances of their existence. In naming ourselves, both individually and collectively, we in effect name not only our reality, but our destiny.

With this in mind, the distinction between American Indians being identified as members of *peoples* understood to constitute *nations* in our own right, and being cast as members of groups commonly perceived as comprising something less—a community, say, or a family, a clan, a "minority group," or a "tribe"— incurs a decisive meaning. Words such as "nation" and "tribe" are *not*, all protestations of government officials and "responsible tribal leaders" notwithstanding, "interchangeable" in either political or legal contexts. To the contrary, phrases such as "tribal sovereignty," currently in vogue in such circles, add up to near-perfect politico-judicial oxymorons, logical impossibilities designed to distort and confuse rather than to inform or clarify discussion of indigenous rights. Referring to someone, or to oneself, as a "member of an Indian tribe" is not, and has never been, a friendly or "value-neutral" act. This essay will endeavor to explain why.

"Tribes" versus "Peoples"

The ongoing significance of Europeans' bestowal of the term "tribes" upon the native peoples they encountered during the period of their expansion across the globe may be apprehended in a meaning of the word which was being developed concurrently. According to the definitive *Oxford English Dictionary* (OED), a tribe is a "group in the classification of plants, animals, etc., used as superior and sometimes inferior to a family; also, loosely, any group or series of animals."[1] There is thus little disparity between categorizing indigenous peoples as tribes, and classifying them as being aggregated into herds, packs, gaggles, coveys, flocks, or any other mode of "lower" animal organization. When applied to specifically human groups, the term takes as its primary focus the lineage of the people included within its rubric, in much the same manner that cattle breeders concern themselves with the pedigree of their livestock. In fact, *Webster's New Collegiate Dictionary* continues to directly associate the term with "*Stock Breeding*" (emphasis in the original), as in "a group of animals descended from some particular female progenitor, through the female line."[2] It is in this light that the balance of the OED's current definition of "tribe" should be considered:

> A group of persons forming a community and claiming common ancestry...A particular race of recognized ancestry; a family...the families or communities of persons having the same surname...A race of people; now esp. to a primary aggregate of people in a primitive or barbarous condition, under a headman or chief.

Or, examine the pertinent language in *Webster's*:"[A]ny aggregation of people, esp. in a primitive or nomadic state, believed to be of a common stock." No matter which way one twists it, to be addressed as "tribal" by English-speaking people—and by speakers of all other major European languages as well—is to be demeaned in a most extraordinarily vicious way. Not only is one's society definitionally restricted from having achieved any level of cultural attainment beyond that of "primitivism" or "barbarism"—both thoroughgoing pejoratives in the Western lexicon—but one is personally reduced thereby to being construed as no more than the product of one's gene pool. Suffice it to say that a more resoundingly racist construction would be difficult to conceive.[3]

Undoubtedly, there are those, non-Indian and Indian alike, who will wish to argue that such an assessment is overly harsh, that it is somehow skewed toward the negative. Use of the term with regard to American Indians in this day and age, they will contend, is actually a positive gesture affording appropriately respectful homage to the uniqueness of Native American traditions, especially the importance of kinship systems in indigenous societies. Despite the surface plausibility of such assertions, they are ultimately vacuous, overlooking as they do the operant realities of traditional native life. While it is true that most indigenous societies were, and in many cases still are, organized along lines of kinship, this hardly implies the pre-occupation with "blood lines" connoted by the term "tribe."[4] Assuming hypothetically that there was ever a genetic structure by which Cheyenne "blood" might have been distinguished from that of a Comanche, Pawnee, or Maidu (a biological impossibility in itself), any such distinction would have disappeared thousands of years ago, entirely as a result of the normal (traditional) functioning of the societies involved. It is no great mystery that most—perhaps all—native peoples customarily incorporated members of other indigenous groups into themselves through various means, most often by marriage, adoption, and the taking of captives; sometimes this occurred through the merger of entire groups into a new whole. Once the invasion of North America began in earnest, the scope of such inclusion was extended by many indigenous peoples to encompass not only Indians of other groups, but considerable numbers of Europeans and Africans as well.[5] In any event, it is clear that Native American traditions most often placed a premium on such things as cultural integrity and allegiance to the group, *as opposed to* lineage per se, in determining social membership and identity.

This may explain why no native language in North America—and surely language must be taken as a key indicator of traditional concepts—contains a word which translates accurately as "tribe." The literal translation of most American Indian people's names for themselves was, traditionally, exactly that: "people." The consistency with which what is at best a mistranslation has been substituted for more accurate terminology cannot be dismissed as something either benign or inadvertent. Consider the relevant portion of *Webster's* definition of most native groups' own self-descriptor:

> **Peo'ple**...**1.** A body of persons united by a common character, culture, or sentiment; the individuals collectively of any characteristic group, conceived apart from the unity of the group as subject to common government (that is, as a *state*) or as issued from a common stock (that is, as a *race* or *tribe*). **2.** A race, tribe, or nation; as, the *peoples* of Europe [emphases in the original].

The OED amplifies this, defining a people as being:

> A body of persons composing a community, tribe, race, or nation; = FOLK...Sometimes viewed as a unity, sometimes as a collective of number...The persons belonging to a place or occupying a particular concourse, congregation, company, or class...Those to whom any one belongs; the members of one's tribe, clan, family, community, association, church, etc., collectively...The common people, the commonality...The whole body of enfranchised or qualified citizens, considered as the source of power; esp. in a democratic state, the electorate...Men or women indefinitely; men and women; persons, folk.

Plainly, there is nothing positive which can be said to be intrinsic to the meaning of "tribe" and not immediately encompassed within the much more broadly delineated term "people." The significance of the Euroamerican's continuing insistence upon referring to native societies as tribes rather than as peoples can thus be located primarily—though not necessarily exclusively, as will be explained below—in the expressly animalistic emphasis embodied in the former, a matter readily contrasted to the fact that the latter relates, as the OED puts it, specifically and "*emphatically* [to] Human beings" (emphasis in the original). It follows that, when indigenous peoples are passed off as tribes, and conditioned to view themselves in this way, they are effectively cast as being subhuman. The upshot is unmistakable. Designation of Indians as tribes provides a near-perfect psychic rationalization/justification of the perpetual, "natural," and "inevitable" subordination of native ("tribal" and therefore "lower," "lesser," or "inferior") societies to their purported European/Euroamerican "betters" ("non-tribal," and therefore, by definition, "superior"). From the imposition of such linguistic subordination, it is but the easiest of steps, both psychologically and physically, to what has always been Eurosupremacism's business-as-usual: the wholesale and systematic expropriation of American Indian assets.[6]

That the term involved functions as a sort of "polite" code for what is actually being said does nothing at all to mitigate or change the situation for the better. Instead, it in many ways makes things worse. Because it to some extent confuses and conceals the nature of the real aspersion being hurled, the code has served as a convenient mask behind which the dominant society's desired (mis)impressions of Native America might be ever more deeply and subliminally imbedded in the popular consciousness, a circumstance extended at this point even to their adoption—as a matter of "cultural pride," no less—by Indians themselves.[7] To be oppressed is one thing, but to be conned into validating that oppression (engaging in outright self-oppression), is quite another and far more insidious proposition.

The Meaning of "Nation"

Nor has "people" ever been the only terminological alternative to "tribe" available to English-speakers, were they to seek to adequately describe the makeup of indigenous groups. The word "nation," for example, is defined by *Webster's* as being properly applicable to a "people connected by supposed ties of blood generally manifested by a community of language, religion, customs, etc....Any aggregation of people having institutions and customs and a sense of social homogeneity and mutual interest...The body of inhabitants of a country united under a single independent government." Or, to take the meaning formulated by the OED, a nation is:

> An extensive aggregate of persons, so closely associated with one another by common descent, language, or history, as to form a distinct race or people, usually organized as a separate political state and occupying a definite territory. In early examples the racial idea is usually stronger than the political; in recent use the notion of political unity and independence is more prominent...a country...The whole people of a country, freq. in contrast to some smaller or narrower body within it [such as a community, clan, family or "tribe"].

This would, in a number of important ways, seem to be the most accurate possible English-language depiction of the functional realities traditionally evidenced by American Indian societies. Indeed, almost as an afterthought, *Webster's* acknowledges that nation is a term which might be correctly applied to any "one of a group of Indian tribes; as, the Six *Nations*" (the reference being to the Haudenosaunee, or Iroquois Six Nations Confederacy, as it is called in English; emphasis in the original). The OED goes a bit further, observing that the word "nation" might best serve to supplant certain archaic or inappropriate terminology, like "Irish Clans" or "tribes of North American Indians," with a more satisfactory and fitting explanation of the social contexts involved.

In the real world, however, suggestions that Indians should actually be referred to as composing nations rather than tribes are often met with rather flippant (or vociferous) dismissal as being "rhetorical," "polemical" or, to borrow a catch phrase presently in vogue among reactionaries, "politically correct."[8] It is frequently asserted—usually by Euroamerican academics, opinion-makers, and politicos having little or no knowledge of the subject matter—that attempting to apply "contemporary" concepts of nationhood to historical indigenous societies is an exercise in "revisionism," a *post hoc* effort to inject a form and dignity into native settings in which it was never really present.[9] A not inconsiderable number of Indian "leaders"—most often those anointed as such, not by their own peoples, but by the dominant society—have joined the chorus, claiming that utilizing "modern" terms like nation would serve to negate much that is of value in the "tribal heritage," notably the forms of native social organization and the primacy of Indian perceptions of themselves as being "natural peoples."[10]

Such arguments are at best absurd. Taking the last point first, it should be noted—as the OED in fact notes—that the term "nation" derives directly from the root words "nature" and "nativity." So much for the alleged conflict between nationalism and naturalism. On the potentially deeper question that some real aspect of indigenous social identity would be lost if a supposedly topical construct like nationality were substituted for tribalism, the example of the Irish clans, posited by the OED as being analogous to American Indian tribes, is instructive. Indisputably, the Irish have, over the past several centuries, advanced an increasingly undeviating emphasis upon a sense of their entitlement to be perceived as a nation. Equally indisputably, they have predicated the articulation of their nationalism on an explicit retention of the kinship structures and other core dimensions of their own traditional ("primitive") social organization.[11] Neither the Irish nor anyone else finds a contradiction inherent to the Irish being, simultaneously, members of their respective clans and citizens of the Irish nation. There is no particular reason why things couldn't work in very much the same fashion for American Indians.

The idea that the concept of national identity is somehow too modern to be applicable to indigenous societies is itself a bizarre revision of historical fact. Even the most cursory reading of the literature of the European colonial period in North America reveals that the colonists and their respective governments understood very well that when dealing with indigenous peoples, they were dealing with other nations. The Spanish record in this connection is ambiguous, but is marked at least to some extent by the Dominican priest Bartolomé de Las Casas's early sixteenth century declaration that "no one may deny that these people are fully capable of governing themselves, and of living like men of good intelligence, and that they are more than others well ordered, sensible, prudent, and rational."[12] The French are known to have entered into a whole series of formal alliances with a large number of Algonkian-speaking peoples—the Montagnais, Micmacs, Etchemins, Hurons, Abenakis, and Algonquins among them—of the sort explicitly reserved for the realm of international affairs.[13] Regarding the brief extension of Dutch colonialism onto the continent, it has been observed that:

> [Colonists and Indians] lived apart physically as well as culturally. They treated each other as separate powers, equal in theory and practice. The Dutch came to America for trade and empire; in seeking these they dealt with the Indians as...political and military powers to be negotiated with, fought as enemies, or courted as allies. The expansion and prosperity—even the very existence of some of the colonies—demanded that these matters be given priority as long as the Indians clung to their independence and their freedom of action.[14]

The English Crown in particular, despite a concomitant and abundant usage of terms such as "tribes" and "savages" (or "salvages," as it was most often spelled in those days) to describe Indians in popular literature, consistently referred to native peoples as constituting nations in their own right.[15] This was intended, not metaphorically, but in a precise and legalistic sense. Examples are legion, but citation of only a few—selected to demonstrate that this appreciation of indigenous national qualities was manifested in geographically diverse locales and over a long period—should serve to illustrate the point. In 1624, for instance, Plymouth colonist William Wood remarked that, among the native societies he encountered in Massachusetts, there were both laws and a relative absence of criminal conduct: "[A]s their evill courses come short of many other Nations, so they have not so many Lawes, though they are not without some."[16] Somewhat later, an anonymous chronicler of Indian/white relations in Maryland recorded native "ambassadors" seeking to school their English counterparts in "ye law of Nations."[17] "No people in the world," wrote English Superintendent for Southern Indian Affairs Edmund Atkin in 1754, "understand and pursue their true National Interest, better than the Indians."[18]

On the whole, England officially and repeatedly affirmed the genuinely national character of most of eastern North America's indigenous societies, forging a complex set of diplomatic relations with them which included numerous trade agreements and military alliances. Career diplomats were committed by the Crown to such purposes—Atkin in the south, for example, and Sir William Johnson in the north— their efforts consummating in a lengthy series of treaties between England and an array of American

Indian peoples. What is important to note in this connection is that the prevailing international custom and convention to which England was then bound held that treaties were instruments of understanding and agreement which could exist *only* between fully sovereign nations.[19] In other words, each treaty effected with Indians legally signified England's formal and unequivocal recognition that its native counterparts embodied the same attributes of nationality evidenced by England itself. As Atkin put it at the time, "[I]n their publick Treaties no People on earth are more open, explicit, and Direct [than Indian nations]. Nor are they excelled by any in the observance of them."[20]

After 1776, the newly-emergent United States followed the English example, conducting its relations with Indians on an explicitly nation-to-nation basis involving formal treaties and other accoutrements of international diplomacy.[21] Between 1778 and 1868, the federal government entered into more than 370 ratified treaties (and several hundred more which were never ratified), each of them conveying direct legal recognition by the United States that one or more indigenous peoples constituted nations in exactly "the same sense as any other."[22] Given that many of these international instruments entailed land cessions by the native peoples involved, and thus constitute the basic title to most of what the U.S. now claims as its own territory, the majority of the treaties remain in force at the present time despite the government's official suspension of treaty-making with Indians in 1871.[23]

Although it has become increasingly fashionable in some circles to insist U.S./Indian treaties never "really" implied any genuine acknowledgement of the national status of the latter peoples, the statements of the federal government's most preeminent legal authorities at the time point to the exact opposite. As Chief Justice of the Supreme Court John Marshall observed in 1831 with regard to the Cherokees: "The numerous treaties made with them by the United States recognize them as a people capable of maintaining the relations of peace and war, of being responsible for their political character for any violation of their engagements, or for any aggression committed on the citizens of the United States, by any individual of their community....[Hence, the] acts of our government plainly recognize the Cherokee nation as a state, and the courts are bound by those acts."[24] More broadly, Attorney General William Wirt framed the matter in the following way in an opinion written in 1828:

> The point...once conceded, that the Indians are independent to the purpose of treating, their independence is, to that purpose, as absolute as that of any other nation. Nor can it be conceded that their independence as a nation is a limited independence. Like all other independent nations, they are governed solely by their own laws. Like all other independent nations, thye have the absolute power of war and peace. Like all other independent nations, their territory is inviolable by any other sovereignty....They treat, or refuse to treat, at their pleasure; and there is no human power that can rightfully control them in the exercise of their discretion in this respect. In their treaties, in all their contracts with regard to their property, they are as free, sovereign, and independent as any other nation.[25]

This was by no means a transient or atypical viewpoint. A generation later, there was still no disagreement among U.S. policymakers as to whether treaty-making with Indian peoples entailed recognition of them as nations, especially among those opposed to the making of any further such treaties. As Indian Commissioner Ely S. Parker stated in 1869, "A treaty involves the idea of a compact between two or more sovereign powers,"[26] a matter which led Commissioner Edward P. Smith to conclude in 1873 that, "we have in theory over sixty-five independent nations within our borders, with whom we have entered into treaty relations as being sovereign peoples."[27] It was this recognition of Indians "as independent nations," and the nature of the rights they were entitled to assert on the basis of such recognition, that had already prompted Secretary of the Interior Caleb B. Smith to demand a "radical change in the mode" of future U.S. Indian policy.[28]

"Nits Make Lice"

That the popular European/Euroamerican discourse on American Indians—most of it government-sanctioned and quite a lot of it literally government-sponsored—continued to rely upon the vernacular of tribalism even while the governments themselves were evolving policies in which Indians were officially recognized as nations may seem entirely contradictory on its face. This apparent paradox can, however, be reconciled by the simple suggestion that the governments involved never intended to honor the commitments they were making to indigenous nations in the first place. It has been demonstrated quite compellingly by Robert A. Williams and others that, far from displaying any real concern with the rights of native peoples, the colonizing powers were preoccupied mainly with the forging of a system of international law which would anchor their relationship *to one another* in such a way as to allow for maximally efficient global expansion.[29] Indians were merely convenient props, or a "laboratory" employed as a means to perfect the desired legal structure.

To the extent that there was a more direct utility to Europe's international diplomacy and treaty-making with Indians (accelerated after the revolution by the United States), it was mainly tactical, to gain certain advantages over them which would serve over the long run to minimize the costs incurred in their total dispossession and, often enough, outright obliteration.[30] In effect, native nations could be readily acknowledged as such because their national rights would, in the future, be extinguished via their physical liquidation (at least as early as 1830, federal statutes are known to contain clauses stipulating Indian lands would "revert" to the U.S. "if the Indians become extinct").[31] Once this end result had been attained by extralegal means, of course, the means themselves could be legitimated through denials that those liquidated had ever possessed bona fide national rights in the first place (the dead, after all, are in no position to debate the point). Eventually, even the process of liquidation itself could be denied, at least in terms of its magnitude and attendant implications. Small wonder that Adolf Hitler would later expressly base his own notions of diplomacy and foreign policy directly on the example offered by "the Nordics of North America."[32]

As a rule, it was the population-at-large—average colonists, "pioneers," and "settlers," not the formal apparatus of the various European states—which was expected to carry out the actual expropriation of native property and corresponding eradication of indigenous populations; the idea often being to make it appear that what was happening was a sort of irresistible "natural" process, something which continued to occur despite the best efforts and intentions of the European Crowns—and later the U.S. government—to display an appropriate *noblesse oblige* with regard to Indians.[33] In order for this to work in practice, it was imperative that the general citizenry of Europe be inculcated with a view of those to be exterminated (or enslaved *en masse*, or simply dispossessed) as something less than themselves, or, preferably, less than human.[34] To this purpose, the nomenclature of tribalism, with all its emphasis of the "animalism" of those thus classified, was ideally suited. The resulting rhetoric of dehumanization directed at indigenous peoples, juxtaposed as it was to a contemporaneous rhetoric of "civilization" by which Europeans were indoctrinated to view themselves as the world's inherently superior "race," quickly evinced a broad popular appeal.[35] In short order, it had become all-pervasive among the inhabitants of a subcontinental protuberance from the Asian landmass who were soon to demarcate themselves, with telling grandiloquence, as occupants of "The Continent."[36]

Thus, during the sixteenth century, the Spanish could lead the way to a new and highly enlightened theory of international legality—all of it based directly in Spain's hypothetical relationship to the indigenous peoples it was encountering in the New World—secure in the absolute certainty that the colonists it was dispatching to America would violate the very same laws at every step.[37] To be sure, the Spaniards who established what the Crown came to call "New Spain" drew the obvious conclusions from their society's general designation of the natives as tribes, customarily referring to Indians as "beasts" and treating them as such.[38] In the Caribbean, this led from the outset to the unremitting horrors documented by Las Casas and the reduction of the regional indigenous population from as many as 14 million to extinction in barely a generation.[39] On the mainland, the story was much the same, although attrition there may have reached "only" into the ninetieth percentile in most cases; in central Mexico, for example, "the population fell by almost 95 percent within seventy-five years following the Europeans' first arrival—from more than 25,000,000 in 1519 to barely 1,300,000 in 1595."[40] In Peru, the drop was from as many as 14 million to about one-half million between 1520 and 1620.[41] And so it went, throughout "Latin" America.

The means and attitudes by which this was accomplished are supremely instructive: "To many of the conquerors, the Indian was merely another savage animal, and [so] dogs were trained to pursue and rip apart their human quarry with the same zest as they felt when hunting wild beasts."[42] In one instance, involving men under command of the celebrated "Discoverer of the Pacific," Vasco Núñez de

INDIANS ARE US?

Balboa:

> The Spaniards cut off the arm of one, the leg or
> hip of another, and from some their heads at one
> stroke, like butchers cutting up beef or mutton
> for market. Six hundred, including the cacique,
> were thus slain like brute beasts...Vasco ordered
> forty of them to be torn to pieces by dogs.[43]

Such scenes were the norm rather than the
exception in Spanish practice, as historian David E.
Stannard recounts:

> Just as the Spanish soldiers seem to have partic-
> ularly enjoyed testing the sharpness of their yard-
> long rapiers on the bodies of Indian children, so
> their dogs seemed to find the soft bodies of
> infants especially tasty, and the accounts of the
> invading conquistadors and the padres who trav-
> eled with them are filled with detailed descrip-
> tions of young Indian children routinely taken
> from their parents and fed to the hungry animals.
> Men who could take pleasure in this sort of thing
> had little trouble with less sensitive things, such
> as the sacking and burning of entire cities and
> towns.[44]

Meanwhile, the English—who had already
acquired considerable recent experience in dealing
with "Tribes of Wild Irish," whom they correspondingly described as "unreasonable beasts"—began
their invasion of North America.[45] Soon, colonial
militias were "running amok," to quote one New
Englander who was there, "killing...wounded men,
women, and children indiscriminately, firing their
camps, burning the Indians alive or dead in their
huts [which were elsewhere likened to "kennels"]."[46]
Puritan leader Cotton Mather directly linked the lat-

ter activity to the cooking of meat, jubilantly referring to the burning of Indians as "a barbeque."[47] Just as in New Spain, "Hunting redskins became...a popular sport in New England, especially since...the personal danger to hunters was very slight."[48] It could be profitable, too, as a bounty was paid by local governments for Indian scalps until there were simply no Indians left to kill.[49] Like their Spanish counterparts, although perhaps to a lesser extent, the English also exhibited a penchant for feeding their "game" to dogs. Massachusetts colonist John Easton, for example, records how the capture of "a very decrepit and harmless [old] Indian" by Puritans precipitated a debate among them: "[S]ome would have had him devoured by dogs," wrote Easton, "but the tenderness of some of them prevailed to cut off his head."[50] In Virginia and Maryland, another writer described how, as a rule, "blood-Hounds were used to draw after" Indian quarry, and "Mastives to seaze them."[51]

By 1763, when Lord Jeffrey Amherst issued his infamous written order to "extirpate this execrable race" through consciously bacteriological means—thereby proving beyond all reasonable doubt that the devastation of native societies by disease was never so necessarily mysterious to or unintended by European colonists as their apologists would now like to pretend[52]—the indigenous peoples of North America's Atlantic Seaboard, once numbering as many as 2.2 million, had been reduced by approximately 99 percent.[53] While it may be that rank-and-file colonists had become so brainwashed by the incessant barrage of anti-Indian propaganda that they were unable to grasp what it was they'd done, the same cannot be said of English officials: The Indians of the East, wrote one of them in a back-channel communication to the Crown, were now "so rowted, slayne and dispersed, that they are no longer a nation."[54]

After it successfully broke away from England, the new U.S. settler state not only perpetuated, but expanded and accelerated the process. Referring to Indians as "wolves"—"both being beasts of prey, tho' different in shape"—George Washington ordered in 1783 that those remaining within the areas of the initial thirteen states be "hunted like beasts," and that a "war of extermination" be waged against those barring U.S. access to certain desired areas, notably the Ohio River Valley.[55] Or, as Thomas Jefferson put it in 1812, Euroamericans should drive every Indian in its path "with the beasts of the forests into the stony mountains"; alternatively, as he'd already stated in 1807, the U.S. should "pursue [the Indians] into extermination, or drive them to new seats beyond our reach"; national policy should be to wage war against each native people it encountered "until that tribe is exterminated, or driven beyond the Mississippi."[56]

Over the next forty years, even as the federal government was acknowledging by treaty hundreds of times over that the peoples at issue were in fact nations of human beings, the "private" sentiments of Washington and Jefferson concerning the implications of their "tribal" nature were being worked out at a more popular level. Andrew Jackson, to take one notorious example, rode into the White House in 1828 on the breadth of public approval attending his standard characterization of Indians as "wild dogs" and his frequent boasts that, in the manner of a trophy hunter, he had "on all occasions preserved the scalps" of the many native people he'd personally murdered.[57] Jackson was, of course, far more than an individual butcher; he was a grass-roots Euroamerican leader who came by this status as the commander of large bodies of volunteer "Indian fighters":

> [He was the] same Andrew Jackson who had supervised the mutilation of 800 or so Creek Indian corpses—the bodies of men, women, and children that he and his men had massacred [at a place called Horseshoe Bend, in Alabama]—cutting off their noses to count and preserve a record of the dead, slicing long strips of flesh from their bodies to tan and turn into bridle reins. The same Andrew Jackson who—after his Presidency was over—still was recommending that American troops specifically seek out and systematically kill Indian women and children who were hiding: to do otherwise, he wrote, was equivalent to pursuing "a wolf in the hamocks without knowing first where her den and whelps are."[58]

By the 1850s, such phenomena had been consolidated into what analyst David Svaldi has termed an outright "rhetoric of extermination," a discourse in which Indians were not simply dehumanized as "beasts," "dogs," and "wolves" in the popular consciousness, but as "vermin."[59] Although such sensibilities were to be, and had been, concretized through an unrelenting series of wholesale massacres like that at Horseshoe Bend, nowhere was it better epitomized than in Colorado Territory. There, in 1863, a local newspaper, the *Rocky Mountain News*, launched an all-out campaign to create a climate in which the citizenry would undertake an unconstrained effort to "exterminate...the red devils," in this case Cheyennes and Arapahoes, whom editors of the *News* described as being "a dissolute, vagabondish, brutal, and ungrateful race" which should be "wiped from the face of the earth."[60] The paper then threw its enthusiastic support behind Colonel John Milton Chivington, a former Methodist minister who served as commander of the territory's volunteer militia.

> Several months earlier Chivington, who [by 1864] was also a candidate for Congress, had announced in a speech that his policy was to "kill and scalp all, little and big." "Nits make lice," he was fond of saying—indeed, the phrase became a rallying cry for his troops; since Indians were lice, their children were nits—and the only way to get rid of lice was to kill the nits as well. Clearly, Colonel Chivington was a man ahead of his time. It would take more than half a century, after all, before Heinrich Himmler would think to describe the extermination of another people as "the same thing as delousing."[61]

Chivington was, however, hardly alone. After he and some 750 of his men staged a surprise attack on a peaceful Cheyenne encampment on November 29, 1864—killing somewhere between 150 and 300 women and children who were there under ostensible government protection, and who had displayed a white flag of surrender when the militia approached—they mutilated the bodies, returned to Denver, and then conducted a triumphal march through the center of the city, proudly displaying "trophies" which included not only scalps, but whole heads and genitalia.[62] The good citizens of Denver went wild with applause, while the *News* proclaimed the whole affair to have been "a brilliant feat of arms" and chuckled that "Cheyenne scalps are getting thick as toads in Egypt....Everybody has got one and is anxious to get another to send east."[63] Three separate congressional and military investigating committees, convened to affect the proper official posture of concern about the "excess" which had occurred in Colorado, condemned what had happened but somehow failed to recommend a single prosecution. President Theodore Roosevelt later went out of his way to rehabilitate Chivington's "honor"—the colonel himself having gone on to become a favorite on the after-dinner lecture circuit—by proclaiming the massacre to have been "as righteous and beneficial a deed as ever took place on the frontier."[64]

It is in this context that a favorite tidbit of Americana, General Phil Sheridan's 1869 observation that the "only good Indians I ever saw were dead," must be understood.[65] The reality bound up in the general's catchy phrasing was a near-insatiable popular bloodlust in which another army officer, Alfred Sully, ordered the skulls of Teton Lakotas mounted as decorations on his headquarters wall;[66] where scalp bounties paid better than buffalo hides for "enterprising citizens" in Texas and the Dakotas until the 1880s;[67] where the entire Navajo Nation was interned in a concentration camp at the Bosque Redondo in New Mexico in 1864, until, after four years and the death of half their number by starvation and disease, they were finally released;[68] where, for "sport," the "early set-

315

tlers and miners" in California drove the state's Indian population (which had once been over a million) downward from 100,000 in 1849 to fewer than 35,000 in 1860, and finally to a nadir of barely 15,000 in the 1890s.[69]

Even after the last great massacre—the Seventh Cavalry's slaughter of about 300 unarmed Minneconjou Lakotas at Wounded Knee in 1890—the popular sentiments demanding total extermination persisted.[70] The *Aberdeen Saturday Pioneer* in South Dakota, to take but one example, recommended in the aftermath of Wounded Knee that "we had better, in order to protect our civilization, follow it up...and wipe these untamed and untamable creatures from the face of the earth."[71] The editor, L. Frank Baum, later to win acclaim as the "kind and decent soul" who authored the *Wizard of Oz*, went on to explain that:

> [Indians are merely] a pack of whining curs who lick the hand that smites them. The Whites, by law of conquest, by justice of civilization, are masters of the American continent, and the best safety of the frontier settlements will be secured by the total annihilation of the few remaining Indians. Why not annihilation?...[B]etter they should die than live as the miserable wretches that they are.[72]

In sum, there can be no question but that the sort of dehumanizing implications of Europe's imposing the mantle of tribalism upon indigenous peoples through popular discourse has contributed greatly to the kind and extent of ill-treatment, often quite literally genocidal, we have suffered since our fifteenth-century "discovery" by Europeans. While it is true that the most overt pattern of behavior by which this was expressed is primarily historical, at least in North America,[73] there is no shortage of indication that certain effects continue to linger: witness the sign on the door of a bar in Scenic, South Dakota—removed only during the late 1980s—which read "No Dogs or Indians Allowed." More importantly, the evidence is overwhelming that much of what was worst in the historical interactions between Europeans/Euroamericans and Indians is being continued in more covert fashion, as a matter of official policy, and under the time-tested rubric of indigenous tribalism.

The Great Revision

For a considerable period, for reasons already mentioned, it was to the advantage of the federal government to maintain its formal relations with indigenous peoples on a reasonably strict international basis, even while allowing (or encouraging) U.S. citizens to exercise a presumed "right" of exterminating the "wild beasts" composing native populations. During this phase of U.S.-Indian relations, the normative legal phraseology defining the status of Indians was as nations, or, at worst, as "nations and tribes." By 1870, however, the need for this tactical excursion into accuracy had largely passed, the military capacity of Indians to defend their lands and rights—and therefore their ability to block what the United States had long since proclaimed as its "Manifest Destiny" to own their territory in its entirety—having been eroded to the point of disappearance.[74] Taking such factors into account, the government commenced an "enlightened" shift from physical to cultural genocide, advancing a policy of "assimilating" (literally, of "digesting") the native survivors of some forty officially acknowledged "Indian Wars" and an uninterrupted sequence of "individual affairs" or "private citizen actions" which had occurred since 1775.[75]

It was at this point that an effort to reconcile official terminology with the semantics of the general public began to emerge, the word "tribe" completely displacing the word "nation" in the legal discourse leading to congressional termination of treaty-making with Indians in 1871. For instance, the sixth section of an act passed on March 29, 1867, pointedly stipulates that: "[A]ll the laws allowing the President, the Secretary of the Interior, or the commissioner of Indian Affairs to enter into treaties with Indian *tribes* are hereby repealed, and no expense shall hereafter be incurred in negotiating a treaty with any Indian *tribe* until an appropriation authorizing such expense shall first be made by law" (emphasis added).[76] Although it was argued at the time that the suspension of treaty-making would not alter the binding effect of existing treaties—a matter presumably including the bilateral recognition of national status embodied in such instruments—events were to quickly disprove such contentions.

Probably the first firm sign of what was to come appeared in the second section of an act passed on March 3, 1883, through which Congress assigned itself authority to impound the "proceeds of all pasturage and sales of timber, coal, or other product of any Indian reservation...not the result of the labor of any member of such *tribe*" (emphasis added) for purposes of allowing the Secretary of the Interior to administer these resources "in trust."[77] This was clearly *not* a prerogative lawfully enjoyed by the federal government with regard to the assets of any other *nation*, but might be considered to be so with regard to lesser entities, particularly the sort of "primitive" and "childlike" condition legally associated with even the most charitable interpretation of "tribalism."[78] With this groundwork laid, Congress moved swiftly, in 1885, to extend its own jurisdiction over the residual territories of all American Indian peoples within its borders,[79] and, in 1887, to rearrange land tenure patterns within the reservations to suit itself.[80] This last set in motion a process culminating in the Indian Citizenship Act of 1924, under provision of which the distinction between national and tribal status was drawn very plainly: Indians were accorded the "privilege" of retaining *membership* in their respective tribes while being recast as *citizens* of the United States.[81]

In this context, following from John Marshall's 1831 pronouncement in *Cherokee v. Georgia* that Indian peoples, while being nations, were "nations of a peculiar type" both "domestic" to and "dependent" upon the United States, the Supreme Court decided that, practically speaking, they should not be treated as nations at all.[82] The high court held, in the 1903 case of *Lonewolf v. Hitchcock*, that, since Indians had been forced into a position of domesticity and dependence vis-à-vis the U.S., the federal government was entitled to exercise "plenary" (full and absolute) power over their property and their affairs. The U.S./Indian relationship was framed, not in terms in any way resembling the nation-to-nation arrangement acknowledged by the Marshall Court, but as that of a "guardian" to a "ward" (usually a child or mental incompetent). Tellingly, the word "nation" is not used with regard to Indians anywhere in the *Lonewolf* opinion. Instead, the terms "tribe," "tribes," and "tribal" are used exclusively, appearing even as substitutes for "nation," "nations," "national" in paraphrases of Marshall's original language.[83]

By the 1950s, continuation of this legalistic and unilateral demotion of indigenous peoples from national to tribal status had resulted in their having been subsumed, not only under the jurisdiction of the federal government, but often that of individual states of the union as well (by now, many have been pushed even lower, placed under the jurisdiction of counties and, in at least some cases, under that of municipalities as well).[84] During the same period, the Supreme Court quietly completed the process of voiding the original legal foundation upon which Indians had been recognized as constituting nations. This took the form, in the 1955 *Tee-Hit-Ton v. United States* case, of the assertion that, since the "tribal" plaintiffs could point to no document by which the U.S. had conveyed land title to them, they could not be said to own—or to *ever* have owned—any land.[85] The opinion completely inverted elements of international law, in effect since Vitoria's mid-sixteenth-century codification of Discovery Doctrine, holding that land title was *always* to be considered as vested in the indigenous nations who were found in occupancy ("ownership") of it until such time as they themselves willingly conveyed title to "discovering" powers like the United States.[86]

The position of the high court in the *Tee-Hit-Ton* case exemplifies a trend in U.S. juridical practice— that of simply ignoring inconvenient historico-legal facts or of actively distorting them into conformity with the notion that Indians had "always been" seen as tribes, never as nations—which became fully congealed during the second half of the twentieth century. Thus, Chief Justice William Rehnquist, writing for the majority of the Supreme Court in 1978, would peremptorily disregard a mass of evidence to the contrary in order to rule that "Indian tribes do not have inherent jurisdiction to try and punish non-Indians" committing criminal offenses within reservation boundaries. Judicial acknowledgement that Indians held any such right, the Chief Justice argued, would be "*inconsistent with their status*" (emphasis in the original) as tribes rather than nations, and had therefore *never* been recognized by the United States.[87] This contention was quite literally false, as Rehnquist had every reason to know. Not only are there numerous instances in which U.S. citizens were required to obtain passports before traveling "abroad" in Indian Country,[88] but even the standard federal handbook on Indian law points out that:

> Treaties defined the boundaries between the United States, or the separate states, and the territories of the various Indian tribes or nations. Within these territories the Indian...nations had not only full jurisdiction over their own citizens, but the same jurisdiction over citizens of the United States that any other power might lawfully exercise over emigrants from the United States. Treaties between the United States and the various [native peoples] commonly stipulated that cit-

izens of the United States within the territory of the Indian nations were to be subject to the laws of those nations.[89]

Such judicial revision of the record to conform to the topical requirements of Euroamerican hegemony dovetails quite neatly with similar techniques applied by European/Euroamerican "scholars" and officials from very early on. The Spanish, for example, attempted to dismiss Las Casas's and other chronicles of their genocide of native peoples as a "Black Legend."[90] The English proved themselves even more heavy-handed in their efforts to deny what they had done (and, by extension, what they were continuing to do). After the extermination of the Pequots in 1637, for instance:

> The word "Pequot" was...removed from English maps: the river of that name was changed to the Thames and the town of that name became New London. Having virtually eradicated an entire people, it was now necessary to expunge from historical memory any recollection of their past existence.[91]

In the United States, as Francis Jennings and others have shown, techniques employed for similar purposes have been more incremental and sophisticated, centering as a matter of first priority on manipulation of information concerning indigenous population size. Discussing the "groundbreaking" work on the matter of historical indigenous demography undertaken by anthropologist James M. Mooney during the early twentieth century, Jennings observes that:

> A hint of Mooney's method appears in the esti-

mates of New England. Mooney wrote that "the original population of New England was probably about 25,000 or about one-half of what the historian [John Gorham] Palfrey makes it." Apparently Mooney had followed the tradition of Palfrey's own acceptance; that is, he took the estimate of a predecessor and discounted it. The same sort of procedure had been used by every generation of scholars since the original data were recorded in the seventeenth century, and by Mooney's time discount upon discount had reduced the accepted figures to a small fraction of what was mentioned in the sources. It is as if one were to estimate the population of white Americans in 1790 by successive slashes of the census data of that year on the grounds that the census takers were probably exaggerating their numbers for undisclosed reasons....It appears that Mooney applied the same sort of logic to his estimates for all of North America, [making] his total 1,100,000.[92]

Given the acceptance of such procedures at the "highest levels" of American scholarship, it is unsurprising that the "Dean of American Anthropology," Alfred Louis Kroeber, would then take Mooney's estimates, unexamined other than to "convert them into [his] own tribal classifications," and then arbitrarily slash them by ten percent across the board, giving the U.S. a quasi-official estimate that the pre-invasion population of Native North America was not more than a million persons.[93] Not only has this figure served to conceal the magnitude of native population attrition which actually occurred—a matter apprehended by contrasting the pre-invasion number to the number of survivors (237,196) recorded by the U.S. Census Bureau in 1900[94]—

but, as Henry Dobyns has noted, it has dramatically distorted resulting contemporary "interpretations of New World civilizations and cultures."[95] Conversely, as Jennings points out, the "idea that scholars hold of New World cultures directly affects their interpretation of the size of aboriginal populations."[96]

> Proponents of the concept of savagery stipulate, among other things, that large populations are impossible in savage ["tribal"] societies. It follows that if aboriginal populations can be shown to have been large, they could not have been savage. A logical approach may thus be made into the whole question of the nature of aboriginal society and culture through the gate of numbers.[97]

Kroeber himself was astonishingly open in this regard, insofar as his explanation of the sparsity of indigenous population he alleged to have existed in North America prior to the invasion was directly predicated in a virulently articulated presumption of Indian tribalism and savagery. Native societies, he asserted, were characterized by "insane, unending, continuously attritional warfare...[in] the absence of all effective political organization, of the idea of the state."[98] From this, he extrapolated the orthodoxy—repeated endlessly in U.S. "educational" texts down to the present moment—that "prehistoric" Indians experienced an essentially "squalid" existence, "wandering perpetually and nomadically" across the landscape as they pursued a "Stone Age hunting and gathering subsistence," a mode of living devoid of anything resembling true cultural attainment, formation of knowledge, or other accomplishments commonly attributed to human endeavor.[99] By the 1980s, such thinking had progressed to the point that "responsible" anthropologists were suggesting that North America's native people had once survived, in part, by consuming their own dung.[100]

That this all-pervasive depiction of Native North America is utterly untrue—aggregate American Indian population north of the Río Grande was actually at least nine million in 1492, and more likely somewhere between 12.5 and 18.5 million, with all the manifestations of advanced civilization such numbers entail—is precisely the point.[101] Euroamerican scholarship's conscientious and "scientific" falsification of precolumbian material and cultural realities over the past hundred years conforms exactly to the requirements of the revised U.S. juridico-political posture vis-à-vis native peoples which has been articulated during the same period. The result is a deliberately contrived contemporary confluence of popular and official mythologies about American Indians, both of them casting the continent's indigenous societies as having been—and therefore as *being*— something we aren't, never were, and in fact could never have been or be.

Unmistakably, the result intended to be fostered through creation of this interlocking and rather Olympian complex of lies, half-truths, and misleading innuendos is the consecration as universal truth of an even greater myth: that no matter how "tragic" or "unfortunate" the carefully minimized costs incurred by Indians in the process of being "subdued," things have "worked out for the best" in the end. This is the case, so the story goes, not only for the victors but also for the vanquished, whose descendants continue to benefit from their ancestors having been propelled, however "reluctantly" and by whatever means, from their own "condition of primitive tribalism" into the "modern age" (as if, left to our own devices, we might somehow have existed, and would go on existing, in another temporal dimension).[102] Hence, not only does Euroamerican society have nothing whatsoever to regret in its enjoyment of spoils deriving from its wantonly genocidal and duplicitous historical behavior—most of which it now feels free to equivocate or deny outright—it is entitled in its own mind to expect those who suffered that behavior to embrace their own consequent subordination and destitution as a symbol of their "gratitude" for what has been done. No more seamless ideological or psychic self-ratification of an imperial status quo is imaginable.[103]

The Language of Liberation

Predictably, even with all this explained, there will be those who will still seek to argue that the points raised, though "interesting" in some respects, are merely an academic and perhaps arcane preoccupation, but certainly not adding up to the sort of issue which displays abiding significance to the real life struggles of American Indians today. Some will obfuscate, insisting that at base questions of terminology reduce to no more than matters of opinion, that things may never have really meant what they seem to mean, and that there is therefore no cause for serious concern. Others will respond that, while what is said above may be objectively true, they have taken as their mission the "redemption" of terms like "tribe" and "tribalism," devoting themselves to "restoring" meanings to the words which were never there in the first place. Still others will stipulate that, true or not, they couldn't care less; the dominant society is at liberty to call them most anything it likes, so long as it provides them "something tangible" in exchange (usually meaning a minor share of the loot deriving from the existing order), thereby "proving" that no harm is intended.

Those inclined to such positions would do well to wonder why, if the vernacular by which indigenous societies are described is essentially inconsequential or irrelevant, representatives of the United States and Canada have spent the past decade adamantly opposing Indians being addressed as "peoples"—they have insisted, emphatically, that we be defined instead *only* as "populations" and/or "tribal" or "ethnic" groups—in the draft of an international legal instrument designed to extend specific United Nations human rights protections over us for the first time.[104] The answer is that the governments of these countries understand quite well, though some of us may not (or do not wish to admit), that there is an umbilical connection between the description imposed upon any group and how it is treated, between the label a group can be convinced to accept as appropriate to itself and the treatment it is ultimately entitled to demand.[105] This is neither an "abstraction" nor "past history."

In contemporary international law, custom, and convention, ethnic population groups—often referred to as "ethnicities" or "racial minorities" (of which "tribes" are but a specifically inferior classification)—have been formally construed as subparts of nations, an internal or "domestic" concern of those countries in which they happen to be situat-

327

ed.[106] Within a fairly well articulated set of parameters, their needs and interests can be, and usually are, legally ("legitimately") subordinated to the "greater good" or "wider interests" of the national entities into which they are incorporated.[107] The menu of their rights is thus very much constricted to falling within whatever they can persuade those who most directly dominate them to acknowledge as appropriate to their structurally subordinated circumstances. Beyond this, they have little legal or political recourse in attempting to improve the conditions under which they live. *Peoples*, on the other hand, are recognized in international law as possessing inherent rights of "self-determination."[108]

> The subjection of *peoples* to alien subjugation, domination, and exploitation constitutes a denial of fundamental human rights, is contrary to the Charter of the United Nations and is an impediment to world peace and co-operation....All *peoples* have the right to self-determination; by virtue of that right they freely determine their political status and freely pursue their economic, social and cultural development [emphasis added].[109]

It follows that peoples hold a legal right to decide for themselves the nature of their relationships to other entities, such as the larger nations into which they would be arbitrarily lumped if they were relegated to the status of ethnic or racial minority populations.[110] Peoples may decide, for instance, to become (or remain) part of a larger nation, giving up, retaining, or regaining some bilaterally negotiated set of rights in the process. Or they may opt, again on the basis of a bilaterally negotiated arrangement, to enter into some "limited autonomy" relationship—"home rule," for example, or a form of "commonwealth" relations—with a larger nation.[111] Or they may elect to (re)assert complete *national* independence in their own right, either alone or as part of some wholly new amalgam (a confederation, say, or some other kind of synthesis) of peoples.[112]

> All states shall respect the right of self-determination and independence of *peoples and nations*, to be freely exercised without any foreign pressure, and with absolute respect for human rights and fundamental freedoms.[113]

Undeniably, then, the word choices involved in describing native peoples—how we describe *ourselves*, first and foremost—hold a contemporary significance in ways which go well beyond considerations of mere gestural insult or esteem (although these, too, are certainly important). The sorts of concrete rights and options attaching themselves to groups officially acknowledged as being peoples is today, as has *always* been the case, far greater than those accorded groups designated as ethnic/racial populations.[114] And, as always, official terminology itself is subject to reflecting conceptions bound up in the popular vernacular, our own included, which is in turn informed by a discourse purporting to embody more academic or "scholarly" attributes. As the Indian Law Resource Center has noted: "History suggests that those who maintain and assert their self-government, their freedom from outside domination, and their own economic, social and cultural development are most likely to eventually gain [or regain] international recognition as peoples who have the right to self-determination, regardless of formal rules" deriving from a history of conquest or colonization.[115] In other words, all is not lost; we retain the capacity to alter the outcomes of what it is that has been done to us up to this point.

But, if we are once again to be treated as peoples, or as nations, we must begin once again to conduct ourselves accordingly. And, if we are to comport ourselves as nations, we can only begin by seeing and referring to ourselves as such. It is not something which will be done for us, most assuredly not by those who have expended generations upon generations' worth of time and energy converting us into what we are in order that they might preside over what was and is ours. We ourselves must seize the initiative, taking the lead in our revitalization, fostering the general understanding that we constitute living nations of people, rectifying an "academic record" which miscasts us as anything less, and thus eventually compelling restoration of official recognition that we are who and what we say we are. From there, we acquire the tools necessary to reclaim not only our own rights, but the rights of our posterity.

The supplanting of one word, or set of words, with another may seem too small a matter to lead to such results. In and of itself this is no doubt true. But, in and of itself, it is a point of departure which is indispensable, a vital break in the carefully constructed web of "false consciousness" within which we have become trapped, a web of illusion which has increasingly prevented our knowledge of ourselves, which has led us inexorably from where we once were to where it is we now find ourselves, which denies us even the possibility of regaining the dignity we formerly enjoyed. As it has been put elsewhere, "the breaching of false consciousness can provide the Archimedien point for a more comprehensive emancipation—on an infinitely small space to be sure, but the chance for change depends upon the widening of such small spaces."[116]

In effect, by naming ourselves, we name our destiny. The choice is simple enough: we either internalize once and for all the language of our oppression, adopting as both our heritage and our future the dominant society's self-serving invention of us as tribes rather than nations, *or* we can pursue a language of liberation, one which preserves and (re)asserts our ancestors' conception, not just of who we were, but of who we are (or should be) at the present moment and who we can become in the years ahead. As tribes, we have no practical alternative to watching helplessly as what little is left of our lands and lives is drained off with leech-like efficiency by the settler population which has established itself upon us, deluding us in our weakened condition into believing against all appearances that we have somehow now become and will forever be an integral part of itself. As peoples, and *only* as peoples wielding internationally acknowledged rights to restore our fully national existences if and to the extent we so desire, we place ourselves in a position to excise the parasite which not only consumes our lifeblood, but which can be expected to go right on consuming it until we die out altogether. Seen clearly, the "choice" is no choice at all. Rather, an imperative is at hand.

Next time, then, instead of inquiring after the fashion of our oppressors as to someone's "tribe," ask instead, "Who are your people?" or "You are part of which people?" Better yet, and perhaps less awkwardly, make it simply, "What's your nation?" Insist that others making such queries do so in the same accurate, appropriate, and respectful manner. Object, and *keep on* objecting, *any* time you hear or see "Indians" and "tribes" juxtaposed as if there were a natural and necessary correspondence between the two. Don't quit, don't back down. We are *not* beasts or lice, congregated into packs or swarms or tribes. We have suffered much, far *too* much, and for far too *long*, as the result of such verbiage and the attitudes it reveals. The long road to liberation—which is to say, the route back to ourselves—begins right there, in our rejection of such naming. And it's long past time we started the journey.

Notes

1. *The Compact Edition of the Oxford English Dictionary* (London/New York: Oxford University Press, 1985). Although the initial meaning of "tribe" pertained to the original three groups of Romans, and later to the Hebrew clans of ancient Israel, by the time it began to be applied to indigenous peoples outside the flow of European history it was beginning to be applied to the "animal kingdom" as well. The relationship between these last two applications in the European mind is thus quite clear.

2. I've used the dictionaries immediately before me on my desk for purposes of this essay. This includes my trusty Webster's dictionary, given to me by my grandfather while I was in high school; *Webster's New Collegiate Dictionary* (Springfield, MA: G.&C. Merriam Co., Publisher, 1949). It was suggested that I cross-reference the "old" definitions obtained therein with those in newer iterations of the same dictio-

nary, to see whether there have been changes. There have, insofar as the language has been rendered in a more "technical" (sterile) manner. As concerns "tribe," *Webster's Ninth New Collegiate Dictionary* (Springfield, MA: Merriam-Webster, Inc., 1983) now phrases the relevant portion of its definition as follows: "a category of taxonomic classification sometimes equivalent to or ranking below a subfamily; *also*: a natural group irrespective of taxonomic rank." Despite the smoke and mirrors, the word continues to carry the connotations I attribute to it.

3. In essence, what is at issue is a direct continuation of the sort of claptrap comprising the core of nineteenth century American "scientific" racism exemplified in Samuel George Morton's *Crania Americana; or, A Comparative View of the Skulls of Various Aboriginal Nations of North and South America, to which is Prefixed an Essay on The Varieties of the Human Species* (Philadelphia: John Pennington Publisher, 1839); for an excellent overview, see William Stanton, *The Leopard's Spots: Scientific Attitudes toward Race in America, 1815-59* (Chicago: University of Chicago Press, 1960). It is well to note, as Stanton does not, that this body of work had a significant influence upon the formation of the subsequent racial perspectives of nazism; see Robert Cecil, *The Myth of the Master Race: Alfred Rosenberg and Nazi Ideology* (New York: Dodd, Mead & Co., 1972).

4. The preoccupation is actually a matter of U.S. policy implementation; a system of identifying Indians in accordance with a formal eugenics code dubbed "blood quantum" which is still in effect at the present time. For analysis of the effects of this, see M. Annette Jaimes, "Federal Indian Identification Policy: A Usurpation of Indigenous Sovereignty in North America," in M. Annette Jaimes, ed., *The State of*

Native America: Genocide, Colonization, and Resistance (Boston: South End Press, 1992, pp. 123-38).

5.   See Gary Nash, *Red, White and Black: The Peoples of Early America* (Englewood Cliffs, NJ: Prentice-Hall Publishers, 1974). Also see Jack D. Forbes, *Black Africans and Native Americans: Color, Race and Caste in the Evolution of Red-Black Peoples* (Oxford: Basil Blackwell Publishers, 1988).

6.   Arguably, this is a crucial dimension of all colonial contexts. A particularly lucid psychological explanation is offered in Albert Memmi, *The Colonizer and the Colonized* (Boston: Beacon Press, 1965). Also see Frantz Fanon, *The Wretched of the Earth* (New York: Grove Press, 1965).

7.   Such conceptual masquerades seem to be an integral aspect of the ideology of domination. For analysis, see J.G. Merquior, *The Veil and the Mask: Essays on Culture and Ideology* (London: Routledge & Kegan Paul Publishers, 1979).

8.   See, for example, Donald A. Grinde's analysis in his newly revised and expanded edition of *The Iroquois and the Founding of the American Nation* (Niwot: University Press of Colorado, forthcoming) of the controversy attending his contention, corroborated by John Adams and other "Founding Fathers" in their own handwriting, that the form of governance exhibited by the Iroquois Six Nations Confederacy influenced the drafting of the U.S. Constitution and consequent establishment of the American republic.

9.   A prime example of each category will be found in James A. Clifton, ed., *The Invented Indian: Cultural Fictions and Government Policies* (New Brunswick, NJ: Transaction Books, 1990); see especially, Allan van Gestel, "When Fictions Take Hostages," pp. 291-312.

10. Most of the books produced by the late Vincent

LaDuke (also known as "Sun Bear") would fill the bill in this regard, as would the articulations of various "shamans" approved by the Euroamerican "New Age" movement.

11. For an interesting assessment of these dynamics, see Ciarán de Baróid, *Ballymurphy and the Irish War* (London: Pluto Press, 1989).

12. Quoted in Lewis Hanke, "The Dawn of Conscience in America: Spanish Experiments and Experiences with Indians in the New World," *American Philosophical Society Proceedings*, No. 107, 1963, p. 90. For elaboration of the legal implications of Las Casas's position, see James Brown Scott, *The Spanish Origins of International Law* (Oxford: Clarendon Press, 1934).

13. Mason Wade, "The French and the Indians," in Howard Peckham and Charles Gibson, eds., *Attitudes of the Colonial Powers toward the American Indian* (Salt Lake City: University of Utah Press, 1969, pp. 61-80). Wade observes on page 71 that, by 1622, "an ever increasing amount" of the time of Samuel de Champlain, Governor of Nouvelle France (as the French New World colony was called), was consumed by "Indian diplomacy," and that in that year he negotiated on behalf of his Crown a formal treaty—an incontrovertibly international instrument—with what he termed "ambassadors" of the Iroquois Confederacy.

14. Allen W. Trelease, "Dutch Treatment of the Indian, with Particular Reference to New Netherland," in Peckham and Gibson, *op. cit.*, p. 51.

15. K. Knorr, *British Colonial Theories, 1570-1850* (Cambridge, MA: Cambridge University Press, 1944).

16. William Wood, *New England's Prospect* (London, 1624, p. 80).

17. Anonymous, *A Relation to Maryland* (London, 1635, p. 43).

18. Quoted in Wilbur R. Jacobs, *The Appalachian Indian*

Frontier: The Edmund Atkin Report and the Plan of 1755 (Lincoln: University of Nebraska Press, 1967, p. 38).

19. Alden T. Vaughn, *Early American Indian Documents: Treaties and Laws, 1607-1789* (Washington, D.C.: University Publications of America, 1979).

20. Quoted in Jacobs, *op. cit.*, p. 38.

21. The United States became the first country to commit to black letter law the relevant international customs pertaining to the making of treaties. Article I, Section 10 of the U.S. Constitution follows Article IX of the Articles of Confederation in reserving treaty-making prerogatives to the federal government exclusively, and then only with other fully sovereign national entities. The Articles of Confederation make specific reference to American Indian relations in this regard.

22. The phrasing comes from Attorney General William Wirt, Opinion of the Attorney General 110 (1828). Texts of 371 of the ratified treaties appear verbatim in Charles J. Kappler, *Indian Treaties, 1778-1883* (New York: Interland Publishers, 1973). Lakota scholar Vine Deloria, Jr., in conducting an as yet unfinished treaty study of his own, has uncovered the texts of a further eight ratified treaties which are not included in Kappler, and has compiled the texts of approximately 400 unratified treaties upon which the United States predicates portions of presumed land title.

23. To abrogate the treaties out-of-hand would have served—and would still serve—to void most U.S. land title in North America. The Act of March 3, 1871 (16 Stat. L. 566), by which U.S. treaty-making with Indians was ended, was therefore very carefully worded: "*Provided*, That hereafter no Indian nation or tribe within the territory of the United States shall be recognized as an independent nation, tribe, or power

with whom the United States may contract by treaty; *Provided further*, That nothing herein contained shall be construed to invalidate or impair the obligation of any treaty heretofore lawfully made and ratified with any Indian nation or tribe." The best intentions of its framers to play both ends against the middle notwithstanding, the statute obviously adds up to a juridical contradiction of the first order: one of the primary obligations lawfully incurred by—indeed, constitutionally required of—the government in ratifying its many treaties with Indians was/is to recognize them as *precisely* the sort of independent entities with which it could continue to treat. There is simply no legal basis for one nation, having recognized the sovereignty of another, to arbitrarily and unilaterally "unrecognize" it, even if it no longer wishes to enter into new treaties with it.

24. *Cherokee Nation v. Georgia*, 30 U.S. (5 Pet.)1, 16 (1831). See Chapter 14, sec. 3

25. Opinion of the Attorney General 110 (Washington, D.C.: U.S. Department of Justice, 1828).

26. *Report of the Commissioner of Indian Affairs* (Washington, D.C.: U.S. Department of Interior, 1869, p. 6).

27. *Report of the Commissioner of Indian Affairs* (Washington, D.C.: U.S. Department of Interior, 1873, p. 3).

28. "Extract from the Report of the Secretary of Interior," in *Report of the Commissioner of Indian Affairs* (Washington, D.C.: U.S. Department of Interior, 1862, p, 7).

29. Robert A. Williams, Jr., *The American Indian in Western Legal Thought: The Discourses of Conquest* (London/New York: Oxford University Press, 1990).

30. We have this in so many words. During the early 1600s, the Council of Virginia advised its diplomats to enter into treaty relations with Indians so that,

when the natives grew "secure upon the treatie, we shall have the better Advantage both to surprise them, & cutt down their Corne"; quoted in George Percy, "A Trewe Relacyon of the Procedeings and Occurrentes of Momente which have hapned in Virginia," *Tyler's Quarterly Historical and Genealogical Magazine*, No. 3, 1922, pp. 272-3. Overall, see Dorothy V. Jones, *License for Empire: Colonialism by Treaty in Early America* (Chicago: University of Chicago Press, 1982).

31. Act of May 28, 1830 ("Indian Removal Act"), 4 Stat. 411, Sec. 3.

32. "Neither Spain nor Britain should be models of German expansion, but the Nordics of North America, who had ruthlessly pushed aside an inferior race to win for themselves soil and territory for the future"; Norman Rich, *Hitler's War Aims: Ideology, the Nazi State, and the Course of Expansion* (New York: W.W. Norton Publisher, 1973, p. 8). For Hitler's own statements in this regard, see his *Mein Kampf* (Boston: Houghton Mifflin Publishers, 1971, pp. 403, 591); and *Hitler's Secret Book* (New York: Grove Press, 1961, pp. 44-8). Also see the memorandum prepared by Hitler's adjutant, Colonel Friedrich Hossbach, summarizing the contents of a so-called Führer Conference conducted on November 5, 1937; International Military Tribunal, *Trial of the Major War Criminals before the International Military Tribunal: Proceedings and Documents*, Vol. 25, 386-PS (Nuremberg: Office of the International Military Tribunal, 1947-1949, pp. 402-13).

33. A classic example of this sort of duplicity occurred in 1875 when President Ulysses S. Grant secretly instructed his military commanders not to meet the army's legal obligation, incurred under the 1868 Fort Laramie Treaty, to prevent U.S. citizens from trespassing in the territory of the Lakota Nation (the

trespassing itself having been fostered by false but widely publicized reports, written under pseudonyms by George Armstrong Custer and other officers, that an illegal army expedition into the Lakota homeland in 1874 had turned up evidence of major gold deposits therein). The resulting presence of large numbers of U.S. citizens in Lakota country by 1876, and an alleged "need to protect their safety," was then used as a pretext by which the Grant administration could claim to be "compelled" to wage a war of conquest against the Indians. On Grant's order and related maneuvering, see the report by E.T. Watkins listed as Executive Document 184 (Washington, D.C.: 44th Cong., 1st Sess., 1876, pp. 8-9). Overall, see John E. Gray, *The Centennial Campaign: The Sioux Wars of 1876* (Norman: University of Oklahoma Press, 1988).

34. A good case can be made that such sentiments, at least insofar as they were cast along racial lines, were a new thing, coming into being only at the point—*circa* 1450-1500—that Europe was consolidating its notion of itself as a distinct cultural/geographic entity, and discovering that it possessed the capacity, potentially at least, of expanding outward at the expense of other peoples. An interesting examination of this thesis may be found in Ronald Sanders, *Lost Tribes and Promised Lands: The Origins of American Racism* (New York: Harper Perennial Publishers, 1992). A somewhat obtuse, but nonetheless useful analysis of the same ideas is offered by Steven Greenblatt in his *Marvelous Possessions: The Wonder of the New World* (Chicago: University of Chicago Press, 1991).

35. To be fair, the same dynamic had been developed earlier, by the Holy Roman Empire (based in Aachen), for use in creating Europe itself. Here, the Church cast itself as the vessel of "Christian

Civilization," a self-assigned status of superiority contrasted to a host of "evil" and inferior "pagan tribes" (the Celts, for example) which occupied the "periphery" of the subcontinent. On this basis, the zealousness of the Christian faithful was channeled into a centuries-long process of conquest, colonization, extermination, and expulsion which resulted in the incorporation of the bulk of the geography of what is now called Europe into a more-or-less culturally cohesive synthesis dubbed "Western Civilization." A very succinct and useful account of this history will be found in the opening chapters of Rodger Cunningham's *Apples on the Flood: The Southern Mountain Experience* (Knoxville: University of Tennessee Press, 1987).

36. It should be noted for the record that Europe is no more a continent than is the subcontinent of India. Arguments that the Volga River and/or the Ural Mountains, located well into the Asian mainland proper, provide a sort of "natural line of demarcation" between Europe and Asia may be seen as the ridiculously flimsy assertions that they are when one considers the much more formidable Himalayan Mountains separating India from the rest of Asia. Nor can the cultures of Europe be more readily distinguished from those of the portion of central Asia it adjoins than can those of India. For further information, see Kenneth C. Davis, *Don't Know Much About Geography: Everything You Need to Know About the World but Never Learned* (New York: William Morrow & Co., 1992, p. 129).

37. Spanish jurists such as Franciscus de Vitoria and Matías de Paz turned out to be excellent formulators of human rights doctrine, as the Laws of Burgos readily attest; see Leslie Byrd Simpson, ed., *The Laws of Burgos, 1512-1513* (Berkeley: University of California Press, 1960). But, as has been observed

elsewhere, "The phrase with which royal officials in the New World received a new law which they did not intend to put into effect—'Let this law be formally obeyed, but not enforced'—has become embedded in all the textbooks as a clear case of Spanish hypocrisy"; Lewis Hanke, "Indians and Spaniards," in Peckham and Gibson, *op. cit.*, p. 3.

38. In "Indians and Spaniards," Hanke recounts how in 1935, "on my way home from archival work, I visited the ancient silver mining center of Potosí and there observed a Bolivian army officer viciously kicking Indian recruits....This officer also called the Indians 'dogs' and other unpleasant names. Later, when philosophically-minded historians eager to split hairs denied that any Spaniard had ever called Indians 'beasts' in the full scientific and philosophical sense of the word, I found it difficult to follow their subtle reasoning."

39. Bartolomé de Las Casas, *The Devastation of the Indies: A Brief Account* (Baltimore: Johns Hopkins University Press, 1992). For population estimates, see Sherburn F. Cook and Woodrow Borah, *Essays in Population History, Vol. I: Mexico and the Caribbean* (Berkeley: University of California Press, 1971); esp. "The Aboriginal Population of Hispaniola," pp. 376-410.

40. David E. Stannard, *American Holocaust: Columbus and the Conquest of the New World* (London/New York: Oxford University Press, 1992, p. 85).

41. Nobel David Cook, *Demographic Collapse: Peru, 1520-1620* (Cambridge, MA: Cambridge University Press, 1981, p. 114).

42. John Grier Varner and Jeanette Johnson Varner, *Dogs of Conquest* (Norman: University of Oklahoma Press, 1983, pp. 192-3).

43. This is from a contemporaneous account by Peter Martyr, quoted in Tzvetan Todorov, *The Conquest of*

America: The Conquest of the Other (New York: Harper and Row Publishers, 1984, p. 141).

44. Stannard, *op. cit.*, pp. 83-4.

45. See, for example, the descriptions of the supposedly "bestial" nature of the "tribal" Irish offered by William Thomas during the 1550s; quoted in Howard Mumford Jones, *O Strange New World: American Culture—The Formative Years* (London: Chatto and Windus Publishers, 1964, p. 169). It is worth noting that, to the extent the more educated English viewed the Irish as being human at all, they emphatically denied that such "wild men" might be considered "White." Hence, until the late nineteenth century, the Irish were officially categorized as being "Black" by their colonizers.

46. Quoted in Richard Slotkin and James K. Folsom, eds., *So Dreadful a Judgement: Puritan Responses to King Philip's War, 1676-1677* (Middletown, CT: Wesleyan University Press, 1978, p. 381). The description of Indian homes as being "nothing more than kennels" comes from Sarah Kembel Knight, *The Journal of Madam Knight* (Boston: David R. Godine Publisher, 1972, p. 22).

47. Quoted in Slotkin and Folsom, *op. cit.*

48. Douglas Edward Leach, *Flintlock and Tomahawk: New England in King Philip's War* (New York: W.W. Norton Publisher, 1958, p. 237).

49. Contrary to myth, scalping was not an Indian practice, but rather something imported by the English. Its origin may be found in Ireland, where the taking of heads was used as a means of identifying slain resistance leaders. The heads were then used to terrorize the population; they were, according to Gilbert Humphrey, who thought up the idea, "laide on the ground by eche side of the waie ledynge to [English encampments] so that none could come...for any cause but commonly he muste passe through a lane

of heddes which [were] used *ad terrorem*" (quoted in Nicholas P. Canny, "The Ideology of English Colonization: From Ireland to America," *William and Mary Quarterly*, 3rd Ser., No. 30, 1973, p. 582). In the comparatively vast and forested reaches of the New World, the taking of whole heads often proved too cumbersome, and so scalping was evolved as proof the "beasts" had been killed.

50. See "John Easton's Relacion," in Charles H. Lincoln, ed., *Narratives of the Indian Wars, 1675-1699* (New York: Charles Scribner's Sons, Publishers, 1913, pp. 14, 16).

51. Quoted in James Axtell, "The Rise and Fall of the Powhatan Empire," in James Axtell, ed., *After Columbus: Essays in the Ethnohistory of Colonial North America* (London/New York: Oxford University Press, 1988, pp. 218-9).

52. For the purpose indicated, Amherst (in whose honored memory a town and university campus in Massachusetts are presently named) ordered a subordinate, Bouquet, to distribute items taken from a smallpox infirmary as "gifts" during a peace parley with Pontiac's Confederacy. The following day, Bouquet reported, also in writing, that this had been done and that he hoped the measure would "obtain the desired result." Upwards of 100,000 Indians died of smallpox in the ensuing epidemic. Although this is history's first documentable instance of biological warfare, the familiarity with requisite techniques displayed by Amherst and his men strongly suggest that the British had engaged in similar methods before; E. Wagner Stearn and Allen E. Stearn, *The Effects of Smallpox on the Destiny of the Amerindian* (Boston: Bruce Humphries, Publisher, 1945, pp. 44-5). Chemical means—poisons—were also regularly employed by English colonists for purposes of mass extermination, from at least as early as 1623; see, for

example, "Bennetes Welcome," *William and Mary Quarterly*, 2nd Ser., No. 13, 1933, p. 122.

53. The pre-invasion population estimate comes from Henry F. Dobyns, *Their Numbers Become Thinned: Native American Population Dynamics in Eastern North America* (Knoxville: University of Tennessee Press, 1983, p. 41); attrition is estimated by Stannard, *op. cit.*, pp. 120-1.

54. Quoted in Axtell, *op. cit.*, p. 219.

55. Quoted in Richard Drinnon, *Facing West: The Metaphysics of Indian Hating and Empire Building* (New York: Schocken Books, 1990, pp. 65, 331-2).

56. Quoted in Ronald T. Takaki, *Iron Cages: Race and Culture in 19th-Century America* (New York: Alfred A. Knopf, 1979, pp. 61-5). Also see Drinnon, *op. cit.*, pp. 96, 98, 116. As Stannard aptly remarks (at p. 120), "Had these same words been enunciated by a German leader in 1939, and directed at European Jews, they would be engraved in modern memory. Since they were uttered by one of America's founding fathers, however, the most widely admired of the South's slaveholding philosophers of freedom, they conveniently have become lost to historians in their insistent celebration of Jefferson's wisdom and dignity."

57. Quoted in Takaki, *op. cit.*, p. 96. As President, Jackson remained true to his (and Jefferson's) views, overseeing the removal of virtually all Indians east of the Mississippi to points west. This was accomplished by forced march at bayonet-point—called the "Trail of Tears" by its victims—often in the dead of winter, and without anything resembling adequate food, shelter, or medical care. The toll on native lives was predictably horrendous, with up to 55 percent of all Cherokees perishing as a result, about half of all Creeks and Seminoles, etc. See Russell Thornton, "Cherokee Population Losses on the Trail of Tears: A

344

New Perspective and a New Estimate," *Ethnohistory*, No. 31, 1984, pp. 289-300.

58. Stannard, *op. cit.*, p. 123. The massacre at Tohopeka (Horseshoe Bend) occurred on March 27, 1814. The slaughter—in which 557 Creek men and 250-300 women and children died by official count—was immortalized as a "great battle" by the Walt Disney Studios in its 1950s movie series about Davy Crockett, one of the volunteers serving under Jackson, who was cast in the film as a "genuine American hero." In reality, Crockett was a sadist who could write glowingly in his diary about "stewing the grease out of" a 12-year-old Creek boy whose arm and leg had already been shattered by musket balls; see Jimmie Durham, "Cowboys and...Notes on Art, Literature, and American Indians in the Modern American Mind," in *The State of Native America*, *op. cit.*, p. 423.

59. David Svaldi, *Sand Creek and the Rhetoric of Extermination: A Case Study in Indian-White Relations* (Washington, D.C.: University Press of America, 1989).

60. Quoted in *ibid.*, pp. 149-50, 172.

61. Stannard, *op. cit.*, p. 131. The quote from Himmler appears in Robert Jay Lifton, *The Nazi Doctors: Medical Killing and the Psychology of Genocide* (New York: Basic Books, 1986, p. 477).

62. For details on all this, see Stan Hoig, *The Sand Creek Massacre* (Norman: University of Oklahoma Press, 1961).

63. Quoted in Svaldi, *op. cit.*, pp. 298-9. It should be noted that, as late as 1991, members of the American Indian Movement in Colorado discovered that two Cheyenne scalps taken at Sand Creek were still being displayed as a "tourist attraction" in a resort near Denver.

64. Quoted in Thomas G. Dyer, *Theodore Roosevelt and*

the Idea of Race (Baton Rouge: Louisiana State University Press, 1980, p. 79).

65. Quoted in Edward S. Ellis, The History of Our Country: From the Discovery of America to the Present Time, Vol. 6 (Cincinnati: Bartlett Publishing, 1900, p. 1483).

66. Edward Lazarus, Black Hills, White Justice: The Sioux Nation versus the United States, 1775 to the Present (New York: Harper-Collins Publishers, 1991, p. 29). Despite its inclusion of this sort of useful information, the book is a work of anti-Indian revisionism.

67. On Texas, see Stiffarm and Lane, op. cit., p. 35. On the Dakotas, see Lazarus, op. cit., p. 28.

68. Lawrence Kelly, Navajo Roundup (Boulder, CO: Pruett Publishing Co., 1970).

69. Sherburn F. Cook, The Conflict Between the California Indian and White Civilization (Berkeley: University of California Press, 1976, pp. 284). Also see Robert F. Heizer, ed., Destruction of the California Indians (Salt Lake City/Santa Barbara: Peregrine Smith, Inc., 1974).

70. For details on the massacre, see Dee Brown, Bury My Heart at Wounded Knee: An Indian History of the American West (New York: Henry Holt & Co., 1970, pp. 415-45). It should be noted that a number of Congressional Medals of Honor for "bravery" and "gallantry" were awarded to the troops who gunned down defenseless women and children.

71. Quoted in Elliot J. Gorn, Randy Roberts, and Terry D. Bilhartz, Constructing the American Past: A Source Book of a People's History (New York: Harper-Collins Publishers, 1991, p. 99).

72. Ibid.

73. The contemporary situation in Central and South America continues to display the same sorts of direct physical genocide of native peoples which marks the

historical reality of North America. In Guatemala, for example, it is estimated that perhaps 60,000 Mayan Indians have been killed, and another 100,000 turned into refugees, since 1970; Amnesty International, *Guatemala: The Human Rights Record* (London: Amnesty International Publications, 1987); Jean-Marie Simon, *Guatemala: Eternal Spring, Eternal Tyranny* (New York: W.W. Norton, 1987). In Paraguay, during the 1960s and early 70s, the bulk of the Aché people were exterminated through the time-honored expedient of hunting them down with dogs, dispatching them with machetes, and selling the survivors into slavery; Richard Arens, ed., *Genocide in Paraguay* (Philadelphia: Temple University Press, 1976). In Brazil, some 150 distinct peoples are presently confronted with the prospect of genocide because of "development" of the homelands in the Amazon Basin; *The Indian People in Brazil, Vols. 1-18* (São Paulo: Center for Documentation and Information, 1978-1981).

74. The U.S. had, at this point, largely defeated the formidable southern plains peoples—the Comanche, Kiowa, Kiowa Apache, Southern Cheyenne, and Southern Arapaho nations in particular—who comprised one of the two major remaining military barriers to its consolidation of the 48-contiguous area; William H. Leckie, *The Military Conquest of the Southern Plains* (Norman: University of Oklahoma Press, 1963). On the northern plains, it was even then preparing to destroy the final obstacle, composed mainly of the Lakota, Northern Cheyenne, and Northern Arapaho nations; Ralph K. Andrist, *The Long Death: The Last Days of the Plains Indians* (New York: Macmillan Publishers, 1964). Other pockets of residual Indian resistance, among the Chiricahua Apaches of southern Arizona, for example, were considered peripheral nuisances rather than serious threats; Odie B. Falk, *The Geronimo Campaign*

(London/New York: Oxford University Press, 1969).

75. The primary definition of "assimilation" offered by *Webster's Ninth New Collegiate Dictionary* (*op. cit.*) is "the incorporation or conversion of nutrients into protoplasm that in animals follows digestion and absorption and in higher plants involves both photosynthesis and root absorption." The official count of U.S. wars with Indians comes from U.S. Bureau of the Census, *Report on Indians Taxed and Indians Not Taxed in the United States (except Alaska) at the Eleventh U.S. Census: 1890* (Washington, D.C.: U.S. Government Printing Office, 1894, pp. 637-8). Some indication of the extent of the impact of what the report calls "individual affairs" and "private citizen actions" may be apprehended in the fact that every one of the 400-odd native peoples within the continental portion of the U.S. suffered acute physical decimation between 1775 and 1885, a period in which official wars were fought against only 40 of them.

76. 15 Stat. 7, 9.

77. 42 Stat. 582, 590; 25 U.S.C. 155. It should be noted that a number of legislative precursors to this act appear in the record. These applied, however, to individual native nations, or specified groups of nations. The 1883 act was the first to be applied on an across-the-board basis.

78. These are terms habitually used by the so-called "Friends of the Indian," a group which lobbied for absolute social and cultural subordination/dissolution of surviving Indians as a "humane" alternative to final extermination during the second half of the nineteenth century. It was they who were mainly responsible for pushing federal Assimilation Policy into existence. For an advocate's recounting, complete with all the rampant paternalism entailed in the assimilationist perspective, see Loring Benson Priest, *Uncle*

Sam's Stepchildren: The Reformation of United States Indian Policy, 1865-1887 (New Brunswick, NJ: Transaction Books, 1942).

79. Major Crimes Act; Sec. 9, 23 Stat. 362, 385 (March 3, 1885); later incorporated, with amendments, in 18 U.S.C. 548.

80. General Allotment Act; 24 Stat. 388 (February 8, 1887).

81. 43 Stat. 253, 8 U.S.C. 3 (June 2, 1924).

82. 30 U.S. (5 Pet.) 1, 16. Actually, Marshall quite deliberately opened the door to this very sort of interpretation of his opinion. His was an exercise in deforming international laws prohibiting wars of conquest to virtually compel them where Indians were concerned. See Ward Churchill, *Struggle for the Land: Indigenous Resistance to Genocide, Ecocide and Expropriation in Contemporary North America* (Monroe, ME: Common Courage Press, 1993); esp. "Perversions of Justice: Examining the Doctrine of U.S. Rights to Occupancy in North America," pp. 33-83.

83. 187 U.S. 553. *Lonewolf* might be viewed as the capstone to a line of cases beginning in 1886 with *United States v. Kagama* (118 U.S. 375): "[T]hese Indians are within the geographical limits of the United States. The soil and the people within these limits are under the control of the Government of the United States...the right to exclusive sovereignty...must exist in the National Government, and can be found nowhere else." This thinking can obviously be traced directly back to Marshall's formulations in the "Cherokee Cases" of the early 1830s; see the aforementioned *Cherokee v. Georgia* and *Worcester v. Georgia* (31 U.S. (6 Pet.) 551 (1832).

84. Public Law 280 (67 Stat. 588, 590; August 15, 1953).

85. 348 U.S. 272.

86. John Marshall can once again be said to have laid

the groundwork for this interpretation, this time in *Johnson v. McIntosh* (21 U.S. 98 Wheat. 543 (1821)). Here, the Chief Justice argued, in effect, that since Discovery Doctrine imparted a legal prerogative to discovering powers to constrain indigenous nations within the area discovered from alienating their land to anyone else, it implied that the sovereignty of the discoverer was to that extent superior to that of the discovered. This is, in fact, the exact opposite of the intent underlying Vitoria's definitive formulation of the doctrine; see Ernest Nys, ed., *Franciscus de Vitoria, de Indis et de Jure Belli: Refleciones* (New York: Oceana Publications, 1947).

87. *Oliphant v. Suquamish Indian Tribe*, 435 U.S. 191 (1978).

88. To take one example, the Treaty of August 7, 1790, with the Creek Nation states that no citizen or inhabitant of the United States would be allowed to "go into the Creek country, without a passport first obtained from the Governor of some one of the United States, or the officer of the troops of the United States commanding at the nearest military post on the frontiers, or such other person as the President of the United States may, from time to time, authorize or grant the same."

89. Felix S. Cohen, *Handbook of Federal Indian Law* (Washington, D.C.: U.S. Department of Interior, 1942, p. 6). Cohen posits numerous precedents to corroborate his point: "Treaty of January 21, 1785, with the Wiandot, Delaware, Chippewa, and Ottawa Nations, 7 Stat. 16; Treaty of November 28, 1785, with the Cherokees, 7 Stat. 18; Treaty of January 3, 1786, with the Choctaw Nation, 7 Stat. 21; Treaty of January 10, 1786, with the Chickasaw Nation, 7 Stat. 24; Treaty of January 31, 1786, with the Shawanoe Nation, 7 Stat. 26; Treaty of January 9, 1789, with the Wyandot, Delaware, Ottawa,

Chippewa, Pattawattima, and Sac Nations, 7 Stat. 28; Treaty of August 7, 1790, with the Creek Nation, 7 Stat. 35; Treaty of July 2, 1791, with the Cherokee Nation, 7 Stat. 39; Treaty of August 3, 1795, with the Wyandots, Delawares, Shawanoes, Ottawas, Chippewas, Putawatimes, Miamis, Eel River, Weea's, Kickapoos, Piankashaws, and Kaskaskias, 7 Stat. 49."

90. As Sanders (*op. cit.*) notes at page 164, the Inquisition banned Las Casas's *Destruction of the Indies* because, to quote the official text: "This book contains a narrative of very terrible and savage events, whose like does not exist in the histories of other nations, committed, says the author, by Spanish soldiers, settlers in the Indies, and ministers of the Catholic King. It is advisable to seize these narratives as injurious to the Spanish nation, since even if they were true it would have sufficed to make a representation to His Catholic Majesty and not to publish them throughout the world, so giving the initiative to enemies of Spain and to heretics!" As late as 1963, Ramón Mendéndez Pidal, one of Spain's most "reputable" scholars, was still toeing this 450-year-old official line, railing against Las Casas for having let the cat out of the bag; *El Padre las Casas: Su doble personalidad* (Madrid: 1963).

91. Stannard, *op. cit.*, p. 115. He is relying on Sanders (*op. cit.*, pp. 339-40) and Paul Carter, *The Road to Botany Bay: An Exploration of Landscape and History* (New York: Alfred A. Knopf Publishers, 1988, pp. 63-8, 326-31).

92. Francis Jennings, *The Invasion of America: Indians, Colonialism, and the Cant of Conquest* (New York: W.W. Norton Publishers, 1976, p. 17). He is referring to James M. Mooney, *The Aboriginal Population of America North of Mexico* (Washington, D.C.: Smithsonian Miscellaneous Collections, LXXX, No. 7,

1928) and James Gorham Palfrey, *History of New England* (5 vols.; Boston, 1858-1890).

93. Jennings, *op. cit.*, pp. 18-9. He is referring to Alfred Louis Kroeber, "Native American Population," *American Anthropologist*, N.S., XXXVI, 1934, pp. 1-25; and "Section 11: Population," in Alfred Louis Kroeber, *Cultural and Natural Areas of Native North America* (Berkeley/Los Angeles: Publications in American Archaeology and Ethnology, XXXVIII, 1939). Kroeber's one million estimate remained the official "truth" pronounced by the federally-sponsored Smithsonian Institution—generally considered the definitive source for such information in the United States—until well into the 1980s. Under heavy pressure during the latter decade, the official estimate has recently been revised upward to two million.

94. U.S. Bureau of the Census, *Fifteenth Census of the United States, 1930: The Indian Population of the United States and Alaska* (Washington, D.C.: U.S. Government Printing Office, 1937). This would make the attrition of Indians in the United States approximately 75 percent by 1900, or "no worse than" that experienced by the Jews at the hands of the nazis.

95. Henry F. Dobyns, "Estimating Aboriginal American Population: An Appraisal of Techniques with a New Hemispheric Estimate," *Current Anthropology*, No. VII, 1966, p. 395.

96. Jennings, *op. cit.*, p. 16.

97. *Ibid.*

98. *Cultural and Natural Areas of Native North America*, *op. cit.*, pp. 148, 149.

99. Dissemination of these key descriptors on a mass basis has occurred primarily via high school and introductory collegiate anthropology texts, and through such print media vehicles as *Time* and *Newsweek*. In the latter regard see the entirety of the

content devoted to the subjects of the Columbian Quincentennial and "Political Correctness" in both magazines during the period 1990-1992.

100. Interestingly, this notion—literally, that "Indians ate shit (and maybe still do)"—was embraced as avidly by sectors of the Euroamerican left as by the right. See Revolutionary Communist Party, USA, "Searching for the Second Harvest," in Ward Churchill, ed., *Marxism and Native Americans* (Boston: South End Press, 1983, pp. 35-58).

101. The low number comes from Russell Thornton, *American Indian Holocaust and Survival: A Population History Since 1492* (Norman: University of Oklahoma Press, 1987, pp. xvii, 28-9, 242). The higher numbers come from Dobyns, "Estimating Aboriginal American Population," *op. cit.*, p. 415; and *Their Numbers Become Thinned*, *op. cit.*, p. 42. For a succinct review of the sociocultural implications attending such figures, see M. Annette Jaimes, "The Stone Age Revisited: An Indigenist View of Primitivism, Industrialism and the Labor Process," *New Studies on the Left*, Vol. XIV, No. 3, Winter 1990-1991, pp. 57-70.

102. For a classic articulation of this thesis, see Kinney, *A Continent Lost—A Civilization Won: Indian Land Tenure in the United States* (Baltimore: Johns Hopkins University Press, 1937).

103. Essentially, what is at issue is a racist rationalization/justification of colonial domination virtually identical to that elaborated on behalf of the British by Rudyard Kipling. For an unintendedly ironic elaboration of exactly this parallel, see Corey Hurbert's effusive endorsement of the policies of Indian Commissioner Charles H. Burke, "He Carries the White Man's Burden," *Collier's Magazine*, May 12, 1923, at p. 13.

104. The issue focuses upon the "Draft Declaration of the

Rights of Indigenous Peoples," intended for submission in 1993 by the United Nations Working Group on Indigenous Populations, a subpart of the Economic and Social Council (ECOSOC), to the General Assembly. The U.S. and Canada, which had earlier insisted on the particular formulation which appears as the title of the Working Group itself, have sought since 1982 to prevent the declaration from referring to indigenous peoples as "peoples." On establishment of the Working Group, its mandate to draft the convention, and related matters, see Gudmundur Alfredsson, "International Law, International Organizations, and Indigenous Peoples," *Journal of International Affairs*, Vol. 36, No. 1, 1982, pp. 113-25. For the Working Group's history since its inception, see Douglas Sanders, "The U.N. Working Group on Indigenous Populations," *Human Rights Quarterly*, No. 11, 1989.

105. This is spelled out in the U.S./Canadian response to the International Labor Organization's "Draft Convention on Indigenous and Tribal Peoples" advanced in 1989 under the I.L.O. Constitution (3(1), 19, 62 Stat. 3485, 4 Bevans 188, 15 U.N.T.S. 35). Both governments finally stipulated, after several years of obstruction, that they would accept use of the term "peoples [in the convention] so long as it is understood that this does not convey the sense of 'peoples' as embodied in its customary legal meaning." For further background on the I.L.O. and its relationship to native rights, see S. James Anaya, "The Rights of Indigenous Peoples and International Law in Historical and Contemporary Perspective," in Robert N. Clinton, Nell Jessup Newton, and Monroe E. Price, eds, *American Indian Law: Cases and Materials* (Charlottesville, VA: The Michie Co., 1991, pp. 1257-76).

106. As the matter is put by the *Harvard Civil Rights-Civil*

Liberties Law Review (No. 509, 1987, pp. 589-602): "It is important from an international legal perspective to distinguish peoples from minorities, since they are granted different political status. A minority does not have the right of self-determination in international law."

107. "Ethnic or racial populations" cannot be lawfully subjected to genocide, for example. It is worth noting in this regard, however, that both the U.S. and Canada served as major obstructions to formulation of the United Nations Convention on Punishment and Prevention of the Crime of Genocide during 1947 and 1948, managing to have its language and scope considerably diluted before allowing its finalization. The U.S. then proceeded to refuse to ratify even the diluted instrument for some forty years after its enactment in 1948. When Ronald Reagan finally signed the convention into U.S. statutory force in 1988 (The Genocide Convention Implementation Act, Title 18, Crimes and Criminal Procedure, Part I, Chapter 50A), it was on the basis of a so-called "sovereignty package" authored in the Senate, by which the United States sought to unilaterally exempt itself from any provision of the convention it found inconvenient. This last has been rejected by other signatories, leaving the U.S. alone among the recognized nations of the world to have never officially acknowledged genocide as a crime in which it cannot freely engage. For background and details, see Lawrence J. LeBlanc, *The United States and the Genocide Convention* (Durham, NC: Duke University Press, 1991).

108. The United Nations Charter declares in its first article that "all *peoples* have the right to self-determination." This principle is amplied and clarified under Articles 55, 56, and 73 of the charter. The same points are articulated elsewhere, as in the

International Covenant on Civil and Political Rights (G.A. Res. 2200A, 21 U.N. GAOR Supp. (No. 16) at 49, U.N. Doc. A/6546 (1966)) and the International Covenant on Economic, Social and Cultural Rights (G.A. Res. 2200A, 21 U.N. GAOR Supp. (No. 16) at 52, U.N. Doc. A/6546 (1966)).

109. Declaration of the Granting of Independence to Colonial Countries and Peoples, G.A. Res. 1514, 15 U.N. GAOR, Supp. (No. 16) at 66-67, U.N. Doc. A/4684 (1960).

110. A people, as defined by the International Court of Justice, is "a group of persons living in a given country or locality, having a race, religion, language and traditions of their own and unified by this identity of race, religion, language and tradition, in a sentimental solidarity, with a view to preserving their traditions, maintaining their form of worship, insuring the instruction and upbringing of their children in accordance with the spirit and traditions of their race and rendering mutual assistance to each other"; *Greece v. Bulgaria* (1930 P.C.I.J. (ser. B) No. 17, at 21 (July 31)). Leaving aside the problematic consideration of "race," such a description would obviously fit American Indian societies. Moreover, the United Nations Special Rapporteur Aureliu Cristescu has simplified the resulting definition to read, "a social entity possessing a clear identity and its own characteristics...[and exhibiting a close] relationship with territory"; *The Right to Self-Determination: Historical and Current Development on the Basis of United Nations Instruments* (U.N. Doc. E/CN.4/ Sub.2/404/Rev.1 (1981), p. 279). This fits even better.

111. This principle has in fact been actualized with regard to indigenous peoples formerly colonized by Denmark; see Gudmundur Alfredsson, "Greenland and the Law of Political Decolonization," *German*

Yearbook of International Law, No. 25, 1980.

112. Ved Nanda, "Self-Determination Under International Law: The Right to Secede," *Case Western Reserve Journal of International Law*, No. 13, 1981.

113. Declaration of the Inadmissibility of Intervention in Domestic Affairs of States and the Protection of Their Independence and Sovereignty, G.A. Res. 2131, 20 U.N. GAOR, Supp. (No. 14) at 11-12, U.N. Doc. A/6014 (1965).

114. As Anaya (*op. cit.*) points out at page 1266, the U.S. would seem to be seeking to perpetuate the notion articulated by noted jurist Lassa Oppenheim in the 1920 edition of his *International Law*—"that the law of nations does not apply 'to *organized wandering tribes*'"—and to ensure that indigenous peoples are seen as falling into this category.

115. Robert T. Coulter, *Handbook for Indians on International Human Rights Procedures* (Washington, D.C.: Indian Law Resource Center, 1984, p. 14).

116. Herbert Marcuse, "Repressive Tolerance," in Robert Paul Wolf, Barrington Moore, Jr., and Herbert Marcuse, *A Critique of Pure Tolerance* (Boston: Beacon Press, 1965).

Index

A

Index

Index

Index

Index

D

E

G

Index

Guerrero, El Zarco: 112n
Gunn Allen, Paula: 148
Gutohrlein, Adolph ("Hungry Wolf"): 257-8n
Gypsies: 12, 73, 265n
   current deportations of: 265n; extermination of: 73, 265n;
   Cinti and Roma groups of: 265n

H

Hague (IV) Convention, 1907: 21
Hamilton, Candy: 205
Handbook of Federal Indian Law: 291
Harding: Christopher: 210
Harjo, Susan Shown: 109n
Hatcher, Eddie: 99
Hayden, Tom: 231, 261n
Hector: 216
Henderson, Hazel: 150
Heston, Charlton: 82
Hiatt, "Sky": 271n
Hiawatha: 95
Highwater, Jamake: 82
Hill, Charlie: 101
Hill, Kevin: 204
Himmler, Heinrich: 28, 29, 30, 238, 242
Hindus/Hinduism: 213
Hitler, Adolf: 28, 36, 52n, 227, 242, 307
Hitler Youth: 26, 52n
HIV virus: 78
   correlation to AIDS: 78; correlation to Hepatitis-A and -B vaccines: 78
Holt, Sabrine: 119
Holy Grail: *see* Arthurian Mythology
Holy Roman Empire, the: 263n, 339-40n
Horowitz, David: 231, 261n
Horse, Hobart: 203
Hossbach, Col. Freidrich: 57n
"Host World," concept of: *see* Fourth World, concept of
Hunt, Ben: 283
Hunter, Randy: 202
Hurd, R.D.: 190

I

ICJ: *see* International Court of Justice
Identity Christianity: 254n
Ihonataria (Huron village): 125, 127
IITC: *see* International Indian Treaty Council
Illich, Ivan: 150
ILO: *see* International Labor Organization

Index

Index

Index

Index

N

O

R

S

Index

T

U

Index

mans), concept of: 12, 74, 130

Urban, Andrew: 118

V

Valentine, Paul: 122, 132n

Variety magazine: 123

Veterans of Foreign Wars (VFW): 284

Victorio: 284

Vienna Convention on the Laws of Treaties: 19

Vikings, the: 222

Village Journey: 149

Vision Quest, the: 212, 219, 279

Vision Quest, Inc.: 253n

Vitoria, Franciscus de: 320, 340n, 350n

Voltaire, François-Marie Arouet: 169

Vonnegut, Kurt Jr.: 142

V-1/V-2 missiles: 146

W

Wagner, Elaine: 200

Wahpepah, Bill: 148

Wall Street: 229

Walt Disney Studios: 345n

WARN: *see* Women of All Red Nations

Washinawatok, Ingrid (Opegtah Matæmoh): 149

Washington, George: 312

Washington Post: 122, 174

Wasi'chu: 204

Wayne, John: 82

Weatherford, Jack: 167-72

Webster's New Collegiate Dictionary: 294, 295, 297, 299

Wellburn, Tim: 116

Westerman, Floyd: 101

Wetcher, Kenneth: 210

Wewelsberg Castle (Germany): 242

Whitaker, Ben: 45, 46, 63n

White, Randy Lee: 96-7, 111n

White Plume, Priscilla: 198

Wilcox, Leo: 190

Wilkinson, Gerald: 255n

Williams, Robert A.: 307

Williams, SA Ronald: 197-81

Wilson, George: 194n

Wilson, Jim: 194n

Wilson, Manny: 194n, 203

Wilson, Richard "Dick"/"Dickie": 175, 183n, 188-9, 191, 194n and GOONs: 175-7, 188-